*Short Histories* are authoritative and elegantly written introductory texts which offer fresh perspectives on the way history is taught and understood in the 21st century. Designed to have strong appeal to university students and their teachers, as well as to general readers and history enthusiasts, *Short Histories* comprise novel attempts to bring informed interpretation, as well as factual reportage, to historical debates. Addressing key subjects and topics in the fields of history, the history of ideas, religion, classical studies, politics, philosophy and Middle East studies, these texts move beyond the bland, neutral 'introductions' that so often serve as the primary undergraduate teaching tool. While always providing students and generalists with the core facts that they need to get to grips with, *Short Histories* go further. They offer new insights into how a topic has been understood in the past, and what different social and cultural factors might have been at work. They bring original perspectives to bear on current interpretations. They raise questions and – with extensive bibliographies – point the reader to further study, even as they suggest answers. Each text addresses a variety of subjects in a greater degree of depth than is often found in comparable series, yet at the same time in a concise and compact handbook form. *Short Histories* aim to be 'introductions with an edge'. In combining questioning and searching analysis with informed historical writing, they bring history up-to-date for an increasingly complex and globalized digital age.

For more information about titles and authors in the series, please visit: https://www.bloomsbury.com/series/short-histories/

T0347897

'Peter Rhodes' expert new history of Ancient Greece (of the archaic through Hellenistic periods) is very clearly and economically written, packing in a tremendous amount of accurate information and making abundantly clear the perennial interest and importance of the subject. Readers looking for a reliable and brief introductory account of the major political, diplomatic and military events and episodes need look no further than here.'

*– Paul Cartledge, A G Leventis Professor of Greek Culture,*
*University of Cambridge*

'This vivid and clearly written account of Greece from the Bronze Age to the Roman conquest will be eagerly welcomed by students and general readers who want to know not only the history of the region but also some of the scholarly debates surrounding the interpretation of ancient texts, inscriptions, coins and archaeological remains. Professor Rhodes' widely acknowledged mastery of the material allows him to compress an immense amount of information into crisp and direct prose without ever sacrificing the most important details.'

*– Jonathan M Hall, Phyllis Fay Horton Distinguished Service*
*Professor in the Humanities and Professor of History and*
*Classics, University of Chicago*

# A Short History of . . .

# A SHORT HISTORY OF ANCIENT GREECE

# P. J. RHODES

BLOOMSBURY ACADEMIC
LONDON • NEW YORK • OXFORD • NEW DELHI • SYDNEY

BLOOMSBURY ACADEMIC
Bloomsbury Publishing Plc
50 Bedford Square, London, WC1B 3DP, UK
1385 Broadway, New York, NY 10018, USA

BLOOMSBURY, BLOOMSBURY ACADEMIC and the
Diana logo are trademarks of Bloomsbury Publishing Plc

First published in Great Britain 2014 by I.B. Tauris & Co. Ltd
Reprinted by Bloomsbury Academic 2019

A catalogue record for this book is available from the British Library.

A catalog record for this book is available from the Library of Congress

ISBN: 978-1-3501-2752-4
ePDF: 978-0-8577-3551-5
eBook: 978-1-7867-3958-2

Series: Short Histories

Typeset in Sabon by Ellipsis Digital Limited, Glasgow

To find out more about our authors and books visit
www.bloomsbury.com and sign up for our newsletters.

# Contents

# List of Maps and Illustrations

## Maps

## Figures

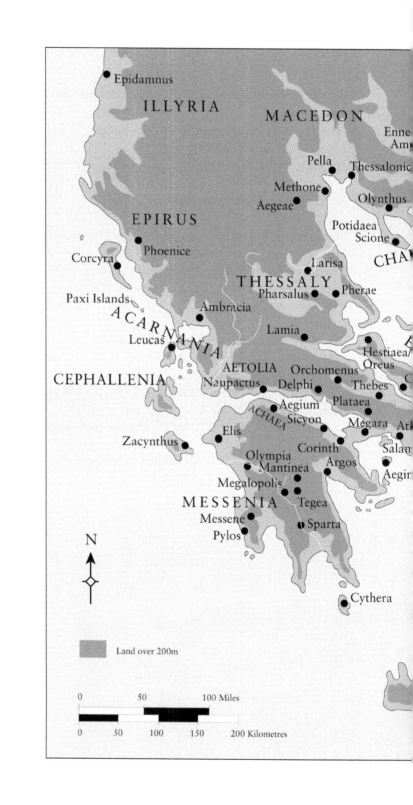

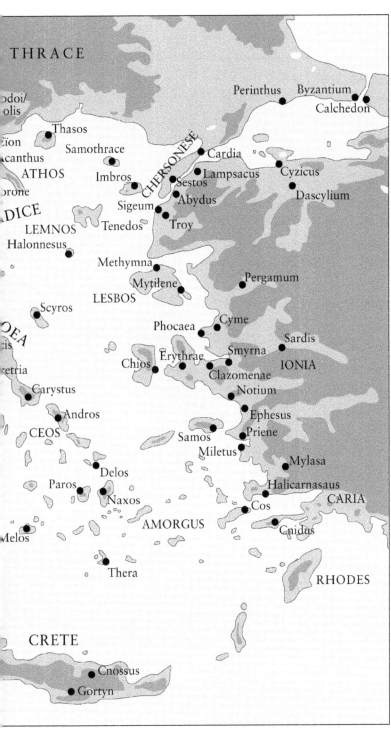

1. Greece and the Aegean

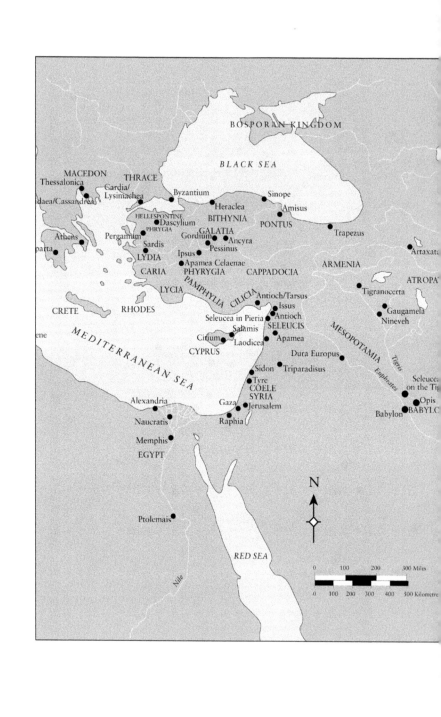

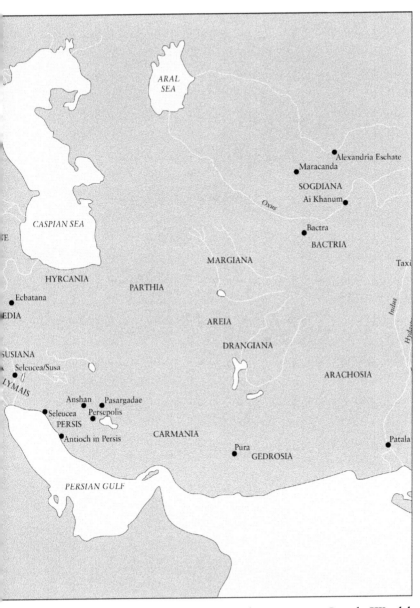

ARAL
SEA

• Alexandria Eschate
Maracanda •
SOGDIANA
Ai Khanum •

Oxus

• Bactra
BACTRIA

CASPIAN SEA

MARGIANA                    Taxi

HYRCANIA

PARTHIA

Indus

Ecbatana •

EDIA                        AREIA

Hydas

DRANGIANA

SUSIANA

Seleucea/Susa •

LYMAIS                      ARACHOSIA

Anshan • Pasargadae •
Seleucea •    Persepolis •
PERSIS                  CARMANIA

Antioch in Persis •                          Patala •

Pura •
GEDROSIA

PERSIAN GULF

2. The Eastern Greek World

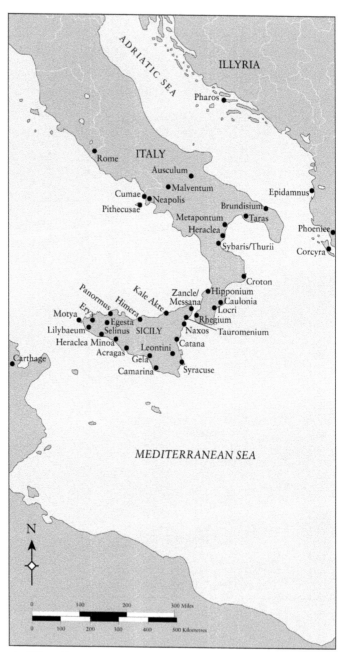

3. The Western Greek World

# Preface

This book, as a contribution to I.B.Tauris' series of Short Histories, in which Ancient Greece well deserves a place, provides an outline of the history of Greece and the Greeks from c.800 to 146 BC, with a prologue and epilogue which look very briefly before and after those dates. To cover this span in a short book I have inevitably had to select and simplify; I have tried to produce an account which will be interesting and intelligible to readers with little knowledge of the subject, and to present enough detail to give substance to the story but not so much as to obscure its main features.

My thanks to Mr A. Wright for inviting me to write this book; to Dr S. English for impersonating a 'general reader', reading a draft and helping me to improve it; and to all who have been involved in the production of the book, in particular those who have supplied and allowed the use of copyright illustrations, and Prof A. J. N. W. Prag, Prof N. B. Rankov and Dr P. C. N. Stewart, who have helped me in connection with illustrations.

# Words and Names;
# References to Sources

There is no universally agreed way of representing Greek words and names in the Latin alphabet. In most cases for words and names printed in Roman type I use Latin forms (e.g. *ae, -us, c*) but for words and names printed in italic type I use direct transliteration (e.g. *ai, -os, k*). In pronunciation the one rule that matters is that *e* after a consonant does not modify the vowel before the consonant, as it often does in English, but always forms part of a new syllable (thus the word *time*, 'honour', is of two syllables).

In citing literary texts I use the following abbreviations:

| | | | |
|---|---|---|---|
| Arist. | Aristotle | Joseph. | Josephus |
| *Pol.* | *Politics* | *A.J.* | *Antiquities of the* |
| Ath. | Athenaeus | | *Jews* |
| *Ath. Pol.* | *Athenaion Politeia* | Lys. | Lysias |
| | (the *Athenian* | Paus. | Pausanias |
| | *Constitution* | Pind. | Pindar |
| | written in | *Pyth.* | *Pythians* |
| | Aristotle's school) | Pl. | Plato |
| Diod. Sic. | Diodorus Siculus | *Resp.* | *Respublica* |
| Hdt. | Herodotus | | (i.e. *Republic*) |
| Hom. | Homer | Plaut. | Plautus |
| *Il.* | *Iliad* | *Mostell* | *Mostellaria* |
| Hor. | Horace | Plut. | Plutarch |
| *Epist.* | *Epistles* | *Demetr* | *Demetrius* |
| Isoc. | Isocrates | *Lyc.* | *Lycurgus* |

| *Per.* | *Pericles* | Thuc. | Thucydides |
|--------|-----------|-------|-----------|
| *Pyrrh.* | *Pyrrhus* | Xen. | Xenophon |
| Polyb. | Polybius | *Hell.* | *Hellenica* |
| Tac. | Tacitus | | |
| *Ann.* | *Annals* | | |

There are translations of all the texts cited, accompanying the original Greek and Latin texts, in the Loeb Classical Library (Harvard University Press), and translations of many in other series such as the Oxford World's Classics and the Penguin Classics. (For Plutarch's *Lives* I subdivide chapters into sections as in the Budé and Teubner editions of the Greek texts: the Loeb edition subdivides the chapters into fewer, longer, sections.)

For inscriptions and a few other texts I cite by editor's name from the series Translated Documents of Greece and Rome (Cambridge University Press):

I. C. W. Fornara, *Archaic Times to the End of the Peloponnesian War* (2nd edition 1983).

II. P. E. Harding, *From the End of the Peloponnesian War to the Battle of Ipsus* (1985).

III. S. M. Burstein, *The Hellenistic Age from the Battle of Ipsos to the Death of Kleopatra VII* (1985).

IV. R. K. Sherk, *Rome and the Greek East to the Death of Augustus* (1984).

And, from outside that series:

M. M. Austin, *The Hellenistic World from Alexander to the Roman Conquest: A Selection of Ancient Sources in Translation* (Cambridge University Press, 2nd edition 2006; the numbering differs from that in the 1st edition, 1981).

# Principal Dates

| | |
|---|---|
| 776/5 | Olympia: traditional foundation date of Olympic games |
| c.735–c. 715 | Sparta: First Messenian War |
| early C7 (?) | Sparta: 'Lycurgan' reforms |
| c.668 (?) | Argos: Pheidon tyrant |
| c.657–c.583 | Corinth: Cypselids tyrants |
| 630s/620s | Athens: Cylon's bid for tyranny |
| 621/0 | Athens: legislation of Draco |
| 594/3 | Athens: archonship and legislation of Solon |
| 582/1 | Delphi: beginning of regular Pythian games |
| c.561/0 | Athens: first coup of Pisistratus |
| 559–530 | Persia: reign of Cyrus II |
| c.556 | Athens: second coup of Pisistratus |
| c.546 | Lydia: Croesus overthrown by Persians |
| 546/5 | Athens: third coup of Pisistratus |
| 530–522 | Persia: reign of Cambyses |
| 525 | Egypt: conquest by Persians |
| 522–486 | Persia: reign of Darius I |
| 514/3 | Athens: assassination of Hipparchus |
| 511/0 | Athens: expulsion of Hippias |
| 498–493 | Asia Minor: Ionian Revolt |
| 491/0 | Gela: Gelon becomes tyrant |
| 490 | First Persian invasion of Greece; battle of Marathon |
| 488/7 | Athens: first ostracism (Hipparchus son of Charmus) |
| 486–465 | Persia: reign of Xerxes |
| 485/4 | Syracuse: seized by Gelon of Gela |
| 480–479 | Second Persian invasion of Greece |

| | |
|---|---|
| 480 | battles of Thermopylae, Artemisium, Salamis |
| 479 | battles of Plataea, Mycale |
| 480 | Carthaginian intervention in Sicily defeated at Himera |
| 478 | Sparta: Pausanias in Aegean, Leotychidas in Thessaly |
| 478/7 | Athens: foundation of Delian League |
| 466/5 | Syracuse: end of tyranny |
| 465– 424/3 | Persia: reign of Artaxerxes I |
| 465/4–463/2 | Delian League: revolt of Thasos |
| c.465/4–c.456/5 | Sparta: Third Messenian War |
| 462/1 | Athens: reforms of Ephialtes |
| c.460–446 | First Peloponnesian War |
| c.460–c.454 | Delian League: campaign in Egypt |
| 454 | Delian League: treasury moved from Delos to Athens |
| 446/5 | Thirty Years' Peace between Athens and Sparta |
| 444/3 (?) | Thurii founded in Italy as successor to Sybaris |
| c.443 | Athens: Thucydides son of Melesias ostracised |
| 440–439 | Athens: War against Samos |
| 435–433 | War between Corinth and Corcyra |
| 432 | Delian League: revolt of Potidaea |
| 431–404 | Peloponnesian War |

| | | |
|---|---|---|
| | 431–421 | Archidamian War |
| | 429 | Athens: death of Pericles |
| | 428–427 | Delian League: revolt of Mytilene |
| | 425 | Athenian success at Pylos |
| | 424/3 | Athenian defeat at Delium |
| | 424/3–405/4 | Persia: reign of Darius II |
| | 422 | Battle outside Amphipolis |
| | 421 | Peace of Nicias |
| 418 | | Spartan victory at Mantinea |
| 416–415 | | Athenian reduction of Melos |
| 415–413 | | Athenian campaign in Sicily |
| 413 | | Spartan fort at Decelea |

P. J. Rhodes

| | |
|---|---|
| 412–411 | Spartan treaties with Persia |
| 411 | Athens: oligarchic revolutions |
| 410 | Athenian victory at Cyzicus |
| 406 | Athenian victory at Arginusae |
| 405 | Spartan victory at Aegospotami |
| 410 | Carthaginian intervention in Sicily begins |
| 405–367 | Syracuse: Dionysius I tyrant |
| 405/4–359/8 | Persia: reign of Artaxerxes II |
| 404–403 | Athens: oligarchy of the Thirty |
| 395–386 | Corinthian War |
| 387/6 | King's Peace = Peace of Antalcidas |
| 382–379/8 | Spartan occupation of Thebes |
| 378/7 | Athens: foundation of Second Athenian League |
| 371 | Theban defeat of Sparta at Leuctra |
| 370/69 | Theban campaign in Peloponnese, liberation of Messenia |
| 362 | Battle of Mantinea |
| 359–336 | Macedon: reign of Philip II |
| 359/8–338/7 | Persia: reign of Artaxerxes III |
| 356–346 | Third Sacred War |
| 346 | Peace of Philocrates between Athens and Philip |
| 344–337 | Sicily: Timoleon fighting against tyrants and Carthaginians |
| 343 | Athens: Aeschines acquitted in Embassy trial |
| 340–338 | Fourth Sacred War |
| 338 | Philip's defeat of Athens and Thebes at Chaeronea |
| 338/7 | Persia: reign of Artaxerxes IV |
| 336–323 | Macedon: reign of Alexander III |
| 336–330 | Persia: reign of Darius III |
| 334–323 | Alexander in Asia |
| | 334 Battle of the Granicus |
| | 333 Battle of Issus |
| | 331 Battle of Gaugamela |
| | 326 Battle of the Hydaspes |
| 330 | Athens: Aeschines unsuccessful in Crown trial |

| | |
|---|---|
| 323–322 | Athens leads unsuccessful Lamian War against Macedon |
| 321 | Conference at Triparadisus apportions territories between Alexander's generals |
| 316/5–289/8 | Syracuse: tyranny of Agathocles |
| 311 | Treaty between Cassander, Lysimachus, Ptolemy I and Antigonus Monophthalmus |
| 307/6–272 | Epirus: reign of Pyrrhus |
| 305–304 | Rhodes resists siege by Demetrius Poliorcetes |
| 301 | Antigonus Monophthalmus killed in battle of Ipsus |
| 283 | Death of Ptolemy I |
| 283 or 282 | Death of Demetrius Poliorcetes |
| 281 | Lysimachus killed in battle of Corupedium |
| 281 | Seleucus I killed |
| 281/0 | Achaea: Achaean League revived |
| 280–277 | Macedon and Greece: invasion by Gallic tribes |
| 277–240/39 | Macedon: reign of Antigonus Gonatas |
| 274–199 | Series of Syrian Wars between Seleucids and Ptolemies |
| *c.*271 – 215 | Syracuse: rule of Hieron II |
| 269/8–263/2 | Athens and Sparta defeated in Chremonidean War against Macedon |
| 263–241 | Pergamum: rule of Eumenes I |
| *c.*244 – 241 | Sparta: reign of Agis IV |
| 240/39–229 | Macedon: reign of Demetrius II |
| *c.*235 – 222 | Sparta: reign of Cleomenes III |
| 229–221 | Macedon: reign of Antigonus Doson |
| 229 | Athens freed from Macedon, realigned with Ptolemies |
| 229–228 | Rome: First Illyrian War |
| 221–179 | Macedon: reign of Philip V |
| 221–217 | Greece: Social War, ended by Peace of Naupactus |
| 219 | Rome: Second Illyrian War |
| 214–205 | Rome: First Macedonian War, ended by Peace of Phoenice |

P. J. Rhodes

# 1

# PROLOGUE

The history of Ancient Greece is interesting in its own right, and for Europeans it is important because it is a significant formative element in our own past. Thanks to the conquests of Alexander the Great, in the fourth century BC, Greek language and culture became the language of the ruling class throughout the eastern Mediterranean and what students of antiquity still call the Near East. Thanks to the absorption of that Greek world by the Romans, in the second and first centuries, Greek language and culture were added to their own by the people who came to rule all the lands surrounding the Mediterranean. Thanks to the inclusion of the land of the Jews in the territory which became first Greek and afterwards Roman, Jews displaced from that land, and Christianity when it was founded, spread westwards into the Mediterranean world more than eastwards into Asia. And, although the Western part of the Roman Empire was eventually overthrown by peoples from the north, who have made their own contributions to the mixture which today's Europeans have inherited, and at one time the south-west of Europe was dominated by Muslim Arabs and at a later time the south-east of Europe was dominated by Muslim Turks, much of what we are familiar with today has come to us from this ancient world of Greeks and Romans, Jews and Christians.

Specifically Greek influence can be found in various aspects of present-day life: political practice and political thought; philosophy; literature, which has reworked Greek *genres* and sometimes reused Greek stories; visual arts, and particularly sculpture; architecture, where 'classical' styles have been fashionable in certain periods. Many of the words which we use are of Greek origin, and reflect ways of thinking which we have inherited from the Greeks: for instance, history; democracy, oligarchy, monarchy; philosophy, and its subdivisions politics, ethics, logic, metaphysics; mathematics, arithmetic, geometry; physics, biology, archaeology, anthropology; epic, lyric, tragedy, comedy, rhetoric.

The Mediterranean Sea is divided into halves by the peninsula of Italy, and its eastern half is subdivided into quarters by the Balkan peninsula, at the southern end of which is mainland Greece. Within mainland Greece a narrow isthmus separates the Gulf of Corinth on the west from the Saronic Gulf on the East, with the Peloponnese to the south and central and northern Greece to the North. In the period on which this book concentrates, the Greek heartland comprised mainland Greece, the Aegean Sea with its many islands to the east of it, and, forming the east coast of the Aegean, the western coastal strip of Asia Minor (present-day Turkey). However, as we shall see in Chapter 2, from the eighth century BC onwards Greeks spread out from that heartland, establishing settlements all round the coasts of the Mediterranean (except the western half of the coast of north Africa) and the coasts of the Black Sea; and later the conquests of Alexander the Great took Greeks into the Near and Middle East.

In this book the primary focus will be on the history of the Greek heartland, but we shall look also at the Greek settlements elsewhere and their interaction with the non-Greeks among whom they settled. I shall say something in this Prologue about the bronze age civilisations of the second millennium BC; but the main body of the book will begin with the emergence of the Greeks from the dark age which followed the breakdown of those civilisations, an emergence which gathered pace in the eighth century, and the book will continue to the absorption of the Greeks into the Roman world in the second and first centuries. Many aspects of Greek life continued without major change for some centuries after that, and we shall look at that period briefly in the Epilogue; but the unchallengeable supremacy of Rome meant that the Greeks' freedom for manoeuvre then was much less than it had been in the previous centuries.

The earliest advanced civilisations of the Greek heartland developed in the third and particularly the second millennium: what have been called the Mycenaean in mainland Greece (Mycenae in the north-east of the Peloponnese was one of its principal centres), the Cycladic in the Aegean (the Cyclades are the islands of the southern Aegean which surround Delos) and the Minoan in Crete (named after Minos, a king of Crete in the classical Greeks' legends about their past). These were based on elaborate 'palaces', from which the agriculture of the surrounding regions was controlled, and which functioned also as religious centres. Writing was used for record-keeping, and, while the Cretan scripts have not yet been deciphered, the Linear B script of the Mycenaeans was deciphered in the 1950s, when it was shown that the Mycenaeans' language was an early form of Greek. In the first half of the second millennium the Minoans were influential in mainland Greece and the Cyclades; in the second half of the second millennium the Mycenaeans controlled Crete, and reached through the Cyclades to Asia Minor in the area of Miletus.

Reliable knowledge of these civilisations is based on archaeology; but the classical Greeks' legends about their past give stories from the history of this period as they imagined it, for instance about a Greek war against Troy. Troy has been identified, in the north-west corner of Asia Minor, and one of the many settlements on the site (VIIa) was destroyed, apparently by human agency, about the time when Greek chronographers dated the war (*c.*1180); but it is doubtful how much authentic memory, if any, lies behind the stories, and much of the background material in the *Iliad* and *Odyssey* attributed to Homer seems to belong not to that period but to the period shortly before the poems were written down, in the eighth century.

From the thirteenth century there were upheavals both in the Greek world and in the Near East; these civilisations broke down, and there followed a 'dark age' of depopulation and migration. It is now somewhat less dark than it used to be, both in that we now know a little more about it than we did and in that the decline was not everywhere as drastic as was previously believed: in particular, a major site has been discovered at Lefkandi, in Euboea between Chalcis and Eretria, which was occupied from the early bronze age until *c.*700, and in the dark age prospered and had connections in various directions. But it remains true that for this period we know less, and what we do know suggests a smaller population and more

3

primitive conditions of life, than for the periods before and after. Some archaeologists now prefer to call this the early iron age, and it is certainly true that it was during this period that techniques for smelting iron were developed, and iron largely replaced bronze (an alloy of copper and tin) as the metal used for a variety of purposes. However, the Greeks of the classical period were not aware of the dark age, but envisaged a continuous advance from primitive beginnings to the heights of their own time.[1]

The bottom of the trough was reached c.1000, and after that a recovery and renewed contact with the wider Mediterranean world began. The peoples to the South and East of the Greek heartland, in Egypt and the near east, were more advanced than the Greeks, and the Greeks were influenced by them in various ways, while the peoples to the north and west were less advanced; Classical Greeks sometimes saw themselves as occupying an ideal position between excessive softness and excessive harshness.[2] Mainland Greece and the islands are mountainous, without large areas of level and fertile land except in the North of the mainland, and western Asia Minor offers only narrow coastal plains before the mountains begin. The communities were essentially farming communities, cultivating particularly the 'Mediterranean triad' of cereals, vines and olives. Early communities were largely self-sufficient, but growth in size and increasing contact with other Greek communities, and contact with and settlement in other parts of the Mediterranean world, made it increasingly practicable for communities to focus on goods which they could produce well and in quantity, and export the surplus, and to import from elsewhere goods which they did not have at all or in sufficient quantity and quality at home.

The bronze age Greek world seems to have been one of fairly large kingdoms, with bureaucracies and hierarchies of titles, but the dark-age population lived in separate small and simple communities, and separate small communities remained the norm in the first millennium. The typical though not universal community was the *polis*, the city state, of which there were about a thousand in the whole Greek world (as opposed to the heartland alone) at any one time down to the fourth century: of these only thirteen had a territory of more than 1,000 km² = 390 sq. miles, while about 60 per cent had 100 km² = 39 sq. miles or less and a correspondingly small population – so the conventional term 'city' can give a misleading impression. Particularly to the North and West, we sometimes find regional entities in which the individual settlements were less substantial and less independent than cities; but in this book I shall sometimes for convenience write of 'cities' when referring to states of various kinds.

While larger and stronger cities tried to absorb smaller and weaker neighbours, and sometimes succeeded in doing so, even the smaller and weaker cities were strongly attached to their separate existence, and resisted absorption, so that the most expansive cities had to find ways to attach others as dependants without directly incorporating them. If at first the cities had kings, as later Greeks believed, these were leading men but not mighty monarchs like those of the near east, and by the time for which we have reliable evidence these kings had been replaced, except in Sparta,[3] by the collective rule of the leading men, who took it in turn to hold short-term (often annual) offices. Each city had its own laws and its own pattern of offices, but underlying the differences in detail was an overall similarity in the problems which the laws confronted and the solutions which they offered, and in the basic structure of governance. Similarly they had their own calendars with their own irregularities (though all with a year based on 12 lunar months with a thirteenth added in some years in order not to stray too far from the solar year); and different parts of the Greek world had different weights and measures, giving different values to units with the same names. (Many cities began their year at midsummer: in this book 594/3 denotes an official year beginning in 594 and ending in 593; 59<u>4</u>/3 or 594/<u>3</u>, with underlining, the earlier or the later part of that year.)

Beyond that, the Greeks will have become increasingly conscious of what united them as Greeks, as, through the trading and colonising discussed in Chapter 2, they had increasing dealings with non-Greeks, 'barbarians' whose languages sounded to the Greeks like *bar-bar*. They were (or believed themselves to be) 'of one blood', they spoke (dialects of) the same language, and they worshipped in the same ways the same gods (with different local cult titles and rituals, though there were also sanctuaries, such as Olympia and Delphi, which attracted Greeks from many places).[4]

At the end of the dark ages the Greeks had no form of writing. The scripts of the bronze age kingdoms, which used characters for syllables and would be learned only by specialist scribes, had died with the kingdoms, and the alphabet, using about two dozen characters to express consonants and vowels, and capable of being learned by anybody, was developed from the Phoenicians' script in the first half of the eighth century. They also had no coins, pieces of precious metal bearing a stamp to guarantee their quality and value. For some time before the introduction of coinage weighed pieces of precious metal could be used to make payments, but coins were first produced in Lydia, in western Asia Minor, about the beginning of the sixth century (in electrum, an alloy of gold and silver), and Greek states began issuing coins (mostly in silver) about the middle of the century.[5]

# Archaic Greece, *c.*800–500

# 2

# THE ARCHAIC GREEK WORLD

Bronze age Greece was prehistoric: we have archaeological evidence but, except in the records in the Linear B tablets, no reliable textual evidence. Archaic Greece is semi-historic. We have archaeology, but it is often hard to relate changes or trends revealed by the physical remains to events recorded in texts. In addition we have poetry, some of it on themes which interest historians, and some other contemporary public and private texts inscribed on stone or another medium;[1] but most of our textual evidence is later, in the works of historians and others writing in the fifth and subsequent centuries, who made what they could, more successfully in some cases than in others, of physical remains, poetry, oral tradition and the like. Our knowledge of this period is of varying, and often disputed, reliability; and it is also patchy, with information about one place at one time and another place at another time but gaps in between. (Similarly my knowledge of London is patchy: I know a number of areas within London, but I travel from one area which I know to another area which I know by Underground, and so I do not know what lies between those areas or how they are related to one another.)

Dates are particularly problematic. Our reckoning of years AD was introduced in the sixth century AD (with a base date which was slightly wrong), and projected back to years BC only in the seventeenth century. In the Greek world every state went its own way, working with regnal years of kings or priests or with an 'eponymous' annual official after whom the year was named, and it was not until the late fifth century that any Greeks attempted to correlate records and work out the implications.[2] Classical Greeks often placed a person or event of the archaic period a certain number of generations ago, but different people in different contexts had figures between 25 and 40 years for the length of a generation, and unawareness of the dark age resulted in a tendency to place persons and events too early in order to fill the gap. Except when archaeological and textual data are firmly linked, as with the buildings on the Athenian acropolis of the second half of the fifth century, archaeology can give us relative dates but not absolute dates. From about the middle of the sixth century onwards our dates are reasonably secure; the earlier we go from there, the less reliable our dates are. In this book I give the dates that are generally accepted; from time to time drastic and widespread downdatings have been proposed, but they have not gained general acceptance.

Among poets who will be mentioned in the chapters which follow are Tyrtaeus, promoting the régime in Sparta in the mid-seventh century; Theognis of Megara, probably in the second half of the seventh century, lamenting the rise of upstarts to challenge the established leading families (but some of the verses attributed to him were written later, by others); Alcaeus, involved in feuding on Lesbos in the years around 600; Solon, commenting on Athens and his own reforms at the beginning of the sixth century.

The first serious historian whose work survives, and as far as we can tell the first serious historian, was Herodotus, from Halicarnassus in Asia Minor, who wrote in the third quarter of the fifth century. His main theme was the wars between the Greeks and Persians at the beginning of the century, and he gives a continuous narrative from 499 to 479, with many digressions on episodes in the earlier history of the Greeks and neighbouring peoples; he seems to have drawn a line about the middle of the sixth century between what could be remembered by the oldest people he had met and the less reliable earlier history before then. In the last quarter of the fifth century Thucydides of Athens wrote a narrowly focused history of the Peloponnesian War between Sparta and Athens, which he began while the war was in progress and which was left unfinished when he died. To justify his view that the truest reason for the war was Athens' power and Sparta's fear of it, he gave a short account of the growth of Athens' power from 479,[3] and to justify his view that the Peloponnesian War was greater than any previous war he gave an account – highly rational, even though on some points he now seems to be mistaken – of the growth of power in Greece down to the Persian Wars.[4]

At the end of the fifth century men started writing local histories of individual cities, which preserved a good deal of legend and oral tradition about the archaic period and earlier. None of these survive, but we have 'fragments' quoted or paraphrased from them by later writers. In the third quarter of the fourth century Aristotle's school in Athens produced *Constitutions* of 158 states: of these the *Athenian Constitution* survives, giving a history of the constitution followed by an account of its working at the time of writing, and we have fragments from some of the others. Ephorus, of Cyme in Asia Minor in the fourth century, wrote a universal history of the Greeks and the near-eastern peoples: from that we not only have fragments, but Ephorus' history was used substantially by Diodorus of Sicily, who wrote a universal history in the first century BC. About a third of Diodorus' history survives, including the section on the Classical period in Greece but not the sections on the archaic period or on the Hellenistic period after 302/1.

Three other writers of the Roman period deserve to be mentioned here for the earlier material which they made use of. Strabo, of Asia Minor in the first century BC and early first century AD, wrote on the geography and history of the Roman world, and he too made use of Ephorus' history along with other sources. Plutarch, of Chaeronea in Boeotia in the late first and early second century AD, wrote essays on a wide range of subjects and *Parallel Lives* of famous Greeks and famous Romans, based on a great variety of sources. Pausanias, of Asia Minor in the second century AD, wrote a description of central and southern mainland Greece, focusing on the buildings and monuments and the stories behind them.

As Greece emerged from the dark age, settlements became larger and more prosperous, and more willing to engage in friendly interaction with one another or to quarrel with neighbours over land which they wanted to add to their own. In what was called *synoikismos*, coming to live together, a process which continued into the classical period but was often resisted by those attached to their local independence, small neighbouring communities might combine to form a single larger community. Sometimes a small plain would be dominated by a single city, built on a defensible hill; larger plains might have several cities, which could quarrel among themselves or combine against an outside enemy. Athens, centred on its acropolis, controlled the surrounding plain, and then exceptionally extended its control to the whole region of Attica, so that the one city had a territory of about 1,000 sq. miles = 2,600 km², and at the beginning of the Peloponnesian War perhaps about 60,000 adult male citizens.[5] Sparta, in the Peloponnese, conquered the whole of its own region of Laconia and then the neighbouring region of Messenia, leaving other cities separate but subordinate to Sparta, and thus gaining a territory of about 2,400 sq. miles = 6,200 km²; stories about distribution of conquered land presuppose a body of 9,000 adult male citizens in the archaic period.[6] By contrast, in Boeotia, to the north of Attica, a region of about 1,150 sq. miles = 2,950 km², a number of separate cities surrounded Lake Copaïs (now drained): over time some of the smaller cities were absorbed by or made subordinate to larger cities, and for most of the time from the late sixth century onwards they were all combined in a federal organisation.[7]

At the end of the dark age the emerging cities were probably much like the cities depicted by Homer: where there was still a king, he was merely the foremost of the leading men; he regularly associated with and consulted the other leading men (those who had emerged from the upheavals of the dark age as the owners of larger quantities of better land); occasionally there would be an assembly of the citizens at large, to communicate information or to obtain support for a war or other major undertaking. In the assembly the poorer men would be expected to know their place, to join in forming an opinion but not themselves to speak or make proposals. The counting of votes had not yet been invented (that seems to be later than the constitutional reform in Sparta which is best dated to the early seventh century);[8] a king was not bound to follow the prevailing view of the council of leading men or the assembly, but he could not afford to defy it often. Citizens were native inhabitants of the city, adult (as still in the modern world) and male (as regularly until the twentieth century AD); free men who had migrated from elsewhere would be rare (mostly men who had fallen into trouble in their own city, for instance in a blood feud); there will also have been some slaves (for instance people who had been captured in war and not ransomed). In some cities there will have been men who were not totally free but were peasants dependent on an over-lord, such as the *hektemoroi* of Athens,[9] or in some form of servitude, such as the helots of Sparta.[10]

There were various articulations of the Greek people as a whole, and of the population within a city. Among the Greeks as a whole three main strands were recognised (though not all belonged to one of these three): Dorians, who lived particularly in the Peloponnese; Ionians, who lived particularly in Athens and Euboea; and Aeolians, who lived particularly in Boeotia and Thessaly. The Greeks had stories of a 'Dorian invasion' of the Peloponnese from a homeland in central Greece, and it does at least seem to be true that in the Peloponnese the Dorians were more recent arrivals than the other Greeks who lived there. As some Greeks moved eastwards through the Aegean to Asia Minor in the tenth and ninth centuries, the three strands had grown in self-consciousness and had settled in different areas corresponding to their location on the mainland, Aeolians to the North, Ionians in the middle and Dorians to the South. Within a city the population was divided into *phylai*, 'tribes', notionally kinship groups, which over time became more so in fact since membership was hereditary: in Dorian cities there were commonly three; among the Ionians six are known altogether, of which Athens had four. We hear also of smaller units, such as *phratriai*, 'brotherhoods'. Tribes and brotherhoods were perhaps groupings formed during the uncertainties of the dark age, which enabled the greater men to provide themselves with dependants and the lesser men to provide themsleves with protectors.

Agricultural communities which aimed at self-sufficiency, and had no writing and no coinage, were fairly static. Wealth consisted primarily of land and the crops grown on it and the animals pastured on it: a family might lose all its sons and die out, or have too many sons who survived to adulthood and be impoverished as the property was divided, but on the whole the families which were the richest in one generation were likely to remain the richest in the next generation. Most families would have some land, as free owners or as dependants, while a few men would work as cobblers and the like; these too would have some land, and most families would expect to live primarily from the produce of their land. Since laws could not be written down and consulted by all who were able to read, in practice the laws of a city would be what the leading men said they were, and it would be hard to challenge them.

## TRADE AND COLONISATION

In more secure conditions more children tended to be born, and they tended to live longer, so there was an increase in population, and therefore a need for more food. Some cities were at first able to bring more land under cultivation;[11] neighbouring cities might both lay claim to land between the two; but some cities reached a state in which, in less good years if not in all years, they could not feed all their population, and so they needed to import food or export people or both. The result was that from the eighth century the Greeks took to sailing around the Aegean and beyond, to find places from which they could import foodstuffs and other commodities which they needed, and in which they could establish colonies (*apoikiai*, literally 'homes away') where their surplus population could settle and produce their own food locally. In addition, some people will have migrated for political reasons,[12] and some will have travelled in a spirit of adventure.

In return for their imports the Greeks will have been able to export olive oil and wine, and from some places silver; but at the beginning of the archaic period they will not have had much to offer, and some Greek human beings may have been sold into slavery abroad. Particular cities came to have a reputation for particular goods: for instance, Athens and Paros for marble, Miletus for furniture and woollen goods, Cos and Amorgus for silk. We should not think of large-scale 'industry' in the producing cities, or of large merchant fleets. Production was at the level of the household, and trade depended particularly on a man who had a ship, on which he carried goods of his own and sometimes goods of other traders too. Herodotus tells of two exceptionally successful individuals, Colaeus of Samos and Sostratus of Aegina,[13] and pots found in Etruria in

Italy with the letters SO scratched on them may have been pots transported by Sostratus.

Coins, pieces of precious metal whose quality and value were guaranteed, were issued by the Lydians from the beginning of the sixth century and by some Greek states from the middle of the century: Aegina, Corinth and Athens seem to have been the first to do so. They were then rapidly adopted as a convenient means of payment both for commercial and for official purposes (whatever may have been the purpose originally envisaged), and by the end of the century many Greek cities though by no means all were issuing their own coins; very probably they had been preceded by the use of weighed pieces of precious metal.[14] The universal container for liquid goods and dry goods was pottery, of different shapes and sizes, sometimes plain and sometimes decorated. Pottery can be broken but not destroyed, and pots of different dates, originating in and found in different places, form a substantial part of our archaeological evidence.

The form which these overseas ventures took varied with the nature of the existing population in the places to which the Greeks travelled. At the eastern end of the Mediterranean, at sites such as Al Mina at the mouth of the Orontes in the south-east of Turkey, traders seeking metals and luxury goods from the east joined in already-existing communities. Greeks went to Egypt for grain, and were obliged by the Egyptians to concentrate their activities in the single city of Naucratis, in the West of the Nile Delta; other Greeks went to Egypt to serve the pharaohs as mercenary soldiers, and some of these left their graffiti on a large statue of Rameses II at Abu Simbel, South of Aswan.[15] In these cases Greeks from Asia Minor and its offshore islands were prominent. Agricultural settlements were founded at Cyrene (figure 1) and other places in eastern Libya by emigrants from Thera, in the southern Aegean, allegedly after a series of bad harvests at home: the native people were nomadic, and in Herodotus' narrative they did not resist at first, but did resist later with support from Egypt, though ultimately unsuccessfully, as the colonies prospered and more Greeks came to join them.

Even during the dark age a trade route between Cyprus and Sardinia had remained in use, and by c.800 goods from Euboea

Figure 1. Cyrene: in the foreground the temple of Apollo (rebuilt second century AD).

were reaching Sardinia. The first Greek settlement in this area was at Pithecusae (now Ischia), an island outside the Bay of Naples, founded in the first half of the eighth century by the Euboean cities Chalcis and Eretria. It had good land for farming, and became a substantial community with a population of some thousands, but the reason for settling there was that it gave access to metals from Etruria. About the middle of the century another settlement was founded at Cumae, on the mainland, and Pithecusae was destroyed by volcanic upheavals *c.*700. To ease contact with Greece, further settlements were founded *c.*730–720 on the strait separating Sicily from mainland Italy, at Zancle (later Messana) in Sicily and Rhegium in mainland Italy. In the 730s we have the first of a series of settlements in Sicily where there was good farming land: by Euboeans again at Naxos in the north-east, the first point reached by coast-hugging ships from Greece; by Corinth at Syracuse, further South on the East Coast with a fine natural harbour (figure 2). These were followed by many other colonies, until by the early sixth century there were Greek settlements all round the coasts except at the western end of the island. To establish these colonies the Greeks had

Figure 2. Syracuse: in the foreground Ortygia, the heart of the city; on the skyline Epipolae, the plateau outside the city; to the left, the great bay.

to dislodge or subject the indigenous peoples, Sicels in the East of the island and Sicans in the West; by the Classical period these had become substantially Hellenised. To strengthen their control of the route to the West, the Corinthians also founded colonies in the north-west of the Greek mainland and on the nearby islands, beginning with Corcyra (Corfu) in the 730s.

Other Greeks went to the south coast of Italy, looking again for land to farm, and also for overland routes to Etruria. Achaeans, from the north coast of the Peloponnese, founded Sybaris and Croton in the late eighth century, after which both of them founded other settlements. Men from Sparta who had been unable to obtain a share in land conquered in the Peloponnese founded Taras shortly before 700.[16] So many colonies were founded in this region that southern Italy, on its own or with Sicily, came to be called Great Greece (*Megale Hellas*).

Further West men from Phocaea in Asia Minor defeated the Carthaginians and founded Massalia on the south coast of France, *c.*600, and other colonies to the East and West of that, looking for metals, including tin, which came there over land from Britain. In return they introduced olives and vines to that region. About 560 they founded Alalia on Corsica, but they abandoned that after an expensive victory over the Etruscans and Carthaginians *c.*540. Towards the end of the sixth century changes in Europe meant that overland trade moved further east and arrived at the head of the Adriatic: Phocaeans then joined in colonies founded by the Etruscans there.

The Greeks did not have the Western Mediterranean to themselves; as the conflicts between the Carthaginians and the Phocaeans indicate, Phoenicians from the coasts of Syria and Lebanon had interests there too. Towards the end of the dark age there are some signs of their presence in the Aegean. Later they founded a series of colonies on the western part of the coast of north Africa, of which the best known is Carthage, on the site of modern Tunis, where the earliest remains are of the second half of the eighth century. From there they moved also to the West end of Sicily, Sardinia, the Balearics and Spain both inside and outside the straits of Gibraltar. The Carthaginians are said to have made a treaty with Rome *c.*509.

In moving across the Aegean to Asia Minor in the dark age the Greeks had not ventured North. In the seventh century Euboeans looking for land and for timber went to the North of the Aegean and founded many colonies in the region (which on account of Chalcis' involvement came to be called Chalcidice), and the three prongs projecting southwards from it. Exceptionally Potidaea, on the isthmus of the western prong, was settled from Corinth *c*.600. Other colonies were founded on the Thracian coast East of Chalcidice, where there were metals as well as timber. The Lesbians in the sixth century occupied the Asiatic mainland nearby, and continued northwards to sites at the Aegean end of the Hellespont. Milesians went further into the Hellespont and beyond it to the Propontis, and in due course to the Black Sea, gaining access to various goods from the East and to grain from the North Coast and Crimea. To gain more land, Megara, in Greece squeezed on the Isthmus between Corinth and Athens, sent colonies to Calchedon on the Asiatic side of the Bosporus, to Selymbria on the Propontis, and finally to Byzantium, best placed to exploit or control trade between the Black Sea and the Aegean.

The period of most active colonisation was from the eighth century to the sixth, but the process did not end then. Athens, for instance, founded Amphipolis in Thrace in 437/6, after unsuccessful attempts there earlier in the fifth century, and to protect its grain trade also set up a colony in the Adriatic in 325/4.

Colonies preserved and on suitable occasions deployed stories about their foundation, stories which were typically based on the sending-out of a colonising expedition from a mother city (or occasionally joint mother cities) under one or more *oikistai*, settlement-founders, often after consultation of the Delphic oracle.[17] What it suits people to remember later is of course not always straightforward truth, and recently some scholars have remarked that the archaeological evidence points to more mixed and haphazard origins for colonies: for instance, at Taras the earliest finds are not noticeably Spartan. It is likely enough that there will have been visits to some sites before the foundation of a permanent settlement there, and that once a settlement had been created a variety of people would get to hear of it and for various reasons

Figure 3. Rome, Museo Nazionale Etrusco di Villa Giulia: Chigi Vase, Proto-corinthian *olpe*, showing hoplites (*c*.675–625: Beazley Archive no. 9004217).

go to join it, but there must still have been a degree of coherence in the original decision to settle in a place and organise a community there, and doubts about foundation stories should not be pushed too far. Sometimes the organisation resulted in what was more clearly a *polis*, a city state, than the communities from which the settlers had come: for instance, the Achaeans, who founded colonies in southern Italy, may not at home have been effectively urbanised in the archaic period. The general Greek understanding was that a colony was a city state in its own right, bound to its mother city by ties of kinship and religion but not formally subordinate to it. Corinth seems to have tried more than most mother cities to claim some kind of ongoing superiority over its colonies, and was still sending annual officials to Potidaea until the 430s.

## TYRANNY

During the seventh and sixth centuries many Greek cities, though as far as we can tell by no means all, underwent a period of rule by a 'tyrant', a man who usurped power and either ruled his city autocratically or kept existing institutions and directed it more tactfully (the notion that a tyrant is by definition a wicked despot is due to the philosophers Plato and Aristotle in the fourth century). Some were able to bequeath their rule to their sons, but none of the archaic tyrannies lasted beyond the third generation. The Greek word for a hereditary king was *basileus* (though in the Mycenaeans' Linear B tablets *basileis* rank below a *wanax*); the word *tyrannos* seems to have been imported from Lydia, and was perhaps first applied to Gyges, who established a new dynasty of kings there *c.*675. Use of the two words was more fluid earlier than it became in the fourth century, and it is likely that many tyrants themselves preferred to be called *basileus*.

Thucydides draws attention to the growth of wealth.[18] What perhaps matters more is that growth in the range of economic activities made it easier for some men to become richer than their fathers and others to become poorer than their fathers, and the newly rich claimed to be as good as those of established families.[19] Coinage will have assisted this process, but as we have seen Greek cities did not issue coins until the middle of the sixth century. Aristotle imagined a military development from aristocratic cities relying on cavalry to more democratic cities relying on 'hoplites' (heavy infantry).[20] It seems that Greek aristocrats used their horses for transport rather than for fighting; but during the Archaic period the Greeks did develop the practice of fighting battles with 'phalanxes' (massed formations) of hoplites (for an early depiction see figure 3), though how rapid and how drastic the development was continues to be disputed, and it seems credible that when more of a city's men played an important part in ensuring its success more of them would feel entitled to a say in its affairs. Some cities seem to have emerged from the dark age with an actual or perceived racial mixture, for instance Sicyon, which seems to have had the three Dorian tribes and one other,[21] and this too may have been a cause of tension. In the eighth century the Greek alphabet made its appearance,[22] and from the seventh cities began to put laws in writing. At first that may have benefited aristocrats wanting to prevent one of their number from stepping out of line more than people lower down the scale: for instance, the earliest surviving written law, from Drerus in Crete in the seventh century, limits any man's tenure of the city's principal office to one year in ten.[23] But written laws did make it possible to challenge powerful men who simply declared what the law was.

We should not think of one all-embracing explanation for tyranny. There had in any case to be a man interested in seizing power; and, whether or not he held some office under the existing régime, he will commonly have been badly enough placed under that régime to want a change but not so badly placed that nobody would see him as a credible leader. He will then have exploited whatever kinds of discontent there were in his own city, which is why many tyrants are said to have been popular at first; but in time his own position will in turn have become a cause of discontent, which is why tyrannies did not last long.

At Argos, in the north-eastern Peloponnese, Pheidon is said to have been a hereditary king who usurped additional power, recovered the possessions in the eastern Peloponnese of his mythical ancestor Temenus, interfered at Olympia and himself presided over the games, introduced standard measures (and perhaps weights and coins), and died when intervening in a disturbance in Corinth. ('Pheidonean' measures of capacity were still used in some places in the fourth century; there may also have been Pheidonean weights; but even the latest date proposed for him is too early for coinage.) Dating him is highly problematic. A story in Herodotus implies a date c.600, but by then Corinth was stronger than Argos. Other texts imply a very early date, many of them before the alleged founding of the Olympic games in 776. Texts recording interruptions at Olympia offer two dates, c.748 and c.668; and Argos (but Pheidon is not mentioned) is said to have defeated Sparta in a battle in 669/8, though the basis for that date is unknown. The date c.668 is the

Figure 4. Corinth: temple of Apollo (*c.*550) with Acrocorinth behind.

least difficult: Olympia was beginning to appeal to a wider Greek constituency,[24] Corinth was approaching the overthrow of the Bacchiads (cf. below), Sparta was perhaps preoccupied with internal problems,[25] and there are signs that Argos was involved in the development of the hoplite phalanx about the early seventh century. This would be a suitable context for the usurpation of power in Argos by an insider as opposed to a comparative outsider. After Pheidon's death the kingship survived for a time, but by the fifth century *basileus* was the title of an annual official.

In Corinth (figure 4) the rule of a king from the Bacchiad clan had given way to collective rule and annual officials, under whom Corinth prospered. In the late eighth century it supplanted Athens as the leading producer of decorated pottery;[26] its position on the Isthmus between the Peloponnese and central Greece enabled it to profit from trade along and across the Isthmus; it was active in founding colonies, especially in the West. Thucydides believed that the trireme, a warship which by arranging its oarsmen in three banks added to its oar-power without adding impracticably to its length (for a modern replica see figure 5), was invented in Corinth, perhaps

Figure 5. *Olympias*, replica trireme.

in the Bacchiad period.[27] He may have been wrong – the trireme may have originated in Phoenicia, and it certainly did not become the Greeks' standard warship until the end of the sixth century – but the belief reflects the Corinthians' reputation as seafarers.

The Bacchiads were overthrown in a *coup* headed by Cypselus, a marginal member of the clan, of whom it is said that his mother was Bacchiad but lame, his father non-Bacchiad and indeed non-Dorian: he is one of the people of whom the story is told that an attempt to kill him at birth misfired.[28] Herodotus (V. 92. ε. ii) makes him a cruel ruler, but in a context in which the Corinthians are arguing that tyranny is wicked; a later writer makes him mild and popular. The sources agree that his son Periander was cruel; Periander's nephew Psammetichus was assassinated soon after succeeding Periander; the conventional dates are Cypselus *c.*657–627, Periander *c.*627–586, Psammetichus *c.*586–583.

Corinth continued to prosper. Cypselus is credited with founding the Corinthian treasury at Delphi, to house Corinthian dedications, and with a statue of Zeus at Olympia. Periander is said to have fought against neighbouring states, and his overseas adventures include a quarrel with Corinth's colony Corcyra and a discussion with Thrasybulus of Miletus on how to be a successful tyrant (they walked through a grain field, and one instructed the other by knocking off the ears which stood out above the others). In his time the *diolkos* was built, a paved track for transporting ships and/or cargoes across the Isthmus, and his reputation was not wholly unfavourable: until the inclusion of a tyrant became politically incorrect he was considered one of the Seven Wise Men of archaic Greece. The tyranny was followed by a mildly oligarchic régime, and it was probably at this point that Corinth was given a new articulation of the citizen body, designed to cut across old distinctions: there were eight new tribes which by the middle of the fifth century had their own subdivisions, and a council of eighty. The temple of Apollo built *c.*570–560, soon after the end of the tyranny, was one of the first all-stone temples in Greece, and Corinth was one of the first Greek cities to issue coins, about the middle of the century.

Megara, on the Isthmus of Corinth, was ruled by a tyrant called Theagenes in the second half of the seventh century: his daughter was married to Cylon of Athens, and he supported Cylon in his unsuccessful attempt to become tyrant of Athens.[29] The Megarian poet Theognis, who deplored the rise of upstarts,[30] was probably active at this time.

In Sicyon, to the West of Corinth, the Orthagorid dynasty ruled probably from the mid seventh century to the mid sixth. The best-known tyrant was Cleisthenes, who ruled at the beginning of the sixth century: after a quarrel with Argos he is said to have undertaken various anti-Dorian measures, including a renaming of the tribes (where Herodotus' story that he gave insulting names to the Dorian tribes and the name Archelaoi, 'ruling people' to his own,[31] is probably a garbled version of what actually happened). He quarrelled also with Periander's Corinth; he was on the winning side in the Sacred War for the control of Delphi when Corinth was on the losing, and was winner of the first chariot race there.[32] A year-long house party to find a wife for his daughter Agariste resulted in her marrying the Athenian Megacles and giving birth to the Athenian reformer Cleisthenes.[33] The tyranny here was ended by Sparta, probably in the 550s.[34]

In Athens, for Cylon in the seventh century and Pisistratus and his sons in the sixth, see Chapter 3.

Information on tyrants in the Aegean and western Asia Minor is scrappy. In Lesbos in the years around 600, after the overthrow of the Penthelidae, there were upheavals in which the poet Alcaeus was caught up; there was a war against Athens over the colony of Sigeum near the Hellespont, ended for a time when Periander of Corinth arbitrated in favour of Athens; eventually a man called Pittacus occupied a position in which he could be called tyrant or mediator. He revised the laws and after ten years resigned. In Miletus Thrasybulus was tyrant c.600 and met Periander; perhaps later, a pair of tyrants was deposed, and there was strife between factions called 'wealth' and 'hand-fighting' until the Parians were called in to arbitrate. However, apart from those faction names, what we hear of tyrannies in the east points more to feuding within the aristocracy than to social tension.

Better attested, but problematic, is Polycrates of Samos in the sixth century. His rule is dated c.532–522, and he was helped in the seizing of power by Lygdamis of Naxos, who himself had been helped by Pisistratus of Athens; but Herodotus considered him the greatest tyrant apart from those of Syracuse,[35] and the achievements attributed to him are hard to accommodate within those ten years. They include the conquest of island and Asiatic mainland cities, at a time when the Persians were ruling on the mainland, and major public works, the great temple of Hera, harbour works and a tunnel through which the water supply was brought to the city. The easiest solution is that the famous man has gained the credit for what the Samians did over a longer period in the sixth century. His rule ended when he was enticed to the mainland and killed by a Persian satrap; his secretary Maeandrius considered resigning but stayed on as an unpopular ruler, until after much bloodshed the Persians installed Polycrates' brother Syloson, and Maeandrius failed to persuade the Spartans to reinstate him.[36]

Lygdamis of Naxos was overthrown by the Spartans in the 520s or 510s. Sparta boasted that it had never been ruled by a tyrant,[37] and had put down tyrannies in other cities. Apart from Lygdamis the best-attested instances are the Orthagorids in Sicyon about the middle of the sixth century and Hippias of Athens in 511/0. It is unlikely that as early as the sixth century the Spartans had a doctrinaire opposition to tyranny: a few years after expelling Hippias they considered reinstating him.[38] More probably tyrannies were in any case coming to an end as Spartan power was increasing, and in some cases a Spartan success was bound up with the fall of a tyrant; and it was particularly the expulsion of Hippias which gave Sparta its reputation in the classical period as an overthrower of tyrants.

In glorifying themselves tyrants tended also to glorify their cities, but their rule was bad for aristocrats, because the rule of one man or family encroached on the power which the other leading families had exercised. A distinction between democracy and oligarchy, and the words to label them, probably did not appear until the fifth century,[39] but most cities after they were freed from tyranny had a form of constitutional government, in which at any rate the citizens who were rich enough to fight as hoplites were at any rate members of a citizen assembly to which the most important issues were referred: the constitutional distinction most important to Herodotus was that between 'freedom' and subjection to a monarch.

## GODS, SANCTUARIES AND FESTIVALS

In Greek cities, and in the ancient world generally, religion was an integral part of a community's life, and, while sacred matters could be distinguished from secular, the city could take decisions about religious buildings, officials and festivals just as it could take decisions about secular buildings, officials and other matters. The Greeks had many anthropomorphic gods. Stories about the gods represented them as behaving and misbehaving as human beings did, but by the sixth century some Greeks were unhappy with that: there was presumably at any one time a spectrum among worshippers of attitudes to such stories. Beyond that, those who worshipped the gods must have had some beliefs, including some beliefs about the gods and human conduct (disasters might be seen as divine punishment for some misconduct), but proper performance of duties to the gods was considered more important than orthodox doctrine about the gods.

Greeks in different places 'worshipped the same gods',[40] though the cult titles, the occasions and the rituals varied from place to place. Thus in Athens the Panathenaea, celebrated in the first month of the year, was an Athenian festival of Athena Polias, Athena the guardian of the city of Athens. Gods were given temples as their homes (symbolised by the presence of a statue), and these were used also as treasuries; they were worshipped by means of sacrifices of animals and other foodstuffs, on an altar in front of the temple, which provided not only food for the god but also a feast for the worshippers. Many temples were built in city centres, for instance those on the acropolis in Athens, but there were also important temples in the countryside, such as the Heraea (temples of Hera) of Argos and Samos, which served to link the countryside to the city. Festivals included not only processions and sacrifices but also activities which in our culture are not connected with religious occasions, in particular various kinds of athletic, poetic and musical contests.

While every sanctuary belonged to its own local community, some succeeded in appealing to a much wider constitutency of Greeks. One was that of Apollo at Delphi, with a much-consulted oracle, a

Figure 6. Delphi: temple of Apollo (rebuilt second half of fourth century).

Figure 7. Olympia: entrance to stadium.

short distance inland from the North Coast of the Gulf of Corinth (figure 6). The site was occupied in the Mycenaean period. The sanctuary is mentioned by Homer; the earliest dedications found there are of *c.*800; the oracle is said to have been consulted in connection with the colonisation of Syracuse in the 730s. The settlement was relocated and the first temple was built in the seventh century. At first Corinth was particularly influential there, but in a sacred war in the 590s Corinth was on the losing side while its neighbour Sicyon and Athens supported the Thessalians of northern Greece (who were particularly powerful in the early sixth century) on the winning side. After that the sanctuary at Delphi and another near Thermopylae were controlled by an amphictyony (league of neighbours) in which Thessaly and the surrounding regions predominated; after a first celebration in 591/0, regular four-yearly Pythian games were held from 582/1 onwards.

At Olympia in the West of the Peloponnese there was a sanctuary of Zeus (figure 7). The site was occupied in the Mycenaean period and earlier, and there were dedications there from the tenth century onwards; the earliest temple, of Zeus' wife Hera, was built *c.*590, and was one of the last major temples to be built not wholly of stone but partly of mud, brick and wood. The traditional foundation date for the four-yearly Olympic games is 776/5, and the lists of victors reconstructed by later Greeks show a credible expansion from local winners at first to the whole of the Peloponnese in the late eighth century and the wider Greek world in the seventh. The people in the immediate vicinity of Olympia were Pisatans, but the people of Elis, to the north, aspired to expand into that region and control Olympia. Different texts give different dates for conflict over Olympia (the intervention of Pheidon of Argos is perhaps to be dated 668), but it seems that Elis finally gained control c.580.

Two other sanctuaries, in the north-east of the Peloponnese, joined Delphi and Olympia as major Greek sanctuaries in the early sixth century. The sanctuary of Poseidon on the Isthmus of Corinth was founded in the eleventh century, and a temple was built in the early seventh century. Two-yearly Isthmian games, controlled by Corinth, were organised perhaps in 583/2: this may reflect a Corinthian reaction to the loss of influence at Delphi. Not far from there, at Nemea, in the North of the Argolid, there was another sanctuary of Zeus: a temple was built in the early sixth century, and two-yearly Nemean games began in 573/2. The sanctuary was controlled at first by nearby Cleonae, later by Argos.

Other sanctuaries appealed not to the whole of the Greek world but to a substantial body of Greeks. The small island of Delos in the middle of the Cyclades was occupied in the bronze age, and a major sanctuary of Apollo for the Aegean islanders and the Ionian Greeks developed there from the eighth century. Athens first took an interest in Delos in the sixth century, in the time of Pisistratus, and controlled it for much of the fifth century (making it the centre of the Delian League) and again after a short interval for much of the fourth.[41] The Panionium, opposite Samos on the mainland of Asia Minor, was a sanctuary of Poseidon common to the Ionian cities of Asia Minor with Chios and Samos.

In Athens itself the Panathenaea was reorganised and expanded in 566/5, with the Great Panathenaea, including games, celebrated one year in four. If the Athenians hoped that this would rank with the festivals at Delphi, Olympia, Isthmia and Nemea they were disappointed – the festival was perhaps associated too closely with the city of Athens – but in the fifth century the member states of the Delian League were made to participate. Athens had more success with the mysteries of Demeter and Kore at Eleusis, in the West of Attica. Mystery cults offered spiritual benefits to those who were initiated, and the Eleusinian mysteries attracted initiates from the whole Greek world. An Athenian decree of perhaps the 430s orders the members of the Delian League and invites other Greeks to send firstfruits of their grain harvest as an offering to Eleusis.[42]

# 3

# SPARTA AND ATHENS

## SPARTA

Sparta, the principal city of Laconia in the southern Peloponnese, lay on the River Eurotas, about 20 miles = 32 km from the sea. There was Mycenaean and earlier occupation nearby; modest occupation of this site began perhaps in the tenth century. The 'city' was still in the classical period an agglomeration of four villages, not fully urbanised,[1] combined with Amyclae, a short distance to the south. Sparta had, and retained until well into the Hellenistic period, two kings: in Greek legend they were descended from twin descendants of the hero Heracles, who had been among the leaders of the 'Dorian invasion' and had received Sparta as their share; in fact they were probably survivals from a stage in the amalgamation of the villages.

Late writers, particularly the traveller Pausanias, provide many details concerning Sparta's expansion into Laconia and (to the West) Messenia, but they are suspect, because, after Sparta had been weakened and Messenia had been liberated in 371–369, places which had no history felt the need to invent one. Whenever the process began, by the second half of the eighth century the Dorian Spartans had conquered the non-Dorians who lived elsewhere in Laconia. Some of these became *perioikoi* ('dwellers around'), living in cities whose local affairs they were still free to run, but in external affairs subject to Sparta and required to fight for Sparta without having any say in Sparta's decisions. Others became helots (*heilotai*, a word meaning 'captives' or perhaps 'slaves'): unlike imported chattel slaves these were local people, and they had a family life, but they were treated as the property of the Spartan state and were required to farm their land for the benefit of the Spartans who now owned it. Sparta declared war against them every year and they were subjected to various forms of humiliation and ill treatment.

In the First Messenian War, probably *c.*735–715, Sparta conquered the Stenyclarus valley in the East of Messenia, and reports that Sparta was helped by Corinth and the Messenians by other Peloponnesians may be true. The Second Messenian War, perhaps a series of conflicts in the mid and late seventh century, began with a Messenian revolt and ended with Sparta's conquest of the whole region; probably more men were made helots and fewer *perioikoi* in Messenia than in Laconia. The poet Tyrtaeus, writing in the middle of the seventh century, referred to the war two generations earlier, and was a commander in the Second War and urged the Spartans to fight bravely as hoplites. By gaining land in Laconia and Messenia Sparta did not need to take part in the colonising process: those who went to Taras shortly before 700[2] were perhaps men born during the first war whose legitimacy was doubted and who were therefore denied a share in the land conquered then.

In the fifth century and later all the institutions of Sparta were attributed to a reformer called Lycurgus (Plutarch admitted that nothing was known about him for certain, but still wrote a *Life* of him, based in part on the now-lost *Spartan Constitution* written in Aristotle's school in the fourth century). Ancient writers placed him at the time of the first Olympic games or even earlier, but it is generally agreed that the institutions he is credited with cannot have been as ancient as that. Not everything is likely to have been introduced by one man at one time, but some reforms are probably to be placed in the first half of the seventh century, between the First Messenian War and the Second. Plutarch quotes and expounds, and Tyrtaeus seems to paraphrase, a document known as the Great *Rhetra* ('saying', a Spartan word for a law):[3] the Spartans' articulation by the three Dorian tribes was combined with an articulation by five topographical units called obes, corresponding to the four villages and Amyclae; the council of leading men was formalised as a *gerousia* (council of elders) comprising the two kings and

28 men over 60 (elected from the leading families for what remained of their lives); a citizen assembly was to have regular meetings and a final right of decision. This is an early example of a pattern which was to become widespread in Greece, though implemented in different ways and with different emphases in different places: prior consideration of business by a council, and final decision by a citizen assembly. In the Spartan version the assembly was comparatively weak: only the members of the *gerousia* and the ephors (below) could speak or make proposals in the assembly, but when they were divided the assembly's right to have the last word was important. As a sign of the early date of Sparta's institutions, voting was a matter of shouting, with men in a windowless hut judging which was the louder shout.

Some writers but not all attributed to Lycurgus the five ephors ('overseers') elected annually from all the citizens. While not abolishing its kings, who remained important in religion, as army commanders and as members of the *gerousia*, Sparta transferred other functions of the heads of state, such as presiding in the *gerousia* and assembly, to these. There was sometimes tension between the ephors and the kings, and they were probably created to counterbalance the kings; later a list was reconstructed which began in 755/4, but no ephor is now known earlier than Chilon, who was influential when serving in 555/4.

Lycurgus was credited also with a distribution of land (or, according to some writers, the first of two distributions), and it is likely that some land was given to Spartan citizens after the First Messenian War and more after the Second. The alleged nine thousand allotments correspond to the notional number of full citizens in the archaic period. In spite of what later Greeks believed, it now seems that once distributed the allotments became ordinary, heritable and disposable, private property, and the citizens were never equal in wealth; the term *homoioi*, 'equals', was perhaps introduced when it became necessary to distinguish these from the *hypomeiones*, men downgraded as 'inferiors'.[4] But they did all now have enough land to live off and helots to work it, so we can assign to this time also the full-time military life of the citizens, eating in messes and until they were thirty sleeping in barracks, which the large body of subjected people made both possible and necessary. The elaborate and harsh system of training for young citizens, based on a series of age-classes, was probably intensified and developed, gradually between now and the classical period, out of a basic structure which was widespread in Greece but was elsewhere becoming unimportant.

Sparta in the archaic period experienced similar growing-pains to other cities. Conquest in Laconia and Messenia made Sparta's solution different from others, but measures such as the reorganisation of the citizen body and the formalisation of council and assembly have parallels elsewhere. Sparta avoided revolution and tyranny, it seems, by a deal between the leading families and the other citizens: by giving the citizens a share in the conquered land and in political power, the leading families gained their support in opposition to the people who were made *perioikoi* and helots.

In the fifth century and afterwards Sparta was notorious for and proud of the citizens' austere lifestyle. However, there were archaic Spartan poets, Tyrtaeus in the middle of the seventh century and Alcman at the end of that century; and archaeology suggests that in the archaic period Sparta was no more uncultured than other cities (its pottery flourished in the first half of the sixth century and its bronze work throughout that century). There must have been some conscious decisions, for instance, in the second half of the sixth century, not to adopt coinage (though Sparta was not the only city to make that decision), but much of the image depends on the contrast between simple, old-fashioned Sparta and luxurious and up-to-date Athens which it suited both cities to cultivate in the fifth century.

In the first half of the sixth century Sparta's ambitions were directed northwards, to Arcadia. Herodotus has a story of ambiguous Delphic oracles, with the Spartans first marching out with fetters to enslave the men of Tegea but being defeated and made to wear the fetters themselves as slaves working the land of Tegea, but later bringing back from Tegea a skeleton said to be that of the hero Orestes, after which success followed. In Greek legend Orestes was a non-Dorian: it appears that Sparta now aimed to become the leader of all the Peloponnesians rather than Dorian overlord of the others, and Tegea later claimed to be Sparta's senior ally. It was through alliances in which Sparta was recognised as the superior partner that by the end of the century Sparta came to dominate the whole of the Peloponnese, except Argos, which would never recognise Spartan superiority (both claimed territory on the East Coast of the Peloponnese, and after a Spartan vistory *c.*546/5 there was perhaps a fifty-year peace treaty), and Achaea on the South Coast of the Gulf of Corinth, whose connections were more with central Greece.

It was in the sixth century that the rise of Sparta coincided with the fall of tyrants in other places, though that was probably not a deliberate policy (cf. above). The earliest well-attested instance is in Sicyon, which a papyrus fragment links with king Anaxandridas II (*c.* 560–520) and Chilon (ephor 555/4).[5] When Anaxandridas' wife did not bear him a son, under pressure from the ephors he took a second wife, apparently from Chilon's family. She bore Cleomenes, who as the eldest son succeeded; the first wife then did bear sons (cf. below).

In the second half of the sixth century Sparta was interested in the wider world. It had an alliance with king Croesus of Lydia in Asia Minor; but it was unable to save him from the Persians *c.*546/5, and it then refused to support the Asiatic Greeks against the Persians, though it sent a ship to investigate, and to forbid the Persians to harm the Greeks.[6] It had contact with king Amasis of Egypt, but did not intervene in 525 when, after his death, the Persians conquered Egypt.[7] There was also contact with Samos (which had perhaps supported Sparta in the Second Messenian War), not always of a friendly kind. In the middle of the sixth century Samos intercepted gifts being sent to or from Sparta; in 525 Sparta and Corinth tried unsuccessfully to reinstate enemies of Polycrates in Samos, and *c.*517 king Cleomenes refused an appeal from Polycrates' former secretary Maeandrius to reinstate him in Samos.[8] Among the tyrants said to have been overthrown by Sparta was Lygdamis of Naxos, in the 520s or 510s.[9]

Cleomenes I succeeded Anaxandridas *c.*520; his half-brother Dorieus, younger but born from Anaxandridas' preferred wife, was got out of the way on colonising expeditions to North Africa and Sicily. In 519 Plataea, in the South of Boeotia and unwilling to join a Boeotian federation headed by Thebes, appealed to him for support; he advised it to appeal instead to Athens, and so began a long connection between Athens and Plataea, and hostility between Athens and Thebes. He intervened in Athens on several occasions between 511/0 and *c.*504:[10] to expel the tyrant Hippias; unsuccessfully, to support Isagoras against Cleisthenes, and later to try to reinstate Isagoras (he took an army from the whole Peloponnese, but his fellow king Demaratus and the Corinthians objected and the expedition collapsed); finally, he was probably responsible for a Spartan proposal to reinstate Hippias, which was rejected when Corinth led the opposition. By this time Sparta's allies were organised in what scholars call the Peloponnesian League, in which the allies had to vote on proposals for joint action made by Sparta: that organisation, and a rule that only one of the two kings was to go on any campaign, were probably reactions to the previous collapse.

In 499 Aristagoras of Miletus asked Sparta and Athens for support in the Ionian Revolt against the Persians, and Athens sent help but in Sparta Cleomenes, allegedly stiffened by his daughter Gorgo, refused.[11] About 494, perhaps after the expiry of a treaty (cf. above), Cleomenes led an attack on Argos: by means of a trick he defeated the Argives at Sepeia, but puzzlingly he failed to follow up his victory, was put on trial in Sparta, and gave a religious explanation, which was accepted. After heavy losses in Argos there was some kind of revolution there, perhaps involving the incorporation of Argive *perioikoi* in the citizen body, but Argos' hostility to Sparta remained unchanged.

A complicated series of events was triggered by the Persian King Darius' demand for the submission of the Greeks, probably in 493/2.[12] Sparta and Athens both refused, but among the states which did submit was Aegina, in the Saronic Gulf, and Athens appealed to Sparta. Cleomenes responded, but again encountered opposition from Demaratus; he induced the Delphic oracle to confirm rumours that Demaratus was not the son of his supposed father, after which Demaratus was deposed and replaced by a distant relative, Leotychidas II, who cooperated with Cleomenes. But Cleomenes' machinations were exposed; he fled into exile and incited the Arcadians against Sparta; but he was induced to return, and allegedly went mad, was put in the stocks and managed to kill himself, c.491/0. The account of him given later to Herodotus was hostile: he was mad, and reigned only a short time (the latter palpably untrue).[13] In fact he seems to have believed in a strong position for himself within Sparta and a strong position for Sparta within the Greek world, but he did not deliver success: he did not upset the régime of Cleisthenes in Athens, and he did not make Argos subordinate to Sparta.

In the Persian Wars Sparta was too late to help Athens in 490, but was accepted as leader of the Greeks opposed to Persia in 480–479. Cleomenes was succeeded by his half-brother Leonidas, who died at Thermopylae in 480, in a battle which, though it was itself a defeat, came to be remembered as a heroic episode in an ultimately successful war.[14]

## ATHENS

The Athenians claimed to be autochthonous, descendants of the original inhabitants of Attica. That cannot be verified, but it is true that, while other sites in Attica were abandoned, the city of Athens was continuously occupied from the Mycenaean period through the dark age to the archaic, and there may be some truth in the Athenians' claim that Greeks migrating from the mainland to the Aegean and Asia Minor went through Athens: Athens was already claiming to be the mother city of the Ionians in the time of Solon.[15] Between the tenth century and the eighth Athens was one of the leading cities as Greece emerged from the trough of the dark age, and one of the main producers of protogeometric and geometric pottery. The countryside of Attica seems to have been reoccupied from Athens, and so Athens like Sparta did not need to found colonies overseas in the eighth and seventh centuries. But from the eighth to the seventh century Athens seems to have fallen behind: the lead in decorated pottery passed to Corinth,[16] and archaeological finds point to upheavals in the seventh century which we lack other evidence to make sense of.

If Athens had once had a king, the position had been downgraded, and by the end of the seventh century there were nine annual archons ('rulers') appointed from the leading families, of whom one was called simply *archon*, another *basileus* ('king') and a third *polemarchos* ('war-ruler'). After their year of office these men became members for life of the council of the Areopagus, named after the hill where it met, north-west of the acropolis.

We have the whole of the *Athenian Constitution* written in Aristotle's school in the fourth century (cited here as *Ath. Pol.*), apart from a few pages at the beginning which dealt with Athens' legendary early history. Plutarch wrote a life of *Solon*, and the partial overlap between these two works points to an earlier work on Solon and the half-century before, used by both of these. For Solon himself that work will have been able to use Solon's poems, some of which deal with affairs in Athens, and the text of his laws. Our evidence for Solon is therefore good, but our sources may have assumed too readily that every item in Solon's laws represented a departure from previous practice.

The first identifiable event in Athenian history was the attempt of Cylon to make himself tyrant in the 630s or 620s. Cylon was an upper-class man, who had won an Olympic victory in 640, and was married to the daughter of Theagenes of Megara.[17] He had an oracle from Delphi, and support from Megara, but not enough support within Athens for his attempt to seize the acropolis to succeed. His supporters sought refuge as suppliants, pleading for divine protection; allegedly it was promised that their lives would be spared but the promise was broken; the man blamed for this was Megacles of the Alcmaeonid family, the current archon. The episode led to ongoing contention, and eventually to a curse on the Alcmaeonids, which could be deployed against them until the time of Pericles, in the second half of the fifth century.[18]

In 621/0 Athens was given its first written laws, including laws about homicide, by Draco. Probably he was largely recording current practice rather than modifying it; his laws were not overtly aimed at clarifying the position after the Cylonian episode, but it is hard to suppose that there was no connection between that episode and the production of written laws shortly afterwards. Draco's laws were remembered as exceptionally severe (hence our word 'draconian'), but, while the laws of Solon which supplanted them may have set a limit to punishments as Draco's did not, Draco's laws were probably typical for their time.

After the time of Cylon dissatisfaction seems to have increased, and Solon's remedies point to two particular grievances. There was a class of dependent peasants called *hektemoroi* ('sixth-parters'), who were not outright owners of their land, but had to pay a sixth of their produce to an overlord, and could be deprived of their land and enslaved if they failed to do so. And increasing economic mobility was enabling some men from new families to become as rich as men from established families, and to challenge the established families' monopoly of political affairs.

After commenting on the state of Athens in some of his poems, Solon was elected archon for 594/3, and given a special commission to undertake reforms. To be made archon he must himself have been from the established upper class, though our sources describe him as a 'middling' man, to match his attempt to strike a balance between the claims of advantaged and disadvantaged. His *seisachtheia* ('shaking-off of burdens') was probably a cancellation not of all debts but of the obligations of the *hektemoroi*, making them absolute owners of their land (but he did not go further and confiscate land directly owned by the rich), and for the future he banned enslavement for debt (but not temporary bondage until a debt was discharged). Other economic measures included a ban on the export of natural products other than olive oil, which points to a shift from the ideal of self-sufficiency to a concentration on what Athens could do well and a willingness to import other goods in return. He was credited with changes in measures of capacity, weights and coinage: perhaps what he actually did was legislate for the use of measures and weights which were already current; coinage did not yet exist in Athens, but when it was introduced coins were named after their weights in silver, so later Greeks thought that measures concerning the 'drachma' and so on concerned coins.

Politically, Solon categorised the Athenians in four economic classes (probably by distinguishing a highest class from three already used for military purposes), and ruled that for the future political rights were to be based solely on membership of these classes, with no account taken of family. Archons were to be appointed by lot from an elected shortlist (to improve the chances of candidates from new families); and, since the council of the Areopagus would still be dominated by the established families for some time to come, he created a new council of four hundred to prepare the assembly's business, and probably as in Sparta this was accompanied by a guarantee of regular meetings for the assembly. Supplanting Draco's laws in areas other than homicide (but doubtless incorporating material from them rather than changing everything), he produced a new body of laws; and his other measures included a distinction between 'private' suits, which only the injured parties and their families could initiate, and a new class of 'public' lawsuits, which any citizens in good standing could initiate (but prosecution by the authorities was rare in Athens), and the right to appeal to a jury against the verdicts of individual officials. He was not a democrat, but still expected the people to follow their leaders;[19] however, by establishing a free, land-owning citizenry and attacking the political monopoly of the leading families he in fact laid the foundation for development towards democracy.

Solon's poems show that he could have been tyrant but refused, and that he tried to be fair both to the advantaged and to the disadvantaged, with the result that he satisfied neither.[20] Trouble over the archonship in the years which followed points to resistance from the leading families, and the ban on enslavement for debt may actually have made it harder for those who needed to borrow to do so. Trouble of another kind arose from regional loyalties: when there was rivalry between men of the plain around Athens, led by Lycurgus (no connection of the Spartan Lycurgus), and men of the coast running towards Sunium, led by Megacles (grandson of the Megacles who had opposed Cylon), a man called Pisistratus, from the east coast of Attica, championed the 'men beyond the hills'. Crude translation into political and economic categories would be mistaken, but Lycurgus' group will have contained the largest number of men from leading families, and Pisistratus' group the largest number of discontented men both from eastern Attica and from elsewhere, while Megacles cooperated at different times with each of the others. It took Pisistratus three attempts to establish himself in power as tyrant (*c.*561/0, *c.*556 and 546/5), but when he died in 528/7 he was succeeded by his eldest sons, Hippias and Hipparchus. (Tyranny was not an office to which a man was appointed, and it is better to think of family rule headed by the two men than to suppose that Hippias as the eldest must have been 'the' tyrant.)

Like other tyrants Pisistratus was popular at first; he is said to have worked through existing institutions rather than rule despotically; members of some leading families were persuaded to acquiesce in his rule and hold office under it (for archons he reverted to direct election, and no doubt counted on the assembly to elect the candidates whom he preferred). He perhaps took some land from opponents and gave it to supporters; he levied a tax on produce (problematic, because taxes levied by tyrants were seen as enriching the tyrants personally) and made grants to poorer farmers. Like other tyrants he simultaneously glorified the city and his own family: various poets were attracted to his court; he is credited with buildings on the acropolis and elsewhere (including the beginning of the great temple of Olympian Zeus, south-east of the acropolis, which was finished only under the Roman emperor Hadrian in the second century AD); some developments in the Panathenaea[21] are attributed to him, and it may have been under the tyranny that the cult of Dionysus was brought to Athens. Silence suggests that he was not on good terms with Apollo of Delphi; but he began Athens' interest in Apollo's island of Delos, 'purifying' it by removing the bodies buried within sight of the sanctuary. His rule had a centralising effect which contributed to the greater unification of Attica: Athens was where the tyrant resided, and therefore where power resided; the rule of a tyrant was bad for other leading families, and in particular by appointing travelling magistrates to deal with local disputes Pisistratus encroached on the power of the other families in their own localities.

During the sixth century Athens returned to prominence in the Greek world after its period of comparative isolation, and Athens once more became the leading producer of decorated pottery: Black-Figure (painted black figures on an unpainted background) from the beginning of the century, and Red-Figure (with a painted black background) from c.525. We do not know whether Athens' first coins, about the middle of the century, were issued while

Pisistratus was in power (though he was from the East of Attica, where Athens' mines were, and he is said to have had access to the silver mines of Thrace between his second *coup* and his third); the change from a variety of designs to the 'owl' design (figure 8) probably belongs to the time of Hippias and Hipparchus. In the years around 600 Athens began to dispute with Megara control of the island of Salamis, very close to both, and Salamis was finally awarded to Athens by Spartan arbitrators *c.*500, with important consequences for the security of Athens' trade and navy. At the same time it challenged Lesbos for control of Sigeum, near the Hellespont, a sign of growing interest in trade with the Black Sea; at one stage Periander of Corinth arbitrated in favour of Athens,[22] but Sigeum had to be reconquered by Pisistratus. In the First Sacred War, in the 590s,[23] Athens (represented by Alcmeon, son of the Megacles who opposed Cylon) was one of the cities supporting Thessaly on the winning side. Pisistratus in his third *coup* had backing from Greeks in various places, including Argos, Eretria, Thebes and Thessaly, and Lygdamis of Naxos,[24] whom he afterwards helped to become tyrant there. Miltiades, from one of Athens' leading families, accepted an invitation to preside over a settlement of Thracians in the Chersonese (Gallipoli), on the northern side of the Hellespont, thus reinforcing Athens' acquisition of Sigeum. Athens broke with Thebes in 519 by supporting Plataea against it.[25]

Figure 8. Athens: 4-drachmae 'owl' coin (*c.*440–420).

Later Greeks wrote of Pisistratus' reign as a golden age but of a deterioration afterwards – but at what point afterwards depended on how they told the story of the ending of the tyranny. At the Great Panathenaea of 514/3 Hipparchus was assassinated by Harmodius and Aristogeiton, and even Thucydides, who claims that until then all was well and their motive was purely personal, leaves some signs of hostility to the tyranny in his version of the story.[26] Hippias survived, and became vindictive. The Alcmaeonids, who had gone into exile after the third *coup* but had later returned, were among those who went into exile now. First they occupied a fort in the mountains between Attica and Boeotia, but were driven out. They had maintained their family's connection with Delphi from the time of the Sacred War, and after the temple of Apollo had been burned down in 548/7 they had taken the contract for rebuilding it and had done a more lavish job than they had undertaken to do: they now persuaded the oracle to include in its responses to the Spartans that they should liberate Athens, and in 511/0, under king Cleomenes, the Spartans did that. Hippias withdrew to Sigeum, then to Lampsacus on the Asiatic side of the Hellespont (whose tyrant was married to Hippias' daughter), and from there to the Persians.

The removal of the tyrant left a political vacuum, and two contenders for supremacy: Cleisthenes of the Alcmaeonid family (who had been archon in 525/4), and Isagoras, probably from the northeast of Attica. At first Isagoras got the better of it, and was elected archon for 508/7; but Cleisthenes then advanced proposals for reform which gained him a surge in popularity. Isagoras, who had established a link with Cleomenes at the time of Hippias' expulsion, persuaded him to intervene in Athens again – presumably by arguing that Cleisthenes was likely to become another tyrant. Cleisthenes and his leading supporters withdrew, but there remained opposition in the council of four hundred, which was threatened with dissolution, and Cleomenes and Isagoras found themselves besieged on the acropolis, and had to withdraw in their turn. Cleisthenes returned, and his reform was enacted.

The essence of the reform was a new articulation of the citizen body, as in Lycurgan Sparta and in Corinth after the tyranny.[27]

The four old tribes and the *phratriai*[28] survived, but there was to be a new organisation on a territorial basis (though hereditary thereafter), on which Athens' political life was to be based. Local units – 139 of them – were organised as demes (a special sense of the word *demos*, 'people'). These were grouped to form thirty *trittyes* ('thirds'), ten in each of the three regions City, Coast and Inland (not the same as the three regions of the time of Pisistratus). Ten new tribes were formed, each comprising one *trittys* from each of the three regions. Demes were natural units, and so were some *trittyes*, but there were also some striking anomalies, by which a *trittys* included some demes distant from and unconnected with the others. Solon's council of four hundred became a council of five hundred, fifty from each tribe with individual demes used as constituencies; generals and many other officials were ten in number, one from each tribe; at some time even the nine archons were made up to ten by the addition of a secretary, so that one of them could be appointed from each tribe.

It is not immediately obvious why this organisation should have made Cleisthenes popular: the best suggestion is that he was offering the Athenians local government, as opposed to the domination of the local leading family, in addition to city government. Beyond that, he was 'mixing up the people',[29] to continue the unification of Attica, and the anomalies in the make-up of *trittyes* suggest that he was particularly interested in undermining old associations, often linked to cult centres (for instance, in the area of Isagoras' probable home in north-eastern Attica). The Alcmaeonid family had not been well placed in that respect, but there are signs that it was to be well placed in the new organisation. Setting up the new organisation will have taken time, and it was perhaps not brought into effect until 501/0.

The ending of the tyranny had probably been hailed with words from the root *iso-*, denoting 'equality' or 'fairness'; and Cleisthenes probably claimed that he was providing still greater *isotes*. Probably what he envisaged was still aristocratic politics, with the active role played by members of what were now the leading families, but the Alcmaeonids well placed under the new rules as they had been badly placed under the old. However, his system required large-scale citizen participation in meetings and office-holding at various levels,

Figure 9. Athens: *ostraka* used for voting against Aristides, Themistocles, Cimon and Pericles.

and, whether he expected and wanted it or not, the Athenians evidently took to this, and in due course were ready for still more citizen participation.[30]

One other institution attributed to Cleisthenes is ostracism, a procedure by which the Athenians had the opportunity each year to send one man into a kind of honourable exile for ten years, voting by writing (or having somebody write for them – but the institution presupposes that the average Athenian had that degree of literacy) on a potsherd (*ostrakon*: figure 9) the name of the man whom they wished to remove, and in a few instances adding some kind of comment: if at least six thousand votes were cast, the man with the greatest number had to go. The sources suggest that this was a measure to prevent tyranny, but a likely tyrant would probably be able to ensure that somebody else received more votes than he did. More probably it was a measure to resolve in a more peaceful way such rivalries as that between Cleisthenes and Isagoras, and after the first few instances that is how it was used (cf. below).

Cleomenes of Sparta did not take his rejection lying down. About

506, in the hope of reinstating Isagoras, he organised a three-pronged attack by the Peloponnesians, the Boeotians and the Chalcidians of Euboea, but the Peloponnesian force was undermined by disagreements, and Athens then defeated the Boeotians and the Chalcidians. About 504 he proposed to reinstate Hippias, but the Corinthians led the opposition to that.[31] With Sparta hostile, Athens looked to Persia, but was offended by a Persian demand for formal submission, and it later protested against Persia's harbouring of Hippias.

In 499 Athens, claiming to be the mother city of the Ionians,[32] and now anti-Persian, agreed to support the Ionian Revolt against Persia when Sparta did not.[33] Twenty ships, a substantial contribution, took part in the campaign of 498, but were then recalled: various explanations are possible, and we should not jump to conclusions about a political shift in Athens. Athens was still or again anti-Persian when the revolt ended unsuccessfully in 494/3. In 493/2 Themistocles was archon, and began the building of the harbour at Piraeus. We should possibly assign to that year also Phrynichus' tragedy on the Persian capture of Miletus, which distressed the Athenians, and the acquittal of Miltiades (nephew of the Miltiades who first went to the Chersonese: he returned to Athens claiming to be anti-Persian at the end of the Ionian Revolt) on a charge of 'tyranny' in the Chersonese: the Athenians would not care how the Thracians were ruled, and perhaps his rule there was seen by his opponents as a remnant of Pisistratid power.

Probably in this same year Athens with Sparta refused Persian demands for submission. When Aegina, against which Athens had been fighting an intermittent war for some years, did submit, Athens appealed to Cleomenes in Sparta. After obtaining a compliant fellow king,[34] Cleomenes took hostages from Aegina to Athens, but after Cleomenes' death Aegina demanded their return. There was then an episode of fighting in which a dissident Aeginetan plotted to betray his city to Athens, but Athens after waiting for additional ships from Corinth arrived too late; then Athens won a first naval battle but Aegina won a second.

For the Persian invasions of 490 and 480–479 see Chapter 4. The invasion of 490 was aimed specifically at Athens and Eretria

P. J. Rhodes

in retaliation for their involvement in the Ionian Revolt: Athens was
supported only by neighbouring Plataea (Spartans came, but arrived
too late), and credit for the victory at Marathon was claimed by
Miltiades. The Persians brought with them the elderly Hippias, and
some Athenians including the Alcmaeonids were suspected of being
in league with them. Afterwards, beginning in 488/7, the Athenians
began using their institution of ostracism. The first victims point to
a witch-hunt against men suspected but not convicted of disloyalty
in 490: a man called Hipparchus who was perhaps a grandson of
Hippias; the Alcmaeonid Megacles (and surviving *ostraka* show that
several other Alcmaeonids attracted votes in the 480s); and an
unknown third victim. The victims of 483/4 and 483/2 seem to be
the losers in a three-cornered political struggle in which Themistocles
was the winner: Xanthippus, with an Alcmaeonid wife (who bore
him Pericles) but distinguished by *Ath. Pol.* from the first three,[35]
and Aristides 'the just' (so called in contrast to the cunning Themistocles). Meanwhile, in 487/6 Athens reverted to Solon's practice of
appointing archons by lot from an elected shortlist: we do not know
who was responsible (though many modern authors allege Themistocles) or why, but this was one stage in the development by which
the archons became routine officials and were overtaken in political
importance by the ten generals (who were elected and could be
re-elected). In 483/2 Athens did particularly well out of its silver
mines, and Themistocles persuaded the assembly not to pay a div-
idend to the citizens but to have a new fleet of triremes built (there
was a precedent for each elsewhere in Greece) – so that in 480
Athens had two hundred. This was the year of Aristides' ostracism,
but we do not know which happened first, and there is no evidence
that Aristides opposed the plan.

In 480–479 Sparta led the Greek resistance to the Persians, but
Athens provided more than half of the Greek fleet. In 480 Themistocles commanded the Athenians, and claimed the credit for the
naval victory at Salamis which turned the tide. In 479 nothing is
heard of him, and the Athenians were commanded by Aristides on
land and by Xanthippus at sea, both recalled from their period of
ostracism: perhaps the Athenians thought that they too should be
given their opportunity. During this campaign the Athenians had

to abandon their city and it was sacked by the Persians, but they emerged from the Persian Wars with an enthusiastic and active citizen body and with pride in their achievements.

# 4

# THE GREEKS AND THE NEAR-EASTERN KINGDOMS

Herodotus' history is an account of the conflicts between Greeks and Asiatics which culminates in the Ionian Revolt of the 490s and the Persian invasions of Greece in 490 and 480–479; from V. 28 to the end he provides a narrative from 499.[1] From the Near East we have no narrative histories, but we have documents of various kinds, ranging from kings' commemorations of their achievements to clay tablets from Persepolis which record administrative details.[2]

While the Greeks settled on the Aegean coast, the rest of Asia Minor was inhabited by non-Greeks. In the south-west corner were the Carians, who became substantially hellenised, and whose history was bound up with that of the Asiatic Greeks. From the end of the second millennium inland Asia Minor was dominated by the Phrygians, whose capital was at Gordium, south-west of modern Ankara. A king called Midas (confused in oral tradition with a legendary figure who had ass's ears and whose touch turned everything to gold), in the late eighth century, had a Greek wife and made dedications at Delphi. From the first half of the seventh century they were supplanted by the Lydians, nearer to the Aegean, with their capital at Sardis, about 55 miles = 90 km inland from Smyrna. A new Lydian dynasty was founded by Gyges,[3] and he and his successors reduced the Asiatic Greeks to some kind of subordination, while making dedications at Delphi and other Greek sanctuaries. It was the Lydians who first issued coinage, about the beginning of the sixth century.[4]

Further East the leading power in the early centuries of the first millennium was the Assyrian Empire (referred to as 'neo-Assyrian' in contrast to two previous periods of power in the early and the late second millennium), whose capital was at Nineveh, on the Tigris near Mosul in northern Iraq. To the south of that was Babylon, on the Euphrates near Al Hillal in Iraq, conquered by the Assyrians in the second half of the eighth century. To the south-east of Assyria was Media, which became united and powerful in the seventh century, with its capital at Ecbatana (Hamadan, in western Iran); to the east of Babylon was Elam, with its capital at Susa, in western Iran; Persia, in the mountains to the East of the Persian Gulf, centred on Anshan, was a dependency of Elam.

In the first half of the seventh century Assyria was still powerful, and it destroyed Susa in 646. However, at the end of the century Assyria was overthrown by a combination of Media and a revived Babylon (the 'neo-Babylonian' kingdom), which destroyed Nineveh in 612. Probably what remained of Elam was absorbed into Babylon, and Persia broke away. The Mediterranean coast was disputed between Babylon and Egypt, with Babylon prevailing, and deporting the Jews by instalments in the 590s and 580s (Jerusalem was destroyed in 587). Persia became powerful under Cyrus II (559–530): Herodotus' representation of him as a vassal of the Medes who revolted against them appears from other evidence to be mistaken; he may well himself have been Elamite, though it may be true that he had some kind of family connection with the Median royal family. He and Nabonidus of Babylon fought against Astyages of Media, who was perhaps the attacker, and were victorious in 550/49 when the Median commander Harpagus deserted to them. In 539/8 he captured Babylon. The Persians were in general supportive of local religions: here Cyrus restored the traditional religion which had been disrupted by Nabonidus, and began the release of the exiled Jews (perhaps to create a bulwark against Egypt).

The downfall of the Medes left a power vacuum in the region, which attracted not only Cyrus but also the king of Lydia, Croesus, who ruled from c.560 and had alliances with Babylon and Egypt. Croesus is said to have consulted the Delphic oracle, made the strongest of the Greeks his ally (his investigations showed that that meant Sparta), and acted on the prediction that if he crossed the River Halys (which flows North to the Black Sea from the Anatolian plateau) he would destroy a great empire. In or about 546 Croesus marched East beyond the Halys, and Cyrus marched North to meet him. After an indecisive battle Croesus retired to Sardis for the winter and called on his allies to support him next spring, but Cyrus followed him, defeated the Lydians and broke into the city: the empire which Croesus destroyed was his own. There are stories of Croesus' being saved at the last minute from being burned alive: probably he did survive, as Nabonidus survived later after the fall of Babylon.

The Greek cities on the coast then fell to the Persians, and Sparta in response to an appeal sent one ship to investigate and to warn the Persians not to harm the Greeks, but did no more than that;[5] some men from some cities fled to colonies elsewhere. Samos and the other island states close to the mainland may have made token submission, but they had not been subject to the Lydians and did not yet become effectively subject to the Persians.

Cyrus died in 530 in a war on his north-eastern frontier, and was succeeded by his son Cambyses. He gained control of the Phoenician coast and Cyprus with their navies; and in 525 he conquered Egypt, after which he made expeditions West to Cyrene and South to Ethiopia but did not gain effective control of them. In 522 his rule was challenged by a man who claimed to be his brother – and who may actually have been his brother, though the story told afterwards was that Cambyses had secretly killed his brother and this man was an impostor. Cambyses himself died on his way back from Egypt, and in a counter-coup Darius I (Cambyses' spear-bearer in Egypt) with the backing of six other nobles killed this claimant and became the next king. Herodotus insists on the authenticity of a debate among the seven over democracy, oligarchy and monarchy,[6] but the debate belongs to the Greek world of Herodotus' own time, and the only question was who should be the next king. The episode provoked various revolts, and Darius in the inscription at Bisitun in which he gives his version of the story boasts of their suppression.[7] He claimed to be from another branch of what he advertised as the Achaemenid family: that may not be true, but he established marriage links with the family of Cyrus and Cambyses and with his fellow conspirators, and from then on important positions went overwhelmingly to members of his family and the families of the others.

Darius emphasised the worship of Ahuramazda; the Old Persian script was perhaps created for him;[8] near Anshan he completed the palace which Cyrus had begun at Pasargadae and himself began a new palace at Persepolis, and he also began a new palace at Susa (which Greek writers generally considered to be the Persian capital). He greatly improved the organisation of the empire in satrapies (provinces, governed by a satrap). Clay tablets at Persepolis preserve records comparable to the Linear B tablets of the Mycenaeans: these and other documents show that Greeks were among the workmen employed on Darius' palaces, and Greeks found their way into other positions also, for instance as secretaries. In the Greek world Darius did gain control of the island states close to the coast of Asia Minor. Polycrates of Samos was killed *c.*522 by Oroetes, the satrap of Lydia; Oroetes tried to set himself up as an independent ruler but was killed by an agent of Darius; Polycrates' brother Syloson was eventually installed in Samos as tyrant by the Persians,[9] and soon died and was succeeded by his son Aeaces. Before long Chios and Lesbos were similarly made subject to Persia; and as in Samos Darius generally controlled the Greek cities through vassal tyrants.

Greeks tended to see the world as divided into Europe and Asia, with Europe as their own domain and Asia as the Persians'. The Persians' first main venture into Europe was aimed not at the Greeks but at the Scythians, north of the Danube, *c.*514: all the peoples to the north of their empire were considered to be Scythians; a Scythian rebel in the east was the last rebel recorded by Darius at Bisitun,[10] and Herodotus has perhaps conflated the expedition of *c.*514 with an earlier one north-west of the Caspian. The Chersonese and Byzantium had already been added to the empire. Darius brought an army from Susa, added the Asiatic Greeks including the islanders to his force, had a bridge of boats across the Bosporus designed by a Samian, advanced to the Danube and had a bridge built there by the Greeks. Whatever he tried to do beyond the Danube, he was unsuccessful. The story which reached Herodotus was that he authorised the Greeks to desert if he did not return within 60 days; he did not return in time, and the Scythians incited the Greeks to break the bridge. The Athenian Miltiades from the Chersonese[11] wanted to break the bridge; Histiaeus from Miletus argued that the tyrants owed their positions to Persian backing; a little of the bridge was broken, but when the Persians arrived they were able to cross.[12] It may be true that the Scythians urged the Greeks to leave Darius stranded North of the Danube, and is certainly true that the Greeks did not do so.

Darius returned to Asia, leaving Megabazus to conquer coastal Thrace, and rewarding Histiaeus for his loyalty by appointing him to found a settlement in Thrace at Myrcinus, near the later Amphipolis. Megabazus transported to Asia a body of Paeonians from the north of the Macedonian region, and perhaps obtained the token submission of king Amyntas of Macedon; but he distrusted Histiaeus, and on returning to Asia persuaded Darius to recall him and take him to Susa. Shortly afterwards Scythian raiders went as far as the Chersonese, and whatever the Persians had gained in Europe was effectively lost.

So far the Persians had shown no sign of wanting to advance further into the Greek world, though Herodotus has a story that a Greek doctor from Italy, Democedes, through Darius' wife urged Darius to attack Greece rather than Scythia, and used a reconnaissance expedition as a means of returning home.[13] However, when a body of rich men exiled from Naxos, the largest island in the Cyclades, appealed to Aristagoras, Histiaeus' successor in Miletus, Aristagoras proposed action to Artaphernes, the Persian satrap in Sardis, and he persuaded Darius, who sent a commander. In 499 a force was sent to attack Naxos, but the Naxians got to hear of it and the attack failed. Aristagoras expected to be blamed, and had been receiving messages from Histiaeus (perhaps that Darius was talking of deporting the Ionians as the Paeonians had been deported), so he decided on what has come to be known as the Ionian Revolt. He resigned his tyranny and arranged for the deposition of the other tyrants, and (retaining some kind of commanding position) he went to Greece, where he failed to convince the Spartans but obtained 20 ships from

Athens and five from Eretria in Euboea.[14] Herodotus focuses on Aristagoras and Histiaeus, but we need to know why the Ionians should have trusted them when they deserted the Persians, and embarked on revolt after half a century of subjection. Tyrants had fallen elsewhere in the Greek world, and perhaps were becoming less tolerable here; the Scythian expedition and its aftermath had shown that the Persians were not invincible; and perhaps a genuine fear of deportation, whether justified or not, had been aroused.

Action began with an attack on Sardis in 498, but the Greeks were pursued and defeated in their return to the coast, and the Athenians then withdrew.[15] In 497 the revolt spread as far as Byzantium in the North and Cyprus (over many centuries poised between the Greek world and the Asiatic world, as it still is in our time) in the South; but, while the Persians did not keep large forces in their provinces, in time they could always send large forces, and they struck back. Aristagoras departed in 496 to Myrcinus in Thrace, perhaps hoping to watch events and make a deal with the eventual winners, but he was killed in a battle with the Thracians. In 495 the Persians prepared for a major assault on Miletus; the Ionians planned to fight at sea, but they were defeated in a battle off the island of Lade, and in 494 Miletus was captured (and men were deported from there to the Persian Gulf). Persia's reconquest of the region continued into 493.

Meanwhile Histiaeus had persuaded Darius to send him to Ionia. He went first to Sardis, but Artaphernes did not trust him; he then went to the Greeks on Chios, from which an attempt to reinstate him in Miletus failed. After a period of piracy in Byzantium he returned to the Aegean, and went to Thasos, off the Thracian coast; but in 493 as the Persians were completing their reconquest he moved to Lesbos, crossed to the mainland, and there was captured by the Persians, who sent his head to Darius. It seems clear that he was trusted by Darius but not by Darius' subordinates; once he had been rejected by Artaphernes his career looks like a series of opportunistic moves, in which he eventually judged wrongly.

Herodotus regarded the revolt as a disaster, but Artaphernes' settlement in 493 (including a reassessment of the tribute paid by the cities) seems not to have been harsh, and in 492 Mardonius replaced the tyrannies in the cities with constitutional government (though we find later that some tyrannies survived or were reintroduced). It was probably in 493/2 that Darius sent demands to Greece for the submission of the cities there – his sights were now set on Greece, and he wanted to punish Athens and Eretria for their support of the Ionian Revolt – and some cities did submit though Athens and Sparta did not.[16] Mardonius advanced into Thrace with an army and navy, and Thasos and the coastal cities, and Macedon, submitted. He may have been intending to continue by the land route into Greece, or to prepare for a later expedition, but his fleet was wrecked off the promontory of Athos and his army suffered heavy losses in a battle, so he withdrew. In 491 there were rumours of revolt in Thasos, but in the face of an ultimatum it backed down.

In 490 the Persians did attack Greece, and Athens and Eretria in particular. They were commanded by Datis (a Mede, unusually, who had been involved in suppressing the Ionian Revolt) and Artaphernes (son of the satrap at Sardis), and this time they took the sea route through the Cyclades. On Naxos, where they had failed in 499, they burned the city and enslaved the inhabitants whom they caught. At Delos the population fled but they did no damage. From other islands they conscripted soldiers and took hostages. Carystus, at the south end of Euboea, originally refused to comply and was besieged until it did. In Eretria the citizens were divided, but they withstood a siege until some men betrayed the city to the Persians, after which the temples were burned and the people enslaved.

Turning their attention to Athens, the Persians landed on the plain of Marathon, in the north-east of Attica: it was close to Eretria, and they had with them the ex-tyrant Hippias, whose family was from eastern Attica;[17] this was a suitable place to wait for treachery, and they camped at the north-east end of the plain. The full Athenian army marched out to Marathon, with the polemarch (military archon) and the ten generals (now the effective commanders), one of whom was Miltiades, who had returned to Athens at the end of the Ionian Revolt.[18] They camped at the south-west end of the plain, about 25 miles = 40 km from the city and guarding the routes towards it. The disagreement among the generals which Herodotus places there may in fact have been an earlier disagreement on whether to go to Marathon or to stay and defend the city. Help came from nearby Plataea, and a runner sent to Sparta obtained a promise that the Spartans would come after holding a festival – not unreasonably: such matters were taken seriously, and the Athenians could be expected to hold out for a time.

But, before the Persians had obtained the betrayal of the city or the Athenians had obtained reinforcements from Sparta, a battle was fought. The Persians had perhaps given up hope of betrayal and started embarking their cavalry to sail round to Athens. Most scholars have placed the battle in the south-west of the plain, near the *soros*, the mound where the Athenian dead were buried, in which case the Persian infantry must have made an advance to which the Athenians responded; some now locate it near the marsh which there was in the north-eastern half of the plain, in which case the Athenians will have taken the initiative. The Athenians were outnumbered, but thinned their centre so that their front matched that of the Persians; and when the Persians broke through their centre their wings turned in and defeated the Persians. Deaths were allegedly 6,400 on the Persian side and 192 on the Athenian, not incredible when hoplites faced inferior opponents.

The Persians then sailed round to the coast near Athens, but when they arrived (probably the next day) they found that the Athenians had returned already, and they withdrew. The story of a runner who hurried back to Athens (the origin of the modern marathon race), announced the victory and then dropped dead had entered the tradition by the fourth century, but is not in Herodotus and is probably invented. Herodotus did know a story that the Alcmaeonids had been signalling to the Persians: he accepted that somebody had been signalling, but with inadequate arguments he denied that the Alcmaeonids could have done so. Votes against the Alcmaeonids in the ostracisms of the 480s[19] show that the accusation was at any rate contemporary.

Miltiades with the whole Athenian fleet attacked the island state of Paros, which had contributed one ship to the Persians; during an unsuccessful siege he was wounded; on returning to Athens he was fined a large sum for deceiving the people by false promises (a charge to which the authors of failed policies were always vulnerable) and fined a large sum. He died from his wound, and the fine was paid by his son Cimon, who was to be a leading figure in the 470s and 460s.[20]

The Persians were now even more in need of revenge on Athens, but the Aegean was simply at one corner of their empire. Late in 486 Egypt revolted; Darius died and was succeeded by his son Xerxes; and by the beginning of 484 the revolt had been put down. There were also revolts in Babylon, perhaps one before 480–479 and one after. But in 485/4 Xerxes began preparations for a large-scale campaign against Greece which he would command himself, this time intending to use the land route on which Mardonius had set out in 492; preparations included a bridge across the River Strymon, which enters the Aegean between Thasos and Chalcidice, and a canal across the isthmus of Athos, to avoid a repetition of Mardonius' disaster.

Unless Themistocles' plan for a new Athenian navy was prompted by expectation of the Persian invasion,[21] the Greeks showed no sign of apprehension until 481, when Xerxes arrived with his land forces at Sardis. There was then a conference of Greeks wanting to resist, perhaps in Sparta. Sparta was accepted as leader; disputes among the Greeks were resolved, notably that between Athens and Aegina; spies were sent to Sardis, where they were shown Xerxes' large forces and sent back to report. Appeals were sent in vain to some Greeks not represented: Argos, which would not accept Spartan leadership;[22] Syracuse in Sicily, which in fact in 480 was to be embroiled in a war at home against the Carthaginians;[23] Corcyra, off the West Coast of Greece, which promised 60 ships which never arrived; Crete, which was not in danger, and at this time was outside the main stream of Greek affairs.[24] In the winter Xerxes sent heralds to demand the submission of the Greeks (perhaps not to Sparta and Athens, which had spurned Darius' demand), but it is not clear how many states did submit before the Persians arrived.

Herodotus, perhaps imagining that Xerxes brought the total manpower of his empire, credited him with over 2,600,000 men in the army and navy plus an equal number of non-combatants: modern scholars reckon between 100,000 and 300,000 men in the army (but attempts to arrive at a figure by reinterpreting some of Herodotus' data are unprofitable). Matching a possible interpretation of Aeschylus' *Persians*,[25] he gave Xerxes a fleet of 1,200 ships, but reduced it through storms to not many more than the Greeks had. His figures for Greek soldiers deployed on different occasions are credible; his Greek fleet of 378 ships was perhaps the total number in use at any time during 480 (Aeschylus had 300 or 310 at Salamis).

Both sides needed to keep army and navy level with each other: triremes needed a friendly shore to which they could put in at night, and if they went ahead of the army they would lack that; while if the army went ahead of the navy the enemy might land men in its rear. Xerxes needed to follow a route which was practicable for a large army; the Greeks needed to resist in narrow places where smaller forces could withstand larger. Neither side had the detailed geographical knowledge which we today take for granted: general information could be picked up, but (for instance) it is entirely credible that neither side knew about the Anopaea path at Thermopylae before arriving there.

Xerxes left Sardis in spring 480, used a bridge of boats to cross the Hellespont, and proceeded along the Thracian coast to Macedon (where King Alexander I was nominally a Persian vassal but was or afterwards claimed to be sympathetic to the Greeks). Some Thessalians appealed to the spring council of the Greek resistance, and an army of 10,000 was sent to hold the gorge of Tempe, through which Xerxes was expected to proceed to the interior of Thessaly. Sparta did not send a king; the Athenians in this and in every episode this year were commanded by Themistocles. But after a few days Tempe was abandoned: they had gone far too soon, the Thessalians were divided, and they found that there were other routes available to Xerxes. After that Thessaly had to submit to the Persians.

The Greeks next decided to send an army to Thermopylae, where there was a narrow coastal strip (much narrower then than it is today) beside the gulf level with the north-west corner of Euboea, and the navy to Artemisium, at the north end of Euboea facing the Gulf of Pagasae. The army under the Spartan king Leonidas comprised 3,000–4,000 men from the Peloponnese and somewhat over 2,000 from central Greece. The Carnea in Sparta and the Olympic festival were approaching, and we need not doubt that this force was considered sufficient for a short time and that more men were to be sent after the festivals. Herodotus has 280 Greek ships at Artemisium, the Athenians arriving in two instalments (perhaps because they were unable to dispatch the whole of their large fleet at once). Here and on other occasions Herodotus has the Greeks first panicking but afterwards fighting bravely.

Probably in late August, for three days there was fighting in both places: on the first two days at Thermopylae the Greeks succeeded in holding back the Persians, at Artemisium the Greeks began small-scale action too late in the day for a full battle to develop. At Thermopylae the Persians then found a guide for the Anopaea path through the mountains which enabled their élite force to descend in the Greeks' rear: Leonidas on learning of the path had sent Phocians from nearby to defend it, who when the Persians came fled homewards. When he realised that he was trapped, Leonidas sent most of his force away, but with the Spartans and the Boeotians (whose cities would now inevitably fall to the Persians) he stayed and fought to the death. At Artemisium the Persians attacked the Greeks, who beat them off but with heavy losses. News from Thermopylae then reached the Greek fleet: there was now no point in their remaining, and they withdrew during the night.

There was nowhere else North of the Isthmus of Corinth where the Greeks could hope to halt the Persian advance: this was a major setback, though afterwards it was presented as a heroic episode in the ultimately successful struggle. The Persians proceeded through Boeotia (where they found collaborators, particularly in Thebes) to Attica, and eventually captured and sacked Athens, obtaining their revenge at last. Apart from a few men who refused to leave the Athenian acropolis, Attica had been evacuated. The Greek navy helped in the evacuation and based itself on the island of Salamis; an army of Peloponnesians started fortifying the Isthmus. Herodotus has a series of meetings at Salamis in which the Greeks considered withdrawing to the Peloponnese and Themistocles argued against: if they did not stay, they would probably disperse, and the Persians would be able to sail past the Isthmus. (In addition, at Salamis the

Greeks were a target in their own right, and it would probably not have occurred to the Persians to use a few of their ships to keep them there while the rest sailed to the Peloponnese.) In the end, the battle, fairly certainly in late September, is said to have been brought about by a deceptive message sent by Themistocles to Xerxes.

For Salamis we have in addition to Herodotus Aeschylus' tragedy *Persians*,[26] produced in 472 whereas Herodotus was writing about the 440s–430s, and on various points Aeschylus is the more credible. For him Themistocles' message was to deceive only the Persians, who spent the night in open water waiting for a Greek escape which did not happen; in the morning the Greeks launched their ships and enticed the tired Persians into the strait between the island and the mainland. For Herodotus Themistocles needed to bring about a battle before the Greeks could escape; and the Persians infiltrated the strait unnoticed by the Greeks during the night but still waited for the Greeks to take the initiative in the morning. Once the battle had begun there was a *mêlée* of many ships in a confined space, where the Persians could not benefit from their ships' greater manoeuvrability and skill. The result was a Greek victory, after which the Persian fleet and Xerxes with most of the army returned to Asia, though Mardonius remained in Greece with part of the army.

Persian attempts to win over Athens were unsuccessful. In 479 the Peloponnesians continued fortifying the Isthmus, but in late summer (perhaps with less difficulty than Herodotus supposed) Athens persuaded Sparta to send northwards an army under the regent Pausanias. (Leonidas had been succeeded by his brother Cleombrotus; but he had died, and his son Pausanias was regent for Leonidas' son.) The Athenian commander was Aristides.[27] The armies faced each other near Plataea, between the Persian base at Thebes and the mountains separating Boeotia from Attica: on the Greek side about 40,000 hoplites and perhaps a similar number of light-armed, and on the Persian side perhaps a comparable force. A first position did not tempt either side to a battle; the Greeks moved to a second position more likely to tempt the Persians, but after some days the Persians made that untenable; a Greek withdrawal towards Plataea, probably less chaotic than Herodotus suggests, did tempt the Persians to a battle, in which Mardonius was killed and the Greeks were victorious. The surviving Persians fled, and the Greeks besieged Thebes.

At sea 479 began with the Persians' fleet based on Samos, and a Greek fleet of 110 ships under the Spartan king Leotychidas based first on Aegina and later, after an appeal from Chios, on Delos. After another appeal, from opponents of Persia on Samos, the Greeks advanced to Samos; and as they approached the Persians withdrew to the south side of the Mycale promontory on the mainland, where they had an army, and sent their Phoenician ships home. The Greeks followed them, landed, and won a battle, perhaps about the same time as Plataea, perhaps somewhat later. After adding eastern Greeks to their alliance they sailed North to destroy Xerxes' bridge of boats across the Hellespont, but found that storms had done that the previous winter. Leotychidas and the Peloponnesians returned home; in a foreshadowing of Athens' future activity the Athenians under Xanthippus[28] and the eastern Greeks stayed on to besiege and capture Sestos, in the Chersonese.

The Greeks had not been united, but those who opposed the Persians fought with patriotic determination, and created a heightened sense of Greek solidarity, while Xerxes had a force pressed into service from all the provinces of his empire. Strategically, the terrain of Greece was in any case unsuitable for a large force, and the Greeks picked points for resistance where the Persians' superior numbers would particularly fail to help them. The Persians had the better ships and crews, but were not given the opportunity to fight in open waters; Greek hoplites were better than the Persians' infantry. The Persians did nevertheless overrun Greece as far as the Isthmus of Corinth. Herodotus thought the perseverance of the Athenians, even after evacuating their own city, was crucial: if they had gone over to the Persians, the Peloponnese could not have been saved.[29]

We now know that the Persians would never invade Europe again; but nobody on either side could have known that at the end of 479, and it must have been generally expected that after a few years the Persians would try to avenge their defeat.

# Classical Greece, *c.*500–323

# 5

# THE *PENTECONTAETIA*, 478–431

## THE ATHENIAN EMPIRE

'Classical' Greece is the Greece of the fifth and fourth centuries. This is a period on which we are comparatively well informed, as we have narratives by contemporaries and near-contemporaries and other contemporary literary texts of various kinds, and an increasing body of texts inscribed on stone or metal. Many of our texts were written by Athenians or by other Greeks active in Athens, and this is a period when Athens was not merely one of the largest Greek cities but was culturally predominant and politically important, to a much greater extent than earlier or later.

Thucydides, the historian of the Peloponnesian War, included in the introduction to his history a sketchy and selective account of the (almost) fifty years between the end of the Persian and the beginning of the Peloponnesian War (the word *pentekontaetia*, 'fifty-year period', is due to an ancient commentator on Thucydides), in order to justify his view that the truest reason for the Peloponnesian War was Athens' growing power and Sparta's fear of it.[1] Later accounts of this period, particularly in the history of Diodorus Siculus (XI. 38 – XII. 32) and Plutarch's *Lives* of Athenians active then, tend on these matters to give more details of episodes mentioned by Thucydides rather than episodes omitted by him, and it is not always clear how reliable this information is. Thucydides gives few chronological indications in his account. Diodorus organised his history by years (though his source for Greek history, Ephorus, did not): he commonly assigned one major story to each year, but where he can be checked his assignments prove unreliable; shorter notes of what happened 'in the same year' seem to come from a table of dates and have a better claim to be considered seriously.[2]

In the early fifth century we have epigrams by writers such as Simonides, and lyric poetry, often for victors in the great games, by writers such as Pindar. Later the main verse form is Athenian drama: tragedy from the 470s onwards by Aeschylus, Sophocles and Euripides, almost always on themes from the legendary past; and comedy from the 420s onwards by Aristophanes and by other writers from whom no complete plays survive, grounded in contemporary public life.

Public inscriptions[3] become more numerous in the classical period, particularly, and probably as a result of deliberate policy, in democratic Athens from the 450s onwards. They provide such texts as treaties between states, laws and decrees,[4] war-related items such as thanksgiving dedications and casualty lists, and financial records of various kinds. In almost all cases they are authentic, in that they are the texts published by the appropriate authorities at the time, but they do not tell the whole story (for instance, decisions tend to be recorded with no explanation or with an uninformatively bland explanation, and there was no indication of whether they were controversial). In addition, only a minority of inscriptions are preserved complete and with every letter legible, and in other cases editors have to make what they can of what survives. Many incomplete texts do not contain a secure indication of their date, and acceptance that a doctrine about changes in letter-forms in Athens which held sway for more than a century was too rigid has added to the uncertainties (in Fornara's collection no opinion is given where different dates have been proposed).

At the end of 479 nobody could have known or expected that the Persians would never invade Europe again.[5] In 478 the two Spartan commanders of 479 exchanged postings: Leotychidas took an army to Thessaly in northern Greece, where he was said to have taken bribes.[6] Pausanias took a fleet first to Cyprus[7] and afterwards to Byzantium, but his arrogant behaviour made him unpopular (this could not have been predicted), and when a new Spartan commander arrived he was rejected. Athens, which after earlier isolation had during the sixth century developed increasing overseas interests,[8] emerged as the leader of a new alliance, known to scholars as the Delian League because its centre was on the island of Delos, sacred to the god Apollo (figure 10).[9] This was a full and permanent alliance, ostensibly to continue the war against the Persians, with member states required to contribute ships for the war or to pay *phoros* ('tribute') which subsidised the Athenian navy. It is not clear how rapidly it grew, but by the middle of the century it included nearly all the islands of the Aegean and cities on its Thracian and Asiatic coasts.

The league was organised by Aristides,[10] but in its early campaigns it was commanded by Cimon, the son of Miltiades.[11] Among early episodes which Thucydides mentions are actions against the Persians and against Greeks who had supported them, including a major land and sea victory against the Persians at the mouth of the River Eurymedon, on the South Coast of Asia Minor, in the early 460s; but also actions of particular benefit to Athens, such as the capture of Scyros, in the northern Aegean with a legendary connection to Athens and lying on the route between Athens and the Hellespont, in the mid 470s (this, together with Lemnos and Imbros, became a mainstay of Athens' control of the northern Aegean). Athens took a permanent alliance to mean permanent warfare, and demanded ships and tribute each year, thus beginning to build up its power over

Figure 10. Delos: Lion terrace (seventh century).

other Greek cities in a wholly unprecedented way (tribute was familiar in the near-eastern empires but not in Greece). This prompted revolts, which were suppressed: in Naxos, perhaps in the late 470s, and in Thasos, in 465/4–463/2; and in the end almost all member states found it less troublesome to pay tribute than to provide ships with their crews each summer. At the beginning it was taken for granted that the members were members of a free alliance; but, as with Russia and eastern Europe in the Soviet period, although Athens never destroyed the formal separate existence of the separate states, it increasingly encroached on their freedom in various ways.

Between c.465/4 and c.456/5 Sparta had to deal with a rebellion in Messenia: Athens under the pro-Spartan Cimon was among the allies which supported Sparta, but in his absence a group of democratic and anti-Spartan politicians became predominant, the Spartans dismissed the Athenians, and the Athenians ostracised Cimon.[12] Under Pericles and others Athens broke with Sparta and made alliances with Argos and Thessaly, and in the 450s, while continuing to fight against the Persians, also set about adding to its power in Greece (in what is sometimes called the First Peloponnesian War). Fighting against Persia took the league first to Cyprus and then to Egypt (where it accepted an invitation to support a rebellion against Persia: Egypt had been attracting Greek traders and mercenaries for two centuries) and Phoenicia; but the campaign in Egypt ended in disaster c.454. Nearer home the Athenians forced Aegina[13] into the league, gained the adherence of Megara, on the Isthmus of Corinth, and campaigned in various places, most notably winning control of Boeotia and of Phocis, the region which included Delphi. Since the beginning of the century they had been developing Piraeus as a harbour town, and they now built long walls linking Athens to Piraeus in a single fortified area with access to the sea.

But, while the campaign in Egypt ended in failure, the expansion in Greece ran out of steam, and it was probably fear of a Persian resurgence that led the Athenians in 454 to transfer the league's treasury from Delos to Athens. A consequence of that was the inscription from 453 onwards of the 'Athenian Tribute Lists', lists of the 1/60 of each year's tribute given as an offering to the goddess Athena and, conveniently for historians, calculated not on the total but on each member's payment. Reconstructing these from the surviving fragments has been a Herculean task, and it would be too much to hope that the current reconstruction is correct in every detail, but they do give a good indication of the amounts paid by different members, and some indication of which members did pay in which years. About the same time meetings of allies seem to have been discontinued: after this league policy was decided by Athens on its own.

Cimon was ostracised in 461 and returned in 451; a five-year truce between Athens and the Peloponnesians was perhaps his doing. He then led another campaign to Cyprus, but was killed, and after that we hear no more of active warfare against the Persians. From the fourth century onwards everybody knew of a Peace of Callias between Athens and the Persians, which excluded the Persians from the Aegean and western Asia Minor.[14] But this is one of a number of purported fifth-century documents for which there is no good fifth-century evidence, and I hold to the minority view that, while active warfare did come to an end, the Peace of Callias was invented after the Peace of Antalcidas of 387/6,[15] to make more vivid the contrast between the glories of the fifth century and the humiliation of the fourth.

What was to become of the Delian League? The first tribute lists show considerable irregularity in payments in the late 450s and early 440s, and if the current reconstruction is right there was no collection of tribute in 449/8. An Athenian decree for Erythrae in Asia Minor, probably of the late 450s, deals with offerings at the Panathenaea, imposes a democratic constitution and refers to men who have fled to the Persians (two reconstructions translated Fornara 71), so at least to that extent Persia seems to have been encouraging defections from Athens. Various signs of Athens' impinging on the allies' freedom appear about the middle of the century: constitutional interference (when provocation and opportunity arose: Athens did not do this systematically, but in the second half of the fifth century democracy and links with Athens, and oligarchy and links with Sparta, tended to go together); the transfer of some categories of lawsuits from local to Athenian courts; allied contributions to Athenian festivals;[16] the establishment of 'cleruchies', bodies of Athenians assigned land in an allied state, and opportunities for richer Athenians to become owners of land in allied territory (whereas normally only citizens of a state could own land there).

If there was a year with no tribute, that may indicate that the Athenians were themselves uncertain what to do with the league; Plutarch mentions an Athenian proposal for a congress which seems intended to enlarge the Delian League into a league of all the Greeks, which did not meet because the Spartans refused to attend;[17] but the upshot certainly was that the league continued, with tribute and Athenian control, even though regular fighting did not. In 447/6 a programme of major building on the Athenian acropolis (figure 11) began, to include the Parthenon as the home of a gold and ivory statue of Athena, the Propylaea as a grand entrance-building, and outside that a temple of Athena Nike (goddess of victory). The Erechtheum was begun perhaps after the Peace of Nicias and finished in the last decade of the century. It is unlikely, though some texts allege it, that until 447/6 temples destroyed by the Persians had deliberately been left in ruins. Among other build-

Figure 11. Athens: acropolis; Propylaea to left, Erechtheum in background, Parthenon to right (all second half of fifth century), Odeum of Herodes Atticus in foreground (second century AD).

ings of this period was the Odeum, below the acropolis to the south-east, specifically attributed to Pericles. Whether there was a direct transfer of funds from the Delian League's treasury for this purpose is uncertain, but by subsidising Athens in other ways the League contributed indirectly if not directly: Plutarch reports that Pericles was challenged on this, and replied that as long as Athens kept the allies safe from the Persians it did not owe them an account of how the money was spent.[18] Some earlier buildings had resulted from private benefactions. Though the Athenians did not bear all the costs themselves, these were public buildings, decided on by the assembly and supervised by boards of publicly appointed over-seers.

In 447/6 Athens faced a series of crises: Boeotia revolted, and was lost to Athens; the cities of Euboea, among the league's first members, followed; and while Pericles was there with an army Megara revolted too, and under the Spartan king Plistoanax the Peloponnesians invaded Attica. Pericles returned; perhaps as a result of private negotiation, the Peloponnesians did not advance beyond the area of Eleusis. Taking bribes was considered wicked, but giving them in a good cause was not: it was believed on both sides that Pericles had bribed Plistoanax; Plistoanax was exiled by the Spartans, but the Athenians were happy to tell the story that Pericles in his accounts for that year had included ten talents 'for necessary expenses'. After the Peloponnesian with-drawal Pericles recovered Euboea. In 446/5 the Thirty Years' Peace was made, by which Athens gave up most of its gains on the Greek mainland, and the division of the Greek world into rival Athenian and Spartan blocs was formally recognised.

Superficially this seemed a victory for Sparta, but after it the Athenians reckoned that, although they could not expand into Spar-ta's sphere, they could continue to expand anywhere else. In the West they reinforced Sybaris in Italy perhaps in 446/5 and refounded it as Thurii perhaps in 444/3, and they were involved in a refoun-dation of Neapolis and made alliances with other cities;[19] in Thrace they founded Amphipolis (after earlier attempts), near the mouth of the River Strymon, in 437/6; in north-western Greece, perhaps in the early 430s, they supported a refoundation of Amphilochian Argos; also in the 430s Pericles led an expedition to the south coast of the Black Sea, and Athens made an alliance with the kingdom of the Cimmerian Bosporus (Crimea), important as a source of grain. Evidence for these episodes is scattered; Thucydides narrates only a war of 440–439 in which Athens supported Miletus against Samos, one of the few members still contributing ships to the Delian League. The Samians obtained some help from Persia (in breach of the Peace of Callias if it existed), and Sparta considered supporting them (in breach of the Thirty Years' Peace) but failed to convince its allies in the Peloponnesian League; but although Athens was seriously challenged it succeeded in regaining control, and probably imposed a democratic constitution.

The empire brought economic gains to Athens, particularly through the tribute and access to land in the members' territory, though probably the Athenians thought primarily of power and glory and the economic gains were a by-product rather than a principal aim. An insistence on the use of Athenian weights, measures and coinage, probably in the 420s,[20] was convenient for the empire as a whole but will have been a blow to the pride of states prevented from retaining their own standards (compare debates on the Euro in recent times). While the member states remained theoretically separate and independent, and Athens did not interfere in their affairs systematically, it was always willing to do so if it seemed appropriate in particular cases. Religion was a part of Greek civic life, and the empire had a religious dimension, with the members required to send contributions to Athenian festivals. Benefits could be conferred on members whose loyalty Athens was anxious to retain: in the 420s Methone, on the Macedonian coast, was given special permission to import a stated quantity of grain from the Black Sea – which implies that other cities were not allowed to do that.[21] Thucydides represented Athenians as speaking hard-headedly about their power, and thought that the members resented their treatment:[22] some modern scholars have thought that only upper-class oligarchs resented it while democrats enjoyed the benefits of membership (including a safe and prosperous Aegean, and possibilities of employment in connection with the Athenian navy). Those who undoubtedly did benefit were democratic leaders who were in a powerful position in their cities and might not have been without Athenian support;

but in general Thucydides' view, though over-simplified, is probably nearer to the truth than the alternative.

## DEMOCRATIC ATHENS

Cleisthenes' new structures gave the Athenians practice in and a taste for political involvement;[23] the large navy created by Themistocles,[24] its success at Salamis and its use in building up the Delian League gave the poorest citizens, who provided many of the oarsmen, a stronger sense of belonging and worth than they had in other cities. After the Persian Wars Themistocles was responsible for resisting Spartan pressure and rebuilding the city and its walls, and there are various stories which depict him in an anti-Spartan light; but he and Aristides, the organiser of the Delian League, were then eclipsed by Cimon.[25] This led to his ostracism, perhaps in the late 470s; after a period in Argos he was accused of involvement with the Spartan Pausanias,[26] and fled first westwards but ultimately across the Aegean to the Persians. He was charged with 'medism', treasonable collaboration with the Persians (Greeks commonly referred to the Persians as Medes), but ironically he seems to have become guilty of it only after being charged with it.

Cimon remained predominant until Athens' war against Thasos:[27] at the end of that war he was accused of taking bribes to spare Macedon, but was acquitted. When Sparta appealed for help against the Messenians[28] he wanted to help, was opposed by Ephialtes, but went with four thousand soldiers. In his absence, in 462/1 Ephialtes, supported by the rising Pericles, attacked the council of former archons, the Areopagus,[29] whose power was becoming harder to justify as the archons were falling in importance[30] and the generals were rising, and transferred from it to other bodies judicial powers of political significance, probably involving the control of officials and major offences against the state. (It was perhaps the Areopagus which had condemned Themistocles and acquitted Cimon.) This was followed during the 450s by the opening of the archonship to all but the poorest citizens, the institution of travelling magistrates to decide lesser private lawsuits locally,[31] the introduction of payment for serving on juries, which was followed by payment for holding various civilian offices and finally, *c*.400, for attending the assembly,[32] and in 451/0, the work of Pericles, a law restricting citizenship to men with an Athenian mother as well as an Athenian father (probably reflecting a view that the benefits of Athenian citizenship should be enjoyed only by those who were genuinely Athenian); at the beginning of the Peloponnesian War Athens had perhaps 60,000 adult male citizens. The changes were controversial. Cimon was ostracised (allegedly for being both pro-Spartan and anti-democratic), Ephialtes was assassinated, and a few years later there was talk of an oligarchic plot, though nothing came of it.

There are reflections of these developments in the tragedies of Aeschylus. *Persians* in 473/2 had Pericles as *choregos*, the rich citizen paying for the production:[33] unusually it deals with the Persians' reaction to their defeat in 480,[34] and it stresses the role of Themistocles though without naming him (whether before or after his ostracism). *Suppliant Women*, probably in 464/3, represents legendary Argos and its king as strangely democratic, and in line 604 the 'powerful hand of the people' (*demou kratousa cheir*) lifted up to vote perhaps reflects the recent coinage of the word *demokratia*. *Eumenides*, in 459/8, features the Areopagus as a homicide court (a role which it retained after Ephialtes' reform), and in lines 681–710 describes it in such a way that scholars have disputed whether Aeschylus supported the reformers (as we should expect) or was turning against them. On the other side, in 469/8, possibly in response to the victory at the Eurymedon,[35] the archon called on Cimon and his fellow generals to judge the tragic competition, and they awarded the prize not to Aeschylus but to the young Sophocles.

Draco, Solon, Pisistratus, Cleisthenes, Ephialtes and Pericles had all contributed to Athens' political development. While much that happened in Athens had parallels elsewhere, by the middle of the fifth century Athens had gone further than other cities, and was self-consciously democratic, capable of imposing democratic changes on member states of the Delian League.[36] I believe that only Ephialtes and Pericles set out to make Athens more democratic; the term *demokratia* was perhaps coined about the 460s, and followed by *aristokratia* and *oligarchia* as favourable and unfavourable terms for non-monarchic régimes which were not democratic. (In contrast to our world, where almost all claim to approve of democracy but the term can be interpreted in various ways, not all Greeks of the Classical period did approve of democracy.) The main characteristics of democracy in classical Greece were that all or almost all (free, adult, male) native inhabitants of a city were citizens with some measure of political power, whereas oligarchic states allowed no power to the poorest, and that the assembly open to all qualified citizens met frequently and took many decisions, whereas oligarchic states limited the power of ordinary citizens in the assembly (e.g. the right to make proposals) and the power of the assembly *vis-à-vis* the authorities (by allowing more power to a small council and/or the officials).[37] Residents who had migrated from elsewhere (in Athens known as metics, *metoikoi*, a term meaning 'migrants' or 'those living with') could become citizens only in exceptional circumstances.

Athens had the standard pattern of council and assembly: the council of five hundred[38] was a representative body appointed for a year at a time. From at any rate the time of Ephialtes the fifty members from one tribe formed the *prytaneis* ('prytany', presiding body and standing committee) in turn for a tenth of the year. The assembly of citizens, probably by the end of the 430s, had forty regular meetings a year and could have additional meetings. It could decide only matters placed on its agenda by the council; but the council could make specific recommendations but did not have to do so, and in the assembly any citizen could speak, and could advance a proposal or an amendment to a proposal already made. Decision was by a simple majority, in most cases not counted but estimated from a show of hands (but ballots were used for decisions affecting individuals, which required a quorum of six thousand). There were no political parties with programmes and discipline: there were leading politicians (inevitably, richer men) who were more active than the average citizens, and who attracted more or less loyal supporters for a variety of reasons ranging from policies to personal connections; no leader, however predominant, could guarantee that the assembly would always vote as he wanted.

Administration was not by professional administrators (apart from a few clerks and public slaves) but by volunteer citizens devoting a year of their life to serving in a particular position. In the fifth century most offices were open to the upper three of Solon's four classes,[39] but none to the lowest (in the fourth century, with a smaller population, that limitation remained in theory but was no longer enforced). The work was divided into many separate jobs, assigned to separate officials or boards (commonly boards of ten, one from each tribe): this provided little scope for a skilful man to do good or an incompetent man to do harm, but involving the citizens was considered more important than finding the best men to do the work. The council was the centre of the administration, and many of the boards were appointed from members of the council. Appointment to the council and to most civilian offices was by lot, with no reappointment to the same position (but, at any rate in the fourth century, men could serve in the council twice; and enthusiasts could serve in several positions over a number of years). Appointment to the generalship and other military offices was by election, with no ban on reappointment: when instituted by Cleisthenes[40] the generals like other officials were one from each tribe; but not every tribe would necessarily be able to provide a good general; from *c.*440 exceptions were possible, and in the third quarter of the fourth century the tribal link was abandoned.[41] Office-holders were subjected to a *dokimasia*, a vetting (of their qualifications as good citizens rather than of their fitness for the position) before entering office, and to a financial (*logos*) and general accounting (*euthynai*) after leaving office.

Taxes were mostly indirect (sales taxes, and the like), and were mostly collected not by state officials but by syndicates of tax-farmers, who would bid for a year's contract and would hope to collect somewhat more than the sum which they were then bound to pay to the state. Rich men each year could volunteer for or have imposed on them the 'liturgies' (public services) of commanding and financing a ship in the navy or directing and financing a group of performers in a festival, the latter commonly in a competitive context;[42] and the rich were liable also, when a need for more money arose, to a property tax called *eisphora* and to appeals for voluntary donations (*epidoseis*).

In the area of justice, Solon's system of appeals against the verdicts of individual officials[43] had developed into a system by which in most cases the official simply checked that the case was in order and then took it to a jury-court (*dikasterion*) in which he presided but did not give a lead. Juries were large (from an annual panel of 6,000: the smallest numbered 201). There were no expert lawyers, but litigants were expected to plead their own cases, though they could employ speech-writers and could share their time with supporting speakers. No trial lasted longer than a day. Solon's distinction remained between public suits in which any citizen could prosecute and private suits in which the injured party or a member of the family prosecuted, and the travelling magistrates[44] decided without a jury private suits for sums up to ten drachmae. 'Common criminals' (highwaymen and the like), if they were manifestly guilty and admitted their guilt, could be dealt with summarily, and there were special procedures for some categories of offence.

This was democracy of a very direct kind: decisions were made in the assembly by as many citizens as wished and were able to attend; they were carried out by a sample picked each year from as many citizens (except the poorest) as wished and were able to take part; judicial decisions depended not on professional lawyers but on amateur officials and litigants and on large juries. Inevitably involvement was easier for those who were richer and/or lived near the centre, but the representative basis of the council and modest stipends mitigated that. From our perspective, the system had weaknesses: not all the decisions of the assembly were in conformity with a coherent policy; the administration set a higher value on involvement than on efficiency; the courts did not necessarily apply the law consistently on different occasions, and for public figures there was not a clear distinction between unlawful conduct and conduct which was unsatisfactory in other ways. But there were also strengths: many citizens were involved (while those who wished and could were able to gain considerable experience over the years, there was not a gulf between a ruling class and the rest); litigation required effort and exposure by the litigants, but it was cheap and quick, and many citizens availed themselves of it. In the fifth century, with tribute from the Delian League paying for things which the Athenians would otherwise have had to pay for themselves, until the last years of the Peloponnesian War, the Athenians had enough money to cover their expenses.

Thucydides saw the Athens of Pericles as 'in theory democracy but in fact rule by the first man'.[45] That was wishful thinking: Pericles (figure 12) was certainly one of the most prominent politicians from the 450s to his death in autumn 429, but in Athens neither he nor anybody else could control policy. He frequently served as general, but as one of a board of ten subject to annual election, and the office gave him little formal power inside the city. He had opponents: Cimon at first; Thucydides son of Melesias (perhaps a brother-in-law of Cimon and grandfather of the historian) in the 440s until he was ostracised *c.*443 (and there were other ostracisms about that time); democrats from families not previously prominent, who attacked him and people associated with him in the early 430s. He had links with men active in various fields: Pheidias the sculptor, who was general overseer of the buildings on the acropolis; Anaxagoras the philosopher. He did not himself make large numbers of speeches and propose large numbers of decrees, but he was involved in things of various kinds done by Athens during those decades, and it is reasonable to assume that, in so far as Athens did pursue coherent policies, they were policies which he approved of and championed.

## SPARTA AND THE PELOPONNESE

While the fact that the Spartan citizens were a

Figure 12. British Museum: bust of Pericles (Roman copy of bronze original).

minority in the population of their region, and the availability of helots, made it possible and necessary for them to concentrate on a military lifestyle, set them apart from other Greeks already in the archaic period, they were not then inward-looking and consciously austere as they became later.[46] In the Persian Wars they promised to help Athens in 490, though they did not arrive in time for the battle of Marathon, and they were accepted as leaders of the Greek resistance in 480–478.[47] However, in 478 King Leotychidas was accused of taking bribes in Thessaly, and after the regent Pausanias made himself unpopular in Byzantium the new Delian League was organised under Athens' leadership and the allies rejected another Spartan commander.[48] The decision may not have been unanimous, but Sparta accepted that rejection, and this is the first sign of a less ambitious Sparta. Pausanias after further adventures in the Aegean was recalled to Sparta again, was accused of treasonable involvement with both the Persians and the helots, and when he fled to a sanctuary was starved to death.

Argos had never accepted Spartan supremacy,[49] and in 480–479 it was one of the states which refused to join the resistance to Persia under Spartan leadership;[50] after defeat but not subjection by Sparta *c*.494 a change which perhaps involved a broadening of the citizen body had not changed the fundamentally anti-Spartan alignment.[51] For the 470s and 460s we have scraps of evidence for upheavals and fighting in which Sparta was embroiled across the Peloponnese from Elis in the west through Arcadia to Argos. In Elis and in Arcadian Mantinea there are reports of *synoikismos*;[52] in Argos the sons of the old ruling class are said to have reasserted themselves; the Athenian Themistocles after his ostracism made Argos his base for a time but (perhaps after that reassertion) did not feel safe there when Sparta accused him of treasonable involvement with Pausanias.[53] Nevertheless, from *c*.462/1 Argos was on good terms with democratic Athens;[54] about that time there was a reorganisation of the citizen body; later in the century Argos claimed to be democratic. Either there was a second change or the returning ruling class accommodated itself to a democratic movement.

Trouble nearer home arose for Sparta *c*.465/4, when an earthquake killed many of the citizens, beginning or accelerating a decline in their numbers which was never reversed,[55] and a rebellion broke out among the helots and *perioikoi* in Messenia. After a war lasting ten years, in which the Athenians were among the allies who came to help Sparta, but were dismissed and then ended their alliance with Sparta,[56] there was a settlement by which many of the Messenians were given a safe conduct out of the Peloponnese and were settled by Athens at Naupactus, on the north side of the Gulf of Corinth. Perhaps because of their continuing involvement in Messenia, the Spartans were not drawn into the opening years of the First Peloponnesian War against Athens;[57] but *c.*457, when they went to the support of their alleged homeland of Doris in central Greece, the Athenians blocked their return, and they did then fight and win at Tanagra in Boeotia. For the Athenians that was a short-lived setback: they returned to Boeotia and conquered it, and soon afterwards an Athenian expedition sailing round the Peloponnese burned the Spartans' dockyard at Gytheum.

In the later 450s Athens was doing less well, and in 451 it made a five-year truce with the Peloponnesians.[58] In the same year Argos made a 30 year peace with Sparta, and it prospered in the period which followed. Conflict over Delphi left the five-year truce technically unbroken, since Sparta and Athens intervened separately and did not fight against each other; but in 447/6, when Athens' problems included the defection of Megara, Sparta led a Peloponnesian invasion of Attica. That was followed by the Thirty Years' Peace of 446/5, in which Athens lost many of its mainland acquisitions but did not feel bound to limit its ambitions in the wider Greek world.[59] Sparta's proposal to break the peace by supporting Samos against Athens in 440–439, rejected by its allies in the Peloponnesian League,[60] showed that many Spartans viewed the unchastened Athens with disquiet.

## SOUTH AND WEST

Crete, closing the Aegean to the South, was a large island with many cities in it, though not the hundred of Homer.[61] On trade routes linking the Near East and Cyprus to the western Mediterranean, it experienced less of a collapse in the dark age than places further

North. It was prosperous in the early Archaic period, though the archaeological record points to a still-unexplained breakdown *c*.600. It was sometimes alleged that Sparta's institutions[62] were copied from Crete: the Cretans of classical times were Dorians, and that was probably a false inference from observed similarities; but it is certainly true that the Cretan cities have been exceptionally productive of inscribed laws. The large code from Gortyn, in the centre of the island,[63] was inscribed in the mid fifth century but largely reproduced older laws.

In the Classical period we have extremely little evidence for the involvement of Crete with other parts of the Greek world, but the few scraps suggest that the silence may to some extent be misleading. Herodotus claims that the Cretans were among those to whom the mainland Greeks appealed for support against the Persian invasion of 480, and that after consulting Delphi they declined;[64] they were themselves not threatened by that invasion. A pair of inscriptions from the middle of the fifth century shows Argos involved in a settlement between the Cretan cities of Cnossus and Tylissus, not simply as an arbitrator but as having an ongoing interest there (with however much or little justification, it was regarded as their mother city).[65] In 429 a squadron of Athenian ships which was needed urgently to reinforce others in the Gulf of Corinth did not go there directly but went to take part in a war in Crete on the way.

Among the Greek colonies outside the Aegean were some at Cyrene and other sites in eastern Libya,[66] between Carthage to the West and the Persian Empire to the East. The land was fertile and the cities prospered: Cyrene was one of only 13 Greek cities with a territory of more than 1,000 km² = 390 sq. miles. The founder, Battus, established a dynasty of kings which lasted until the middle of the fifth century, after which a form of constitutional government was instituted. Otherwise we know hardly anything of the history of these cities in the fifth century, except from victory odes of the poet Pindar and ancient commentaries on them. Telesicrates of Cyrene won the foot-race in the Pythian games of 474.[67] Anaxilas IV, the last king of Cyrene, won the chariot race in the Pythian games of 462:[68] before that he had suppressed a revolt by one Damophilus, who had fled in exile to Thebes, and Pindar tried to bring about a reconciliation (we do not know whether he was successful); after it he won the chariot race at Olympia in 460. Beyond that there are tantalising scraps. Athenians who survived the disaster in Egypt c.454[69] escaped via Cyrene; Peloponnesians sailing to suppport Syracuse in 413 went via Cyrene and Euesperides, which they supported in a war against the indigenous Libyans, but an individual Cyrenaean gave help to Athenians who survived their defeat in Sicily;[70] some of the Messenians evicted from Naupactus[71] by Sparta at the end of the Peloponnesian War made their way to Cyrene and its neighbours.

More is known about the Greeks in Sicily and southern Italy.[72] In Gela, on the South Coast of Sicily, a tyranny was established in 505/4, and in 491/0 power was seized by Gelon, a member of one of the city's leading families. In 485/4 he gained control of Syracuse, on the east coast (figure 2), built it up by various transfers of population and made that his principal city (it was one of the 13 Greek cities with a territory of more than 1,000 km² = 390 sq. miles). From then until the mid 460s Sicilian history was dominated by Gelon and his brothers in Syracuse, in alliance with Theron and his family in Acragas (figure 13), to the West of Gela, and in oppo-

Figure 13. Acragas: 'temple of Concord' (c.430).

sition to Himera on the North Coast and Rhegium on the toe of Italy. When Acragas captured Himera, the northern alliance appealed for help to Carthage (which had small interests at the west end of Sicily but had not tried to build on them), and in 480 Carthage sent a large force, making it impossible for Syracuse to help the Greeks of Greece against the Persians, even if it might otherwise have done so.[73] Carthage and its allies were heavily defeated; Rhegium was brought into the Syracusan orbit, and Thrasydaeus, a son of Theron, took over at Himera.

In Syracuse Gelon was succeeded by his brother Hieron (who at some stage had trouble with another brother, Polyzalus, which threatened to lead to war between Syracuse and Acragas, but that was averted); in 474/3 he won a famous victory over the Etruscans of northern Italy; but in the late 470s and early 460s the tyrannies collapsed. Thrasydaeus, who had succeeded Theron, was driven out of Acragas *c.*472; Hieron died in 467/6, and within a year his last brother, Thrasybulus, was driven out of Syracuse; the tyranny in Rhegium was ended too. Although they did not give themselves grand titles, these Western tyrants were grand rulers: they won victories in the great games, commissioning Pindar and others to write odes for them, and they made dedications at the great sanctuaries. Hieron expelled the population of Catana, north of Syracuse, and refounded it as Aetna for his son Dinomenes to rule: for the inauguration Pindar wrote his *Pythian* i (in 470) and Aeschylus wrote a tragedy, *Women of Aetna*. The cities were prosperous, and some of the most imposing temples of the Greek world were built in Sicily, not only under the tyrants but over a longer period beginning before them and continuing after.

After the overthrow of the tyrants, it took time for the upheavals to subside, for the various population movements to be undone and for constitutional governments to be established, but it was in the end achieved, with Syracuse remaining the strongest and most ambitious of the cities. In the 450s and 440s matters were complicated by a Sicel (indigenous Sicilian) leader, who built up considerable power in the interior of the island, but after a defeat in battle fled as a suppliant to Syracuse, which sent him to Corinth and as a result found itself at war against Acragas. Syracuse defeated Acragas; Ducetius took advantage of that war to return to Sicily, but he died before he could build up his power again.

In southern Italy the famously rich city of Sybaris (whence the word 'sybaritic') was destroyed in 510 by Croton.[74] There were various attempts at refounding it, the last, perhaps in 446/5, with Athenian support. Conflict between the earlier inhabitants and the newcomers was won by the newcomers, and a fresh start with the new name Thurii was made under Athenian auspices, perhaps in 444/3.[75] Athens had not previously been involved in the western Greek world, though there are slight signs that Themistocles was interested in the west, but about the same time it took part in a refoundation of Neapolis (Naples), and it made alliances with Rhegium and with Leontini in Sicily which it reaffirmed in 433/2.[76] Thurii fought unsuccessfully against Sparta's colony Taras;[77] in the 430s after consulting Delphi it broke its foundation link with Athens. Perhaps in opposition to Thurii, Croton (founded from Achaea) attached other cities to it in an 'Achaean' league.

# 6

# THE PELOPONNESIAN WAR, [435–]431–404

## ORIGINS

Thucydides treated the background to the Peloponnesian War in book I of his history, and in books II–VIII gave a narrowly-focused narrative as far as the autumn of 411. At that point, though he lived beyond the end of the war, the surviving text ends,[1] and since other historians began their accounts there what we have must be all that was ever made public. One continuation survives intact, the *Hellenica* (Greek history) of Xenophon, an Athenian who spent much of his life in exile as a dependant of the Spartans, which runs to 362 (to the end of the Peloponnesian War, I – II. 2). For the whole war we have the narrative which Diodorus Siculus (XII. 33 – XIII) based on Ephorus, essentially a rewriting of Thucydides to 411 but independent of Xenophon afterwards, and for the late fifth century and the early fourth derived ultimately from what seems to have been a good and detailed history, of which fragments survive on papyrus (the *Hellenica Oxyrhynchia*, the Greek history found at Oxyrhynchus in Egypt). As before, we have *Lives* by Plutarch of some of the leading figures; and we have inscriptions. Also we have Athenian drama; and some Athenian lawcourt speeches survive from *c*.420 to *c*.320, though not many are earlier than 404.[2]

Thucydides distinguished between openly mentioned 'grievances and disputes' leading to the war, for which he provided a narrative of the years 435–431, and what he considered the concealed 'truest reason', Athens' power and Sparta's fear of it, to justify which he interrupted the other narrative with his account of the *pentekontaetia*.[3] He gives detailed accounts of two 'grievances and disputes' and allows two others to emerge in the debates of 432–431.

Corcyra (Corfu), off the West Coast of northern Greece, had been colonised by Corinth,[4] and had later joined with Corinth in colonising Epidamnus, on the mainland further North. Dissension in Epidamnus had led to the exile of some upper-class men, who joined with the local population in attacking the city; Epidamnus appealed to Corcyra, which refused to help (it presumably had stronger links with the exiles), and then to Corinth, which responded. In 435 Corinth and its allies, on their way to reinforce Epidamnus, were defeated in a naval battle between the south end of Corcyra and the mainland. Epidamnus capitulated to Corcyra, and drops out of the story; but Corcyra and Corinth prepared for a further encounter. Corcyra had previously avoided alliances with other states, but in 433 appealed to Athens; Corinth tried to dissuade Athens; Athens supported Corcyra, but only with a defensive alliance (Corinth was a member of the Peloponnesian League, and Athens hoped to avoid an open breach of the Thirty Years' Peace) and a few ships.[5] In a second battle in the same area as the first Athens had to intervene to save Corcyra, but when further Athenian ships arrived the Corinthians withdrew.[6]

Potidaea, on the western prong of the Chalcidic peninsula in the north-western Aegean, was a tribute-paying member of the Delian League but a colony of Corinth and (surprisingly) was still sent annual officials from Corinth. Worried about the influence of king Perdiccas of Macedon, Athens had already started to put pressure on Potidaea, and now it demanded hostages, demolition of part of the city wall and an end to the Corinthian officials. In 432 Potidaea revolted from Athens, and Perdiccas encouraged neighbouring towns to migrate into Olynthus, a short distance to the north. Athens sent an expedition, and an expedition from Corinth and the Peloponnese went to support Potidaea (the Corinthians were not an official force but volunteers: this time it was Corinth which was trying to avoid an open breach of the peace). The Athenians won a battle, and settled down to besiege the city (it surrendered in 430/29); Athenians and Corinthians had now fought against one another twice.[7]

A meeting of the Spartan assembly was addressed by Corinthians and other allies, and by unrepentant Athenians who 'happened to be there'; in the Spartans' own debate king Archidamus wanted to proceed gradually but the ephor Sthenelaïdas won support for prompt action against Athens as being in breach of the peace. In this debate Thucydides' two other 'grievances and disputes' surfaced: Aegina[8] claimed that Athens was not allowing it the autonomy promised in a treaty, and Megara[9] complained that it was being subjected to economic sanctions by Athens (probably a breach of the spirit of the Thirty Years' Peace but not of the letter).[10] A formal congress of the Peloponnesian League decided on war. Sparta was not ready to strike immediately, so the winter of 432/1 was devoted to an exchange of propaganda, which included an attempt by Sparta to undermine the position of Pericles in Athens by invoking the curse to which he was subject as an Alcmaeonid on his mother's side.[11] In the spring of 431 there was an unsuccessful attempt by Thebes, the leading city of Boeotia and an ally of Sparta, to get control of Plataea, on the Boeotian side of the border but a long-standing ally of Athens:[12] this allowed Athens to claim that the Peloponnesians were in breach of the peace.[13]

Thucydides remarked of the Athenians' decision to support Corcyra in 433 that they were expecting a war against the Peloponnesians, for which Corcyra's navy would be useful and to which the West would be relevant,[14] and it appears that this is not simply due to hindsight but is correct. It was probably in 434/3 that the Athenians repaid outstanding debts to the sacred treasuries, wound up the acropolis building programme and for the future diverted expenditure to the dockyards and walls;[15] and in 433/2 they reaffirmed existing permanent alliances with Rhegium and Leontini.[16] Their behaviour in these years was not calculated to turn away wrath: they seem to have realised that unless they gave up their ambitions conflict with Sparta would come, and to have behaved provocatively but not incorrectly so as to bring about that conflict in circumstances in which they were better prepared and could claim to be in the right. Thucydides the Athenian emphasised two of his 'grievances and disputes' but not the other two: partly, I suspect, to distance himself from those who said that Athens had to fight because Pericles was intransigent over Megara, and partly, perhaps, because Athens' conduct was easier to justify in the episodes on which he concentrated.

The war formally began with a Peloponnesian invasion of Attica in early summer 431: the Thirty Years' Peace had lasted about 14 and a half years.

## THE ARCHIDAMIAN WAR, 431–421

The first phase of the war is known as the Archidamian War, after the Spartan king Archidamus, who led the invasion of Attica in 431 and again in 430, 428 and 427 (in 429 he instead led the Peloponnesians in an attack on Plataea). It was to be a war between Athens as a naval power with large cash reserves and Peloponnesian agricultural communities strong in soldiers but short of ships and cash (and failing to realise how far Athens surpassed them not simply in the number of ships but in skill in using them); and much of the Greek world, beyond the blocs recognised in the Thirty Years' Peace, was drawn into it. The Peloponnesians' original strategy was to invade Attica in force, expecting the Athenians to fight and be beaten. Pericles refused to play that game: the people were withdrawn inside the walled area of Athens and Piraeus[17] (the crowded conditions aided between 430 and 426/5 the spread of a plague which killed about a third of the population) and relied on their access to the sea to import what they needed and raid the Peloponnese while the Peloponnesians raided Attica. In one respect Pericles miscalculated (perhaps, as the Peloponnesians expected Athens to submit, he expected the Peloponnesians to admit that Athens could not be beaten). The Athenians were able to borrow money accumulated in their sacred treasuries, keeping detailed records and intending to repay with interest, but at the beginning of the war they ran down these funds at an unsustainable rate, and after Pericles' death in 429 they had to reduce expensive campaigning and to increase their income, both by levying *eisphorai*[18] on rich Athenians and by collecting more tribute from the Delian League: an inscription survives of a decree of 425 ordering major increases and of the resulting assessment.[19]

The Peloponnesians' best hope of winning a war which required time and money was to abandon half a century of enmity and gain support from Persia; and the Athenians needed if not to obtain Persian support at least to ensure that the Peloponnesians did not obtain it. From the beginning both sides made approaches to Persia; but Persia was likely to insist on the return of the Greek cities of Asia Minor as the price for its help, while Athens for half a century had posed as their champion against Persia and Sparta now claimed to be fighting for the freedom of the Greeks. Athens seems to have made a non-aggression pact with Darius II soon after his accession in 424/3; but it was only in 412, after Athens had been weakened by its unsuccessful Sicilian campaign of 415–413, that Sparta agreed to pay Persia's price and did gain Persian support.[20]

In their opening strategies neither side was likely to be defeated: the Peloponnesians invaded Attica but the Athenians did not meet them in battle; the Athenians sailed to the Peloponnese but withdrew when faced by susbtantial forces. Naval battles in the Gulf of Corinth in 429 made the Athenians' superior skill evident, and when afterwards the Peloponnesians planned to attack the unguarded Piraeus they lost their nerve; when Mytilene with most of the cities of Lesbos (among the last remaining ship-providing members of the Delian League) revolted against Athens in 428–427 the Spartan attempt to support it was a fiasco. In 427 the Peloponnesians captured Plataea and killed those of the population who had not been evacuated to Athens earlier, but that did not significantly affect the course of the war. From 431 to 426 each side tried to support its friends in north-western Greece, an area which contained several colonies of Corinth but which could be reached by the Athenians by sea: Athens got the better of the fighting, but its ambition alarmed its friends, who ended by making a hundred-year treaty amongst themselves. In 427 a bitter civil war began in Corcyra, provoked by men captured by the Corinthians in 433 and sent back to stir up trouble: it continued to 425, with Athenians when present not trying to restrain their friends' cruelty, and left the pro-Athenian democrats victorious but the community exhausted.

After Pericles' death the Athenians attempted strategies which offered a better chance of positive victory rather than avoidance of defeat. In 427 they accepted an invitation to intervene in Sicily, to support Leontini[21] against Syracuse and, Thucydides says, to prevent the transport of grain to the Peloponnese (which would allow Peloponnesian farmers to devote more of their time and effort to fighting against Athens). What began as a fairly modest expedition grew in size and ambition, but in 424 Hermocrates of Syracuse persuaded the combatants that they (like the north-western Greeks) would be better off without outside interference (and with nobody able to put up strong resistance to Syracuse), and a treaty was made in which the Athenian generals had to acquiesce. Leontini was taken over by Syracuse; in 422 Athens sent envoys with a couple of ships to Sicily, but they achieved nothing.

In 426 the Athenian Demosthenes was based on Naupactus, where Athens had earlier installed fugitive Messenians,[22] and set out from there to the north-east, into Aetolia. In the same year other Athenian forces attacked Boeotia by land and sea from Athens: some have thought that Demosthenes planned to reach Boeotia from the West and join those other forces (cf. 424/3, below), but there were too many uncertainties for this to be plausible. In fact he was trapped by light-armed Aetolians, and had difficulty in extricating his survivors and returning to Naupactus.

But in 425 a run of Athenian successes began. Demosthenes, sailing with an Athenian force bound for Corcyra and Sicily (cf. above), had permission to use that force *en route*, and built a fort by the north entrance to the large bay of Pylos on the Messenian coast (where the island of Sphacteria closes the bay with a small gap to the North and a larger to the South; the modern Pylos is on the mainland by the south entrance; this is where the battle of Navarino was fought in in 1827 in the Greek War of Independence). Spartan ships recalled from Corcyra arrived first, entered the bay and landed some men on the island; but the main Athenian force then returned, leaving the Spartans trapped. In a truce for negotiation the Athenian Cleon[23] took a hard line; he was manoeuvred into accepting a command himself and took reinforcements to Demosthenes, and they succeeded in capturing most of the Spartans on the island. By threatening to kill these they put an end to the invasions of Attica, and (as an instance of *epiteichismos*, the establishment of a hostile fort in enemy territory) they installed at Pylos Messenians from Naupactus who were able to raid the countryside (but did not achieve as much as the Athenians hoped and the Spartans feared). Another Athenian commander, Nicias, in 425 campaigned in the Argolid and installed a garrison at Methana on the north-east side – but Argos, with a 30 year peace with Sparta,[24] stayed out of the war until 421 (below). In 424 he captured the island of Cythera, just off the coast of Laconia, to add to the pressure on Sparta.

But after this Athens' successes gave way to failures. Since autumn 431 Athens had been attacking Megara twice a year, and in 424 Megarian democrats plotted to betray the city to Athens, but the plot misfired and Megara ended up in the hands of pro-Spartan oligarchs. In winter 424/3 a plot with Athenian sympathisers in Boeotia failed too: Athenian forces were to enter Boeotia from the south-east and south-west and there was to be a rising in the North, but there were failures in timing, and when the main Athenian force had occupied Delium (the sanctuary of Delian Apollo) in the south-east the Boeotians were free to attack and defeat it on its homeward march.

The Spartan Brasidas had already shown himself to be unusually enterprising, and in 424 he responded to an invitation from the Chalcidians of Olynthus and from king Perdiccas of Macedon[25] and took a force of mercenaries and helots (who were subsequently liberated) to the north of the Aegean, an area which contained many cities included in the Delian League but which could be reached by land. After falling out with Perdiccas (who frequently switched allegiance between Sparta and Athens) he set about winning over cities in the Chalcidian region, insisting that he was a genuine liberator who would not substitute Spartan control for Athenian or support one party against another (but that if the cities did not join him voluntarily he would treat them as hostile). A striking gain, in winter 424/3, was the Athenian colony of Amphipolis:[26] the historian Thucydides, an Athenian general and at the time in Thasos, was too late to save that (and was consequently exiled until the end of the war) but did save the coastal city of Eïon.

Many Spartans after their failure at Pylos had been anxious for peace, and in spring 423 a year's truce was negotiated, which it was hoped would lead to a more lasting settlement. However, the city of Scione went over to Brasidas after the truce had been made but before news of it arrived, and so the war continued in the North; but the truce was observed elsewhere, and in 422 was prolonged until late summer. When it did expire Cleon had himself sent North with an Athenian force. He began with successes, but from Eïon, while waiting for allies, he risked a reconnaissance march towards Amphipolis and was caught off guard and defeated by Brasidas. Cleon and Brasidas were both killed in the fighting; Amphipolis remained opposed to the Athenians, and they never recovered it.[27]

Cleon and Brasidas had both been eager to continue the war, but after their deaths those in favour of peace prevailed, particularly Nicias in Athens and king Plistoanax in Sparta.[28] What scholars call the Peace of Nicias was made in the spring of 421: essentially it involved a return to the situation of 431, with special guarantees for some but not all of the cities in the North, and it was to last for fifty years. If it had been fully implemented, it would have fulfilled Pericles' war aims for Athens – Sparta was making peace after ten years of war in which it had failed to weaken or destroy the Athenian empire – but it was not. Sparta's particular interest in peace after the episode at Pylos was not shared by its allies; Boeotia, Corinth, Megara and Elis refused to participate because territorial demands of theirs were not met, and when Amphipolis resisted being handed back to Athens the Spartan governor there acquiesced. To reassure Athens, Sparta added a 50 year alliance between Sparta and Athens, and the Athenians then gave up their hold on Sparta by returning the prisoners captured at Pylos. That was a mistake: they ought not to have been so easily satisfied with a flawed treaty.

## AFTER THE PEACE OF NICIAS, 421–413

The uncertainty following the Peace of Nicias was compounded by the expiry of the 30 year peace between Sparta and Argos.[29] Corinth took the lead in building up a combination of cities disaffected with Sparta, in alliance with Argos. In winter 421/0 two of the new Spartan ephors encouraged a plan to bring Boeotia into that alliance and align the alliance with Sparta, but the Boeotian officials did not explain that to their fellow citizens, who refused to join the alliance because they saw it as anti-Spartan. Further misunderstandings and crossed wires followed. In Athens Alcibiades,[30] offended because in spite of his family's connections he had not been used in negotiating the Peace of Nicias, was eager to wreck the peace, and in 420, allegedly after sharp practice in the assembly over a Spartan deputation trying to save the peace, he made an alliance for Athens with Argos, Mantinea and Elis (while Corinth refused to join and returned to the Spartan side). This offered the prospect of fighting against Sparta on land in the Peloponnese, which had not been feasible during the Archidamian War.

After lesser campaigns in 420 and 419, the major encounters came in 418. First Sparta and its allies (including Corinth and Boeotia) under king Agis II, son and successor of Archidamus, set out to attack Argos from the North; while they were approaching Argos by various routes the Argive army set out to resist them; and the result was a situation in which no battle was fought but the commanders made a truce, but each side reacted angrily and thought its commanders had thrown away an opportunity of victory. The Argive alliance moved to Mantinea, in Arcadia, in order to attack Tegea, to the South, and Agis went to support Tegea. When Agis eventually marched north he was caught unprepared by the enemy marching south (a wood may have prevented them from seeing each other). The battle of Mantinea was the largest hoplite battle in the Peloponnesian War, with 10,000 or more on each side. At first each army was too far to the right for a direct clash with the other; Agis' attempt to adjust his formation left a gap in the middle of his line, and if the Spartans were to be defeated in a hoplite battle it ought to have happened now. But it did not: even here the Spartans' skill and discipline were too much for opponents who had little experience of fighting together, and they were victorious. The challenge had failed, and Sparta was able to reassert its dominance in the Peloponnese. Even in Argos oligarchic Spartan sympathisers[31] gained agreement for a treaty which seemed to envisage a leadership of the Peloponnese shared between the two cities; but in 417 pro-Athenian democrats returned to power, and in 416 Argos renewed its alliance with Athens; fighting in the north-eastern Peloponnese continued.

For other areas we have scraps of information. Athens withdrew the Messenians from Pylos, but, as the peace was not fully implemented, retained the site, and in 419/8 it declared Sparta to be in breach of the peace and reinstated the Messenians. In the North, in 421 Amphipolis avoided being handed back to Athens (cf. above), but the Athenians captured Scione, killing the men and enslaving the women and children. A few other incidents are mentioned; Perdiccas died c.413, and his successor Archelaus was consistently pro-Athenian, but, as Athens was then weaker, on his own terms.

One episode treated in detail by Thucydides was Athens' capture of the south Aegean island of Melos in 416.[32] Almost from the beginning of the war it had been the only Aegean island outside the Athenian orbit; in 426 it withstood an Athenian attack; in 425 the Athenians assessed it for tribute,[33] but that does not prove that they were in a position to require payment; an inscription listing financial contributions to the Spartan side includes the Melians, probably somewhat before 416.[34] Thucydides does not indicate what Melos had done since 421 to provoke the Athenians; but they sent a force to the island, and he gives us a dialogue between Athenian envoys and Melian officials, in which the Athenians talk the language of power politics in a manner starker than but not fundamentally different from speeches elsewhere in Thucydides' history,[35] while the Melians appeal to justice, the gods and the Spartans. In the end Melos was betrayed, and the men were killed and the women and children enslaved. The episode became notorious, partly because Thucydides wrote it up to contrast it with the Athenians' overreaching themselves in Sicily immediately afterwards: we should at least note that immediately before he reported in one sentence that the Spartans killed all the free inhabitants of a town in the Argolid.[36]

Various hostile acts had taken place which were in breach of the Peace of Nicias, but the Spartans had not entered Athenian territory and the Athenians had not entered Spartan territory, and it did not suit either side to claim that the peace was at an end. Finally in 414 Athens joined Argos in a raid on eastern Laconia, and the Spartans did regard that as the definitive breach of the peace.

Meanwhile a major campaign was under way in Sicily,[37] which was to prove the turning-point in the war. In the west of Sicily Egesta, an ally of Athens, was at war with Selinus, which gained the support of Syracuse. Egesta appealed to Athens, and is said to have deceived Athenian envoys about its ability to pay for Athenian help; in Athens Alcibiades was eager to go, and saw this as the starting-point for expansion in the West, while the cautious Nicias considered long-term success impossible (rightly: controlling Sicily would be greatly different from controlling separate Aegean islands) and thought Athens faced enough problems nearer home. But Nicias' anxieties led to the Athenians' sending in 415 a larger force, with greater confidence and ambition, than was originally envisaged. Nicias and Alcibiades were two of the three commanders – probably not, as Plutarch thought, so that each should moderate the excesses of the other, but because Nicias, though lacking enough support in the assembly to prevent the venture, did have enough support to secure his own appointment. In Syracuse Hermocrates had opponents who distrusted him, but by the end of the campaign he was in an influential position.

When the Athenians arrived, they found that they were generally less welcome than they had hoped and that Egesta did not have the promised funds; and Alcibiades, recalled to face prosecution in Athens,[38] escaped to Sparta and incited the Spartans against Athens. From a base at Catana they sailed to Syracuse and won a battle, but were unable to follow it up. In 414 they sailed back to Syracuse, established themselves on the plateau outside the city, and set about blockading it by building walls to isolate it; they began well, but did not complete their walls in time to prevent the entry of a Peloponnesian force commanded by the Spartan Gylippus. By now Athens' third commander had been killed, and Nicias was on his own, demoralised and ill. The Athenians refused to relieve him of his command, but in 413 sent another substantial force (one of the commanders was Demosthenes, who had been energetic though not always successful in the 420s). A night-time battle to regain control of the plateau ended in failure for the Athenians; their ships did not manage to fight their way out of the great bay; and when they finally tried to withdraw by land they were caught by the Syracusans. What began with high hopes ended in disaster; many men and ships were lost, and much money had been spent in vain; and for the first time it seemed credible that Athens could be beaten.

## THE END OF THE WAR (413–404)

In 413 the Spartan king Agis led a Peloponnesian force which established a fort at Decelea, in the north of Attica (another instance of *epiteichismos*[39]), and he remained with a garrison until the end of the war, depriving the Athenians of the use of their countryside and silver mines all year round. The previous year Athenians had invaded Laconia (cf. above), and the absence of large numbers of Athenians in Sicily lessened the risk of the enterprise.

The Athenians resolved to fight on. Sparta was now approached by various members of the Delian League to whom defection now seemed feasible, and by the Persian satraps in western Asia Minor, Tissaphernes at Sardis and Pharnabazus at Dascylium. A Hellespont strategy was ultimately to win the war for Sparta (cf. below), but in 412, attracted by the prospect of naval support from Chios and by Alcibiades' connections with Miletus, they decided to focus on the Aegean, and they made the first of a series of treaties with Tissaphernes and the Persians, by which Persia was to recover territory which it had possessed in the past. The Athenians sent ships to Samos, and this was to be their naval base in the Aegean to the end of the war.

Alcibiades was falling out with the Spartans: he was rumoured to have fathered a son by the wife of the absent Agis.[40] He made his way to the court of Tissaphernes, contacted the Athenians, and suggested that if they changed from democracy to oligarchy and recalled him he could induce the Persians to support Athens rather than Sparta. For the resulting upheavals in Athens see below.[41] During the winter of 412/1 there was friction between the Spartans and the Persians, but Alcibiades failed to align the Persians with Athens (probably there was never a serious likelihood of that, though some Athenians continued to hope for it until 407), and the Persian alliance with Sparta was reaffirmed in spring 411, now explicitly limiting Persia's territorial claim to mainland Asia Minor but making it absolute there. In autumn 411 the Spartans wasted an opportunity to attack Athens while it was in disarray;[42] their Aegean fleet moved to the Hellespont, and the Athenians followed and defeated it at Cynossema. After this Thucydides' narrative ends, and we have to work with the divergent accounts of Xenophon and Diodorus:[43] although there are problems with Diodorus' account, there is reason to think that on many points what lay behind his account was preferable to that of Xenophon.

Alcibiades joined the Athenian navy, and in the years which followed the Athenians won a series of successes in the North. In 410 they decoyed and defeated the Spartans and killed their commander Mindarus in a sea and land battle at Cyzicus, in the Propontis, after which the survivors sent the message to Sparta in eleven words of Greek, 'Ships gone; Mindarus dead; men starving; don't know what to do'. A peace offer from Sparta was rejected by Athens.[44] It was probably after this that the full democracy was restored in Athens.[45] The fleet achieved less in 409, but in 408 it recovered Calchedon on the Asiatic side of the Bosporus, Selymbria on the Propontis, and finally Byzantium on the European side of the Bosporus. In 407, while one squadron recovered Thasos in the northern Aegean, the main fleet returned to Athens, Alcibiades for the first time since he had gone into exile in 415.[46] He was cleared of the charges on which he had been convicted and, uniquely, given a special position as Athens' commander in chief.

Meanwhile, Sparta had succeeded in further negotiations with Persia, obtaining the King's younger son Cyrus (aged 16) to take charge of a more energetic campaign against Athens, and perhaps an agreement that after the war the Greeks of mainland Asia Minor were to pay tribute to Persia but in other respects to be autonomous. Sparta's admiral for 407/6, Lysander, established a good relationship with Cyrus, and they refitted the Spartan fleet at Ephesus. Alcibiades took an Athenian fleet to Notium, on the mainland north of Ephesus. Early in 406 he left Notium, leaving in charge Antiochus, a friend, whom he ordered not to risk a battle until he returned; but Antiochus and Lysander each attempted a version of the decoying tactics which had worked for the Athenians at Cyzicus, and this time the Spartans were successful. Alcibiades returned and offered battle again, but the Spartans refused; and without waiting to be prosecuted he withdrew into exile in Thrace near the Propontis.

Spartan admirals now served for one year with a ban on reappointment. Lysander's successor for 406/5, Callicratidas, disliked fawning on the Persians and relying on Persian help to fight against fellow Greeks. He took his fleet North to Lesbos and captured the city of Methymna; Conon with the Athenian fleet arrived afterwards and Callicratidas blockaded him in the harbour of Mytilene. The Athenians made a special effort to equip and man another fleet: gold dedications were melted down for coinage, slaves willing to row were liberated, and all eight available generals went with the ships. In late summer 406 Callicratidas had to divide his forces to contain Conon and encounter the newcomers; he was defeated and killed by the newcomers near the Arginusae Islands between Lesbos and the mainland; but the weather was bad and the Athenians were unable to pick up their survivors on wrecked ships and their dead.[47]

Unable to reappoint Lysander for 405/4, the Spartans appointed a figurehead and made Lysander his secretary. He again revived the Spartan fleet at Ephesus with Persian money, while Cyrus departed to his father's deathbed and a succession dispute; and he then moved North to the Hellespont, capturing Lampsacus on the Asiatic side. The Athenians occupied the open beach of Aegospotami, opposite. Alcibiades turned up, criticising the Athenians' position and offering the help of his Thracian friends, but the Athenian generals would not trust him again. The battle perhaps resulted from the Athenians' again attempting a decoy but not being ready with their remaining ships when Lysander responded with the whole Spartan fleet. Conon with a few Athenian ships escaped to Cyprus, but most of the Athenian ships were captured or destroyed.

Lysander recaptured Byzantium and Calchedon, and then proceeded to Athens, which during the winter of 405/4 was blockaded by land and by sea. In the spring the Athenians accepted Sparta's terms (though some of Sparta's allies would have liked Athens to be destroyed): Athens had to demolish the long walls and the Piraeus walls, give up its overseas possessions and all but twelve ships, take back its exiles (mostly oligarchs from 411–410)[48] and become a subordinate ally of Sparta. In the last phase of the war both sides

had been hampered by internal disagreements, Athens between oligarchs and democrats, Sparta between those happy to pay Persia's
price and those not, and Athens did better for a longer time than
most would have expected in 413. But, thanks to the Athenians'
overreaching themselves in Sicily and to the Persians' enabling the
Spartans to persevere until the Athenians could not, the Spartans
had finally achieved their war aim: the Athenian Empire was at an
end. The demolition of Athens' walls was celebrated as 'the beginning
of freedom for Greece'; Lysander received extravagant honours,
including the 'navarchs' dedication' at Delphi, a statue group which
showed him being crowned by the god Poseidon, and games named
after him at Samos (which he captured in 404). This did not, of
course, result in a Greece free from problems, as we shall see in
Chapter 8.

## ATHENS DURING THE WAR

Except in 411 (below) Thucydides' narrow sense of relevance did
not let him include much on Athens' internal affairs. Throughout
the war we have tragedies by Euripides, younger than Aeschylus and
Sophocles, showing awareness of the horrors of war, and more apt
to leave modern readers, at least, feeling that the resolutions of his
stories are problematic. We have abundant material in the comedies
of Aristophanes, who began writing in the 420s: because they are
comedies it is not agreed how humour which had to be popular to
win him the prize was combined with serious points, or whether his
attacks were aimed at all worthwhile targets or have a consistency
which reflects an identifiable point of view; but it can be maintained
that he was more sympathetic to traditional than to upstart political
leaders (cf. below), and, while not pro-Spartan or pacifist, found
some Athenians too belligerent. Another work from the 420s is the
pamphlet of the 'Old Oligarch', the *Athenian Constitution* preserved
with the works of Xenophon: this takes the line that democracy is
bad in principle because it favours the worse people rather than the
better, but is appropriate to Athens as a naval power and successful
there (whereas by 411 the balance had changed so much that the
democracy actually was overthrown: see below).

The plague of 430–426/5[49] killed about a third of Athens' population, including Pericles, who died in autumn 429. Thucydides in his final verdict exaggerated his power in Athens, and exaggerated the distinction between Pericles who controlled the people and subsequent politicians who competed in pandering to the people.[50] Nevertheless, Pericles' death does mark a change. He accepted the democracy but was from the class which had dominated Athens since the time of Solon; most of the leading politicians after him were from families which had become rich but had not previously been dominant; and some of them (for whom the term *demagogos*, 'people-leader', was coined) adopted an ostentatiously populist style which was new to Athens. Leading politicians of the previous half-century were commonly elected as generals, but politicians of the newer kind tended not to hold office year after year, while other men, such as Demosthenes, served frequently as generals but were not so active in politics.

The most prominent politician in the 420s (perhaps already active in the 430s) was Cleon, whose father owned a tanning business. Thucydides, who disliked him,[51] described him as 'most violent' and 'most persuasive', and Aristophanes represented him as apt to make wild accusations against opponents and wild promises. The cautious Nicias, whose wealth came from the silver mines, was likewise a newcomer to politics, but one who tried to copy the style of the earlier politicians. It had probably not occurred to Cleon that he might be a general until he was forced into it in connection with Pylos:[52] in the assembly he taunted Nicias for his feebleness, and Nicias invited him to take over his generalship; he promised to bring back the Spartans from Pylos or kill them within twenty days, and he succeeded (Thucydides comments that sensible men thought he was more likely to die in the attempt).[53] Exceptional in this period was Alcibiades, prominent after 421: he was from the old political class (related to Pericles, who acted as his guardian after his father's death) but flamboyant and selfish, trying to beat the demagogues at their own game.

Cleon was killed at Amphipolis in 422,[54] and Hyperbolus, who aspired to succeed to his position, was for reasons which are not made clear considered particularly contemptible. Nicias wanted to uphold the peace which he helped to make in 421, while Alcibiades was against it, but his Peloponnesian alliance failed to bring success.[55] Alcibiades championed the Sicilian expedition of 415, while Nicias unsuccessfully opposed it.[56] They were rivals in other ways too. In 426/5 Athens had 'purified' Delos by removing all bodies buried on the island, and it instituted or revived a major festival there: Nicias led the Athenian delegation in 417, with great show. More selfishly, at the Olympic games of 416 Alcibiades entered seven teams in the chariot race (there was a dispute about the ownership of one of his teams), and came first, second and fourth.

It was probably in the spring of 415 that Hyperbolus proposed an ostracism, intending that the people should choose between Alcibiades and Nicias. But the supporters of Alcibiades and of Nicias combined to vote against Hyperbolus: he was ostracised, and Alcibiades and Nicias were left in Athens to continue their rivalry. This was probably the work of Alcibiades, getting rid of Hyperbolus and placing Nicias under an obligation to him. Ostracism remained on the statute book, but was never used again: lawsuits aimed at particular men were more likely to hit their targets.

Shortly before the Sicilian expedition was due to set out, in a single night most of Athens' herms (busts of the god Hermes on a plinth with an erect phallus) were damaged. When an enquiry was set up, information was given about mock celebrations of the Eleusinian mysteries in private houses, in which Alcibiades was said to be involved. There was talk of a plot against the democracy: that seems unlikely, but a plot to discredit Alcibiades and create bad omens for the expedition is more credible. Alcibiades failed to secure a trial before setting out, in which he hoped to be acquitted. When he was recalled he escaped to Sparta;[57] he and many other men were condemned on one charge or both, and property confiscated from them helped to provide funds for the campaign in Sicily.

The failure in Sicily in 413 had a disastrous effect on the Athenians' manpower, navy and finances, and on their morale; but they decided to fight on, while Sparta had a fort in Attica at Decelea and gained the support of some of the Delian League members and of the Persians.[58] By the end of 412 Alcibiades had fallen out with the Spartans and was at the court of the satrap Tissaphernes, suggesting to sympathisers in the Athenian fleet at Samos that if Athens' democracy were replaced by oligarchy and he were recalled he could persuade the Persians to support Athens instead of Sparta.[59] Negotiations between Athens, Samos and Sardis failed to gain Persian support, but men in favour of oligarchy decided to go ahead without the Persians and without Alcibiades: about April/May 411 the Athenian assembly was persuaded to vote for a constitution based on a powerful council of four hundred and a restricted citizen body notionally of five thousand, and this régime tried without success to reach a settlement with Sparta. Those who overthrew the democracy will have had a mixture of motives: hopes of defeating Sparta or of ending the war, a desire to save money by abolishing the stipends on which the democracy depended, views about the merits and demerits of democracy, belief or distrust in Alcibiades; and the absence of the fleet will have upset the social balance inside Athens. The most visible agent of change was Pisander, while in the background was the orator Antiphon;[60] Theramenes was among those setting up the oligarchy but also among those working later for the change to the intermediate régime. While the oligarchs came to power in Athens, the Athenians at Samos, as a kind of city in exile, declared in favour of democracy, and Alcibiades joined them.

The régime of the Four Hundred turned out to be more autocratic than many of those who had voted for it expected. In September, when the Four Hundred were having a fortress built at Piraeus, there was a mutiny among the men working on it. A Spartan fleet coming across the Saronic Gulf did not go to Piraeus but went round Attica to the Euripus, the strait between the mainland and Euboea; an Athenian fleet followed it and was defeated. The Spartans did not then seize the opportunity to attack Athens, but the episode led to the overthrow of the Four Hundred and the establishment of an intermediate régime based on the Five Thousand. This régime persevered with the war, and cooperated with the fleet at Samos and Alcibiades. The return to democracy happened beyond the point at which Thucydides' text ends and is not mentioned by Xenophon, but is probably to be placed in 410 after the victory at Cyzicus[61] had reminded the men in Athens of their need for a successful navy.

For a time there was friction betwen men strongly committed to democracy and men less so, and the position of Alcibiades was anomalous: his condemnation of 415 was still in force, but he served as a general with the fleet because the fleet allowed him to do so. After the run of successes in the North he returned to Athens in 407: he was formally cleared of the charges, and he paid his debt to the Eleusinian goddesses by escorting with soldiers a traditional procession from Athens to Eleusis (while the Spartans were at Decelea the procession had travelled by sea). Uniquely, he was made not one equal general among ten but commander in chief, and he returned to the Aegean, but after the defeat of Antiochus at Notium 406 he withdrew into exile again.[62] His attempt to rejoin the Athenians at Aegospotami was rebuffed;[63] after the end of the war he made his way to the Persians, but Pharnabazus had him killed.

When Conon was blockaded by the Spartans in Mytilene in 406 the Athenians made a special effort to fund, equip and man another fleet: at a time of heightened tension this fleet defeated the Spartans off the Arginusae Islands but on account of bad weather was unable to retrieve survivors and corpses from the ships which were wrecked.[64] In Athens relief at the victory was mingled with anger at the aftermath: there were furious recriminations in which trierarchs in charge of some of the ships (including Theramenes, but we should not see this as a conflict between oligarchs and democrats) and the generals tried to pass the blame, until an irregular assembly in a single decision condemned the eight generals who had been involved, and the six who had returned to Athens were put to death.

Euripides' latest tragedies have been seen as escapist and melodramatic. Aristophanes' *Birds*, in 414 (in the middle of the Sicilian venture), was still light-hearted. His *Lysistrata*, in 411, seems to reflect a genuine desire for peace. His *Frogs*, in 405, was a reaction to the recent deaths of Sophocles and Euripides but turned into a contest between Aeschylus and Euripides; the first question put to the two poets was, 'What is to be done about Alcibiades?'

The leading demagogue in this period was Cleophon, son of a man who had served as general. He introduced the *diobelia*, a two-obol grant perhaps paid to citizens with no other means of subsistence while the Spartans were at Decelea; and was implacably opposed to peace with Sparta, both after Cyzicus when Sparta sought peace and after Aegospotami when Athens had no means of continuing to fight. After he had been eliminated on a technical charge of desertion, it was Theramenes who negotiated peace with Sparta in 404. The democracy had lost the war; in the foreseeable future the navy was going to be unimportant; the Spartan Lysander was particularly fond of extreme oligarchy. It is no surprise that Athens' capitulation was followed by another bout of oligarchy.[65]

# 7

# LIFE IN THE GREEK WORLD

## FAMILIES AND OCCUPATIONS

In Ancient Greece, as generally until recent times, it was assumed that there were separate roles for men and for women (though in the poorest households the distinction will not always have been upheld): the men's world included farming and hunting, athletics and warfare, and politics; the women's world was focused on the household and indoor duties, though there were some priestesses and some religious festivals were limited to or included women. Typically a man aged 25 or over would marry a woman aged 15 or under, who would bring a dowry with her; and one reason for keeping a woman at home was to ensure that her husband was the father of her children. It was desirable to have several children, since not all might survive to adulthood, but not too many, for reasons of property. Property belonged primarily to men, and when a man died his property was shared among his sons; in Athens a woman with no brothers would be found a suitable husband to perpetuate the family and its property, but in some other cities women's position with regard to property was less disadvantageous. Education was generally a private matter; but for Spartan citizens the decision to rear a baby or expose it to die was a public decision, and from the age of seven both boys and girls embarked on an elaborate public training programme. Because Spartan citizens spent much of their life with their fellow men, women had more freedom there than in most states.[1]

Cities were communities of citizens, free adult males of citizen parentage – but the requirement in Athens of both an Athenian father and an Athenian mother[2] was a particularly strict requirement in a state whose citizenship was particularly desirable. Citizenship could be conferred on foreigners for good services, and states which were short of citizens would be generous, but there was no general right to apply for citizenship in the state where one lived. Most states will have had some, and Athens had a significant number of, free non-citizen residents (*metoikoi* in Athenian parlance). These were subject to such rights and duties as the citizens chose to give them; unless specially privileged they could not own land and houses in the state's territory.

There were also people in various states of unfreedom, ranging from chattel slaves to inferior classes within the local population. Chattel slaves if not born to slave parents often became slaves through capture in war; but Greek captives were commonly ransomed, and most slaves were non-Greek. These were the property of the state or individual who owned them: conditions, and prospects of eventual liberation, were comparatively good for some with particular skills, but were very far from good for such men as those who worked in Athens' silver mines. In Athens only the very rich would own large numbers of slaves and would not themselves need to work for their living, but only the poorest citizens would own no slaves at all. The best known of the groups of indigenous men and women in a servile state were the helots of Sparta,[3] but there are signs of such categories elsewhere, and Athens had dependent peasants known as *hektemoroi* until they were liberated by Solon.[4] While most Greeks were not idle parasites, it would not have been possible for so many to devote so much time to public life without wives and children, metics and slaves, to do much of the work of other kinds.

The Greek ideal, or at any rate the upper-class Greek ideal, was the citizen farmer, owning and living off the produce of his land. By the classical period states obtained some of their needs by trading rather than locally (and for local produce the difference between a good year and a bad year could be considerable), and will have had such men as cobblers, potters and builders whose primary source of livelihood was not farming. Athens as a large and prosperous city, in which many men received cash payments, will have had a more diversified and a more monetised economy than most others, but even there a high proportion of citizens will have owned some land and have lived partly off their own produce. Rich men will have owned a number of separate plots rather than large, continuous estates, and in the smaller states most men will have lived in the city and have gone out from there to work their land (in Athens the demes spread through Attica[5] were local centres of habitation). Crafts were practised in small workshops with a few workers, not in large factories; building projects relied not on substantial contractors but on large numbers of individual suppliers and workers. Overseas trade was conducted not by merchant fleets but by individual ships whose owner/captain would carry goods of his own and goods of a few other traders; and, although state action occurred where vital interests were concerned (such as the grain supply and materials for shipbuilding, and regulations to prevent dishonest practices in the markets), states did not exercise an overall control of trade. Athens' economic sanctions on Megara in the 430s[6] were probably without precedent, at least on a large scale.

## CULTURAL LIFE

Although Greeks could distinguish the sacred from the secular, their religion was 'embedded' as an integral part of the community's life, as Christianity used to be embedded in European societies and some other religions are still embedded in some societies; the state could take decisions on religious matters (such as buildings, priesthoods, festival regulations) just as it took decisions on other matters, and religious appointments were not seen as fundamentally different from or incompatible with appointments of other kinds. There was a large number of gods and goddesses, and while there was an overall similarity across the Greek world particular gods were worshipped under different cult titles and with different rituals in different places:[7] for instance, on the acropolis of Athens one could find Athena Polias, the patron goddess of the city, Athens Promachos, 'who fights in front', and Athena Nike, 'victory'. Additional cults could be imported into a city from another Greek city or from a non-Greek source: Athens imported the healing god Asclepius in 420/19, and expanded the cult of the Thracian goddess Bendis *c*.410.[8] In the body of Greek legend gods and goddesses were seen as similar to men and women, and as behaving and misbehaving as men and women did, though from the sixth century onwards there were intellectuals who attacked that view of them (cf. below). Religion depended on belief, but there was not a body of sacred texts or orthodox doctrines which had to be accepted, and what was most important was maintaining a good relationship with the gods, by taking part in the right observances in the right ways on the right occasions.

The typical act of public worship was the sacrifice, of slaughtered animals or other foodstuffs, often preceded by a procession to the altar; and often it was conducted in a way which produced not only smoke for the god but a feast for the worshippers. Festivals also included activities which in our culture are not normally linked to religious celebrations, particularly competitions in musical and poetical performance and in athletics. (Gymnasia at which men could exercise were widespread, and from the fourth century they tended to become intellectual centres too.) Mystery cults, such as that of Demeter and Kore at Eleusis, involved revelations to initiates, and were more concerned with the spiritual welfare of individuals. Some sanctuaries became sources of healing, where sufferers would visit for a night and hope to depart cured in the morning. Some sanctuaries, such as that of Apollo at Delphi and that of Zeus at Olympia, attracted not only the local people but a wider constituency; in Athens the Panathenaea was perhaps too much of an Athenian civic festival to achieve that, but the mysteries at Eleusis did have a wider appeal (barbarians were excluded, but even slaves if they were Greek were admitted).[9]

Meetings of councils and assemblies began with a religious ritual and a prayer for success, but the gods did not issue orders to states: their will could be made known through oracles and omens, but it was left to human beings to decide when and where to seek the will of the gods, and how to interpret unclear responses.

The oldest surviving Greek literature is epic poetry: the *Iliad* and *Odyssey* attributed to Homer, telling two stories connected with the legendary Greek war against Troy,[10] are highly accomplished works written down probably in the late eighth century as the culmination of a tradition of oral poetry. From Hesiod, perhaps slightly later, we have the *Theogony*, on the origins and genealogies of the gods, and the *Works and Days*, giving advice for a life of honest work. From the seventh century to the fifth we have a body of various forms of lyric poetry, from which some passages have been cited as source material in the preceding chapters. Some poems were written for choral performance on public occasions: hymns to the gods, songs for weddings and funerals, celebrations of athletic victories (e.g. Pindar and Bacchylides) and military engagements (e.g. Simonides, an uncle of Bacchylides; military engagements were marked also by epigrams inscribed on monuments). Others were intended for performance by an individual, often at upper-class *symposia* (drinking-parties), and might focus on the poet's own life or on public concerns, the latter sometimes generic but sometimes rooted in a particular context (e.g. Tyrtaeus in Sparta, Theognis in Megara, Alcaeus in Lesbos, Solon in Athens). Sappho of Lesbos (seventh century) was a woman and wrote about women's loves.

Athens was the cultural centre of Greece in the fifth and fourth centuries, as it was not earlier or later. The distinctive form of fifth-century poetry is Athenian drama, performed in competititons at festivals of the god Dionysus. Tragedy (accompanied at the competitions by the more earthy and humorous satiric drama), was of high seriousness, with plots (in all surviving instances except Aeschylus' *Persians*, but that had parallels in some plays now lost) taken from the Greeks' legends of the heroic period; tragedies survive from the three writers who quickly achieved classic status, Aeschylus, Sophocles and Euripides. Comedy in its fifth-century form ('old comedy') used fantastic plots to focus on political and intellectual topics and individuals in the contemporary world, while using a good deal of bawdy slapstick humour, and from the 420s to the 380s we have a series of plays by Aristophanes. 'Middle comedy', in the early and middle fourth century, seems to have been somewhat more restrained and did less to integrate the chorus in the drama; the only instances preserved complete are the two latest surviving plays of Aristophanes, *Ecclesiazusae* (assembly-women) and *Plutus* (wealth). 'New comedy', in the late fourth and the third century, used to be known principally from Latin adaptations by Plautus and Terence, but more recently papyri have given us a substantial body of material by Menander (late fourth and early third century: he was not the most successful writer in his time): these plays are set in the contemporary world, but deal with domestic matters such as foundling babies and lovers' misunderstandings, not with public topics, and they develop from middle comedy the restraint and the disengagement of the chorus.

The earliest surviving Greek prose literature is from the second half of the fifth century: Herodotus (from Halicarnassus in Asia Minor, but exiled), in the third quarter of the century, wrote a wide-ranging and intellectually lively history culminating in the Ionian Revolt of the 490s and the Persian invasions of Greece in 490 and 480–479, and fragments quoted from the otherwise-lost works of his predecessors suggest that he represents a great advance on them; Thucydides of Athens, in the last three decades of the century, wrote a magisterial and penetrating but except in its introduction narrowly focused history of the Peloponnesian War.[11] After that histories proliferated. Some writers deliberately set out to continue the unfinished history of Thucydides: the *Hellenica* (Greek affairs) of the Athenian Xenophon runs from 411 to 362.[12] Other writers covered the Greek world or more during a longer or shorter period (the fourth-century Ephorus, of Cyme in Asia Minor, served as the main source of the first-century Diodorus Siculus for his surviving material on the fifth century and the first half of the fourth), while others chose a narrower field, such as the history of a particular city (a series of *Atthides*, histories of Athens, was written between the late fifth century and the early third, but none have been preserved). Aristotle's school, in the third quarter of the fourth century, produced studies of 158 *Constitutions*, of which the *Athenian Constitution* survives, giving a history of the constitution followed by an account of its working at the time of writing.[13] For histories of Alexander the Great see p. 147: several were written in the decades after his death, but the earliest to survive is book XVII of Diodorus Siculus.

Expertise in public speaking was valued from the late fifth century onwards, and we have a large body of Athenian oratory, mostly for law court cases but also a few speeches for meetings of the assembly or other occasions, written between *c.*420 and *c.*320. Authors include Antiphon, Andocides and Lysias at the beginning of the period, Demosthenes, Aeschines and Hyperides at the end. In the courts litigants had to plead their own cases, but could employ speech-writers and be backed up by supporting speakers.[14] How closely the speeches transmitted to us (as models of oratory rather than as historical sources) match the speeches originally delivered is not clear; there are few instances of speeches on both sides of the same case, and often we do not know the outcome. Isocrates, who lived for nearly a hundred years from the 430s to the 330s, wrote a few law court speeches in the 390s but after that wrote political pamphlets in the form of speeches and taught other speakers. Other men also wrote pamphlets, and one which survives is the *Athenian Constitution* of the 'Old Oligarch', preserved with the works of Xenophon but very probably written in the 420s.[15] Rhetoric, the art of composing suitable speeches for different occasions, became an essential ingredient in upper-class education. Gorgias, of Leontini in Sicily, served on an embassy to Athens in 427 and impressed his hearers with his carefully worked-out style; *Rhetoric* is one of the many books by Aristotle, and the *Rhetoric to Alexander* preserved with Aristotle's works is probably slightly earlier and by Anaximenes of Lampsacus.

Philosophy, asking questions about the cosmos and about gods and mortals in terms other than those of traditional legend, began in the sixth century in Asia Minor, particularly in Miletus. Thales, early in the century, was a cosmologist, who thought that the earth floats on water; Anaximander identified the infinite as the origin of all things; Anaximenes thought that air was. Pythagoras, who migrated from Samos to Croton in Italy, was a mathematician, interested particularly in musical pitches (and his name survives in 'Pythagoras' theorem' about right-angled triangles). These approaches could not be reconciled with the traditional anthropomorphic religion: Thales believed that 'all things are full of gods'; Pythagoras and others objected to stories about the behaviour and misbehaviour of the gods. Traditional values were questioned too: Heraclitus of Ephesus thought there was a single divine law from which human laws ought to be derived, but in fact rulers imposed their will and called that law.

In the middle and late fifth century there were travelling intellectuals known as sophists (practitioners of wisdom); not all were

Athenian but many spent some time in Athens. Many of them claimed to teach the skills needed for success in public life, especially that of formulating arguments and making speeches; and they were fond of contrasts such as that between *physis*, 'nature', which cannot be other than it is, and *nomos*, the word for 'law' but in this context 'convention', what happens to have been decided in one way by a particular human community but could be decided otherwise. If the traditional values and their justifications were abandoned, others were needed: Protagoras, of Abdera on the Thracian coast, in the middle of the century, thought laws were a human convention but necessary to facilitate life in cities; but others, such as the Athenian Antiphon (probably but not certainly a different man from Antiphon the orator),[16] thought they were an undesirable device to prevent able men from living as nature would allow.

The Athenian Socrates was caricatured in Aristophanes' *Clouds* (423), and represented as a great teacher by Xenophon and Plato in the fourth century. He may at one time, as in *Clouds*, have been interested in celestial phenomena and rhetoric. For Xenophon and Plato he was engaged in dialectical argument: for Xenophon he defended a traditional understanding of virtue; for Plato he was more given to exposing the weakness of other men's views than to propounding his own, but he seems to have identified virtue with knowledge (so that those who act wrongly do so because they fail to understand what is right). Among the young men who associated with him were some, such as Alcibiades and Critias, who were involved in the oligarchic movements of the late fifth century; and that is part of the reason why he was condemned and executed, formally for impiety, in 400/399.

After the upheavals of the Peloponnesian War fourth-century Greeks looked for certainties. Plato, an aristocratic Athenian related to the oligarch Critias,[17] founded an institution at the Academy, north-west of the city, and wrote dialogues exploring ethics and politics, knowledge and the soul; he also tried to intervene in the affairs of Syracuse.[18] His pupil Aristotle, from Stagira in Chalcidice, after acting as tutor to Alexander the Great returned to Athens and established the Lyceum, East of the city. He wrote on a wide range of subjects, including natural science and literature as well as what we should consider philosophy and logic, and often worked by generalising from a large number of observed instances.

One topic which interested philosophers was the governance of cities. The oldest distinction was between tyranny[19] and constitutional government. In the first half of the fifth century a threefold division into monarchy, oligarchy or aristocracy and democracy was adopted.[20] For the sophists forms of government belonged to the realm of convention: there was no universally right form but each man preferred the form which benefited himself. Plato in his *Republic* offered a new typology, ranking aristocracy, timocracy (based on ambition for honour), oligarchy, democracy and tyranny in descending order; he elsewhere and Aristotle distinguished good and bad versions of the three traditional forms.

As for the visual arts, monumental temples, with a central room or rooms and columned porches or a colonnade, were first built at Corinth and the Isthmus in the seventh century, and from the sixth century onwards were normally buillt wholly of stone. This form reached its climax in the Parthenon built on the acropolis of Athens between 447/6 and 433/2 (figure 11).[21] By then there were major public buildings of other kinds: in Athens the council house (end C6), the *tholos* (round house) as headquarters of the *prytaneis* (*c.* 460) and a series of stoas (open porticoes: late C6 – late C5) in the agora; the Pnyx where the assembly met (first version perhaps late C6), and the odeum of Pericles. Many grand temples were built in the west between the late sixth century and the late fifth (for a temple at Acragas in Sicily see figure 13); but other places in Greece and the Aegean were in the fifth century overshadowed by Athens, though in the middle of the century the temple of Zeus at Olympia and the temple of Apollo at Bassae in Arcadia were built. Fourth-century buildings include at Athens a new council house and two remodellings of the Pnyx, and the first monumental theatre of Dionysus (figure 14) and the stadium (both *c.*330); elsewhere a new temple of Apollo at Delphi (figure 6) and a new temple of Asclepius and other buildings at Epidaurus in the Argolid. The Mausoleum at Halicarnassus (*c.* 350: figure 15), one of the seven wonders of the Ancient world, combined Greek and Near Eastern elements and was

Figure 14. Athens: theatre of Dionysus (*c*.330).

Figure 15. Halicarnassus: reconstruction of Mausoleum (mid fourth century) (Museum of Ancient Art, Aarhus University.)

perhaps intended as the hero-shrine of the Carian dynast Mausolus.[22] Private houses, in Athens and in Greece generally, seem to have been generally modest until the middle of the fourth century, but after that rich men began to build grander houses. A site which is particularly informative on domestic buildings is Olynthus in Chalcidice, rebuilt in 432 and unoccupied after it was destroyed by Philip of Macedon in 348.[23]

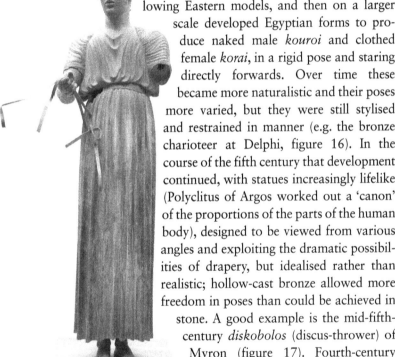

In the Archaic period sculpture began with the 'Daedalic' style of small-scale figures following Eastern models, and then on a larger scale developed Egyptian forms to produce naked male *kouroi* and clothed female *korai*, in a rigid pose and staring directly forwards. Over time these became more naturalistic and their poses more varied, but they were still stylised and restrained in manner (e.g. the bronze charioteer at Delphi, figure 16). In the course of the fifth century that development continued, with statues increasingly lifelike (Polyclitus of Argos worked out a 'canon' of the proportions of the parts of the human body), designed to be viewed from various angles and exploiting the dramatic possibilities of drapery, but idealised rather than realistic; hollow-cast bronze allowed more freedom in poses than could be achieved in stone. A good example is the mid-fifth-century *diskobolos* (discus-thrower) of Myron (figure 17). Fourth-century sculpture had a greater softness (e.g. the Hermes with Dionysus of the Athenian Praxiteles, figure 18), and Lysippus of Sicyon modifed the canon to produce more elegant figures. The earliest surviving sculptures which look like por-

Figure 16. Delphi: statue of charioteer (470s).

115

Figure 17. Rome, Museo Nazionale delle Terme: Myron, statue of *diskobolos* (Roman copy of mid-fifth-century bronze original).

Figure 18. Olympia: Praxiteles, Hermes with child Dionysus (Roman copy of mid-fourth-century original).

Figure 19. Aegeae small tomb: Hades abducting Persephone.

traits of individuals are from the Mausoleum, representing Mausolus and Artemisia or perhaps ancestors of theirs.

Highly accomplished large-scale wall paintings have survived from the Greek civilisations of the bronze age. In Classical Greece large-scale painting, normally on wooden panels, is reported in such buildings as Athens' Painted Stoa (second quarter C5) and Stoa of Zeus (420s), hardly any have survived apart from the fourth-century tomb paintings at Aegeae (Vergina) in Macedon (figure 19). Three-quarter views are said to have been invented by Cimon of Cleonae (*c*.500); Polygnotus of Thasos and Micon of Athens (second quarter C5) used different groundlines and groupings to indicate position; and about the same time Agatharchus of Samos began scene-painting for the theatre at Athens. The paintings at Aegeae are frescoes, painted directly on the walls, with skilful composition (including perspective) and use of colour.

Pottery can be broken but cannot easily be destroyed, and very large quantities of painted pottery survive from the Greek world. There was again high quality and varied work in the bronze age, particularly in the Minoan civilisation of Crete. As Greece emerged from the dark age after *c*.1000 the first style was protogeometric, particularly but not only in Athens, and that was followed by the more elaborate geometric style, beginning after *c*.900. Renewed contact with the wider world led to Eastern influences and an Orientalising style somewhat before 700, particularly in Corinth, which took over the lead from Athens: at first depictions of animals were popular, often in combination with abstract ornaments; later some painters turned to human figures (e.g. the Chigi Vase, from Corinth in the seventh century, figure 3). The Corinthians used painted figures against an unpainted background, and that was the principle followed in the black-figure style which regained the lead for Athens in the sixth century. Towards the end of the sixth century the Athenians switched for most purposes to the more flexible red-figure style, with a black background, and black lines used to provide the details for otherwise unpainted figures (figure 20). As in sculpture there was increasing variety of poses and increasing naturalness in the depiction of figures, and these Athenian styles overwhelmingly dominated the market (but there was independent production in the west in the late fifth and the fourth centuries). Towards the end of the fifth century there was a move in Athens towards gaudier effects, with white paint and gilding, which modern taste finds less attractive; and about the end of the fourth century this kind of decorated pottery went out of fashion.

Figure 20. Voronezh University, Russia: Athenian red-figure *pelike*, showing Orpheus and a Thracian, by Villa Giulia Painter (*c.*475–425: Beazley Archive no. 207206).

# 8

# AFTER THE PELOPONNESIAN WAR, 404–c.360

## INSTABILITY IN THE GREEK WORLD

Xenophon's *Hellenica* continues to 362, and this period is covered also by Diodorus Siculus, XIV–XV.[1] We have *Lives* by Plutarch of the Spartan *Agesilaus* and the Theban *Pelopidas*, Athenian lawcourt speeches, and inscriptions of various kinds of public documents.

With Athens' defeat in the Peloponnesian War, the Athenian empire was at an end. Immediately Sparta did not return the Asiatic cities to Persia in accordance with its treaties of 412–411, but took them over along with the rest of the empire, and collected tribute from them. Lysander was particularly fond of narrow oligarchies, and decarchies, cliques of ten men, were installed in some cities, and the Thirty in Athens.[2]

Darius II died in 405/4 and was succeeded by Artaxerxes II. Cyrus, Artaxerxes' younger brother, assembled an army including ten thousand (in fact, at the beginning thirteen thousand) Greek mercenaries to challenge him, but in 401 was defeated and killed at Cunaxa on the Euphrates; Xenophon's *Anabasis* tells the story of that campaign and the Greeks' return through Armenia to the Black Sea. Tissaphernes returned to Sardis and laid claim to the Asiatic Greeks: they appealed to Sparta, which agreed to fight for them; this is most easily explained if it had obtained a revision of the earlier treaties in 407.[3] At first the fighting was on a small scale, with Spartans other than kings as commanders and men other than Spartan citizens as soldiers (including eventually the survivors of the ten thousand), and was punctuated by truces to consider a compromise on the status of the Asiatic Greeks. In 396 King Agesilaus II, half-brother and successor of Agis,[4] was given the command. He tried, like Agamemnon in the legendary Trojan War, to sacrifice at Aulis in Boeotia, but the Boeotians interfered with his sacrifice; in 395 he won a victory near Sardis (having penetrated further inland than the Athenians in the time of their empire); but in 394 he had to return to Greece.

Sparta's allies in the Peloponnesian War were unhappy with Sparta's conduct at and after the end of the war, and in 395 a border dispute in central Greece led to the outbreak of the Corinthian War (much of the fighting took place near Corinth), in which Boeotia, Corinth and Argos were joined by a reviving Athens in fighting against Sparta. Lysander was defeated and killed at Haliartus in Boeotia in 395; Agesilaus was recalled in 394 and fought his way through Boeotia to the Peloponnese. Meanwhile the Athenian Conon, who had escaped to Cyprus at the end of the Peloponnesian War,[5] had been building up a fleet for Pharnabazus, the Persian satrap at Dascylium, and in 394 they defeated a Spartan fleet off Cnidus, ending Sparta's supremacy in the Aegean. This was in fact a Persian victory over Greeks who had been opposing Persian domination, but the Athenians celebrated Conon and his Cypriot friend Evagoras (from the Greek dynasty which ruled the city of Salamis) as champions of Greek freedom against Spartan tyranny.

The wars dragged on, in Greece and in the Aegean. In Greece Sparta's enemies were brought Persian money by Pharnabazus and Conon; to keep Corinth more firmly anti-Spartan, some kind of union between Corinth and Argos was instituted. In 392 Sparta turned to diplomacy, sending Antalcidas to Tiribazus, the current satrap in Sardis, and the other states involved in the Corinthian War sent envoys too (Athens sent Conon, whom Tiribazus arrested). It was proposed that the Asiatic Greeks should after all be returned to Persia and all other cities and islands should be autonomous; but Sparta's enemies would not accept that. At a conference in Sparta in winter 392/1 a concession was offered to Athens, that it should keep its three north Aegean islands of Imbros, Lemnos and Scyros, which it had possessed for most of the fifth century, and had lost at the end of the Peloponnesian War but had since regained;[6] but Sparta offered no concession on the Boeotian federation[7] or the union of Corinth and Argos, and there was still reluctance to return the Asiatic Greeks to Persia, so again no treaty was made.

In 390 a campaign under the Athenian Thrasybulus[8] seems to have attempted to revive connections and practices of the Athenian empire. He was killed in 389, and his successors did not keep up the momentum, but Athenian decrees of 387/6 for Clazomenae and Erythrae (Harding 26, 28) show Athens still in a buoyant mood. However, in 387 Antalcidas as Spartan admiral was able to regain control of the Hellespont for Sparta and so put Sparta in a strong enough position to obtain the treaty it wanted. In 387/6 the King's Peace, or Peace of Antalcidas, imposed the terms proposed in 392/1: mainland Asia Minor was to belong to Persia (along with Cyprus, where Athens had been supporting Evagoras in extending his power and rebelling against Persia); Athens was to have its three islands; and all other cities were to be autonomous (Athens had also lost Delos after the Peloponnesian War, recovered it in the 390s, lost it again under the King's Peace, but recovered it again soon afterwards). Sparta had obtained the terms and Persia's backing, and Sparta decided what were the entities to which those terms applied and what was to count as autonomy: the Boeotian federation had to be dissolved (though some federations elsewhere in Greece were left intact), and so did the union of Corinth and Argos. This was not simply a treaty to end the Corinthian War, but was envisaged as a 'common peace' for all the Greeks, and it could be invoked with reference to Greeks anywhere in the heartland of mainland Greece and the Aegean: it is not clear how many states not involved in the Corinthian War swore to it, though presumably distant states such as those in Sicily, Italy and North Africa did not.

The Peace was a fact of life, and was to provide a background for Greek inter-state relations for the next half-century. Athens after a period of uncertainty found a way forward in 384, making an alliance with Chios which was purely defensive, and stated to be on a basis of freedom and autonomy and within the framework of the Peace,[9] though c.380 Isocrates in his *Panegyric* (IV), when reasserting Athens' claim to leadership in Greece, contrasted this humiliation with the glories of the fifth century.[10] Sparta proceeded to interpret the Peace in its own interests. In 385 it split Mantinea into the component villages which had united nearly a century earlier.[11] From 382 to 379 it fought against the Chalcidian federation being built up in the North by Olynthus, in response to an invitation from cities which did not wish to be incorporated in that federation; and in 382 it installed a garrison and pro-Spartan régime in Thebes, apparently on the pretext that Thebes was refusing to join in enforcing the Peace against the Chalcidians. Theban opponents of Sparta fled to Athens, and returned from there and recovered control in winter 379/8.

Finally provoked by a raid by Sphodrias, the Spartan garrison commander in Thespiae (west of Thebes), in 378/7 the Athenians founded their Second League, a body of states linked in a defensive alliance modelled on that with Chios. We have an inscribed prospectus, accompanied by a list of members to which names were added in instalments until (probably) 375.[12] The League continued to grow after that: we do not know why additions to this list ceased. Various promises were made to the members – there were to be no constitutional interference, garrisons, governors or tribute, and no Athenian-owned property in allied territory – partly to guarantee that Athens would not behave as it had behaved in the Delian League, and partly to spell out what 'autonomy' was taken to mean. There was a council (*synedrion*) of League members, permanently in Athens: Athens was not represented in that, and it cooperated with the Athenian council to present matters to the Athenian assembly for final decision. The promises were not wholly kept: in the 370s Paros was treated as a colony and required to send offerings to Athenian festivals, and in the 360s revolts in Ceos were put down and some lawsuits were made transferable to Athens; some garrisons are attested (first in Abdera in 375, when the citizens probably welcomed it as a defence against the Thracians); cleruchies[13] were established in Samos and Potidaea when they were acquired,[14] and although these were not members of the League this development might well have alarmed states which were members. Most strikingly, although the Athenians never collected *phoros* ('tribute') from the members, after perhaps relying at first on voluntary payments they did, perhaps from 373, collect *syntaxeis* ('contributions'), though never on a scale which would enrich them.

In the next few years, while Athens was recruiting members for the League, fairly successfully, since the cities were worried more by the current behaviour of Sparta than by memories of the Delian League, Sparta under king Agesilaus tried without success to regain control of Thebes. In 376, when Agesilaus was ill, the other king, Cleombrotus I, was less energetic against Thebes, and a Spartan naval squadron which tried to interrupt Athens' grain supplies from the Black Sea was defeated off Naxos in the first Athenian naval victory since the Peloponnesian War. In 375 a Spartan army in Boeotia was defeated at Tegyra by a Theban army including the 'sacred band', a newly-established élite body of professional citizen soldiers; and to distract Sparta Athens began a war in the West, and defeated a Spartan fleet off Alyzia, opposite Leucas. Jason, the tyrant of Pherae, was becoming powerful in Thessaly, and when Pharsalus asked Sparta for support against him Sparta was unable to respond.

In 375 there was a renewal of the King's Peace, prompted probably by Persia's desire for Greek mercenaries to fight in Egypt.[15] Athens celebrated with a cult and statue of Eirene (peace). But almost immediately the war in the west resumed: it ended in 372 with victory for Athens and the democrats of Corcyra. Thebes meanwhile was building up a new Boeotian federation. The federation of the late fifth and early fourth century had been based on electoral units, organised so that the greater cities accounted for one unit or more than one while others shared in one unit and yet others were dependent on one of those cities and not formally represented. The new federation was based on an assembly which met in Thebes and was dominated by Thebes, and during the 370s Thebes took military action against some Boeotian cities which it perceived as hostile, destroying Plataea and Thespiae.

In 371 the Thebans threatened the neighbouring region of Phocis, and Sparta sent an army under Cleombrotus to defend it. Athens, increasingly uncomfortable with the growing power of Thebes, instigated a conference in Sparta to discuss another renewal of the King's Peace. Originally a treaty was agreed, with the Thebans included as 'Thebans'; but afterwards they returned and asked to be included as 'Boeotians', and after an altercation between Agesilaus and the

Theban leader Epaminondas they were excluded. Cleombrotus was ordered to attack Thebes if it would not leave the Boeotian cities autonomous, and at Leuctra, in the south-west of Boeotia, the Thebans attacked not from the right as was normal with hoplite armies but with a strengthened left wing, and they defeated the Spartans and killed Cleombrotus. This was one of the pivotal moments in Greek history: it had been assumed by everybody that Sparta's hoplite army was better than any other, but the reality no longer matched the image.

After the battle there was another renewal of the common peace, this time organised by Athens. There followed a period of instability in the Peloponnese, as Sparta was no longer able to insist on régimes which it found congenial in the other cities, and no other Peloponnesian city was strong enough to fill the gap. In particular, Mantinea recreated the single state which Sparta had dismantled in 385, and joined with other cities in creating an Arcadian federation, with a new capital at Megalopolis, near the borders of Laconia and Messenia. Arcadia joined with Elis and Argos in an anti-Spartan alliance, and with support from Thebes in winter 370/69 invaded Laconia and liberated Messenia, a loss which Sparta was never prepared to accept. Thebes and other states in central Greece had left the Athenian League, and Thebes was building up a league of its own; in 369 Athens saw that as the greater threat and (not quite ten years after founding its anti-Spartan league) made an alliance with Sparta. In a frustrating decree of 369/8, when Mytilene had asked about Athens' change of policy, the leading politician Callistratus[16] replied that when Sparta was threatening the Greeks in contravention of the peace Athens resisted and called on the other Greeks to join in resistance, but – and the rest of the text is lost.[17]

As with the Delian League in the middle of the fifth century,[18] Athens could not bring itself to disband the League when it no longer pursued the original objective. During the 360s it turned its attention to the North, and fought a series of campaigns in a vain attempt to recover the Chersonese, in order to protect its grain supplies from the Black Sea, and its colony of Amphipolis, lost in 424/3.[19] It was more successful in capturing Samos from the Persians in 366–365 (which under the terms of the Kings' Peace Persia ought not to have possessed); but rather than liberate Samos Athens turned it into an Athenian cleruchy, and a few years later Potidaea was acquired in the course of Athens' northern wars and became another cleruchy.[20]

In northern Greece Jason of Pherae was assassinated in 370 while preparing to attend the Pythian games; other members of his family followed him in quick succession, and were unpopular. The Aleuadae, the leading family of Larisa, first in 369 appealed to Alexander II of Macedon, but he took over Larisa and Crannon for himself. They then appealed to Thebes: dealings with Macedon led to the young Philip's spending some years in Thebes as a hostage; and, after a series of campaigns against Pherae (which was supported by Athens), in 364 the Theban Pelopidas defeated Alexander of Pherae but was himself killed, and a Theban relief army consolidated the victory. Alexander had his power limited to the city of Pherae and was made a subordinate ally of Thebes.

In 367 Thebes tried to obtain a new common peace treaty to its own advantage. Having knocked out Sparta it hoped to knock out Athens too, and the terms which Pelopidas proposed to the Persians included the disbanding of the Athenian navy. It was probably after this that the Athenians deleted from their League's prospectus the clause which referred favourably to the King's Peace – but left undeleted the previous clause which specified the League's anti-Spartan objective.[21] Other proposed clauses offended other Greek states, and no treaty was made; but in 365 a treaty was made which (while perhaps claiming to be a common peace) embraced Thebes and a number of states in the north-eastern Peloponnese, and effectively marked the end of the Peloponnesian League. (This and other treaties stipulated that Messenia was to remain independent, so Sparta regularly refused to join.) In 366 Thebes managed to gain possession of Oropus, a region facing Euboea which was claimed both by Boeotia and by Athens. Epaminondas is said to have planned to build a new Theban fleet and to win over Athens' Aegean allies: the fleet may not have been built, but there was a Theban campaign in the Aegean in 364, and in 362 and 361 Alexander of Pherae turned to attacking Athens.

The Peloponnese in the 360s saw continuing warfare and shifting allegiances. In 365–364 there was a war between Elis and Arcadia, and in 364 the Olympic festival was celebrated by the local people, the Pisatans, and a battle in the sanctuary failed to dislodge them. However, in 363 a division opened within Arcadia, with Mantinea making peace with Elis and transferring its allegiance to Sparta, while Tegea and Megalopolis headed a faction which remained committed to Thebes. In 362 Epaminondas took an army to the Peloponnese, and Thebes and its allies fought against Sparta and its allies at Mantinea: Epaminondas tried to repeat the success of Leuctra but was killed as the Thebans were gaining the upper hand. The division in Arcadia persisted. Xenophon ends his *Hellenica* with the despondent remark that the battle which might have resolved the power struggle resulted in even more indecisiveness and confusion than before.[22]

Persia had gained from the King's Peace the Asiatic Greeks and recognition of its right to Cyprus. Its war against Evagoras ended in 381, when he agreed to obey the Persian King 'as a king to a king' but not 'as a slave to a master'; he survived until 374/3 and his dynasty lasted until 310. Egypt had rebelled against Persia *c.*404/3, and the Persians were not to recover it until 343/2.[23] It was not mentioned in the King's Peace, so the Athenian Chabrias, who had been supporting Evagoras, moved there. In 380/79 Pharnabazus (transferred from Dascylium) was preparing to lead a Persian campaign against Egypt, and protested to Athens, which recalled Chabrias and instead sent Iphicrates to fight on the Persian side. Preparations took several years. and it was probably to increase the availability of Greek mercenaries that the Persians renewed the King's Peace in 375.[24] The invasion finally took place in 374, but Iphicrates fell out with Pharnabazus and returned to Athens, and the campaign petered out.

In the 360s the western margins of the Persian Empire were troubled by the Satraps' Revolt. This began with Datames, satrap of Cappadocia (eastern Asia Minor), and Ariobarzanes, who had succeeded his father Pharnabazus at Dascylium but whose position was claimed by his half-brother Artabazus; it was joined by Mausolus, of a local dynasty which had been in charge of a separate satrapy of Caria since the 390s.[25] When Thebes gained Persian support, Sparta (under King Agesilaus) and Athens supported the rebels

(Athens' capture of Samos was one result of this). The rebels also made contact with Tachos, the current ruler in Egypt, and in 362/1 the Athenian Chabrias (as a free-lance) and the Spartan Agesilaus (officially) went to support him; but the revolt collapsed, and Agesilaus died in 360/59 on his way back to Sparta. Artaxerxes II died in 359/8, and was succeeded by Artaxerxes III.

## SPARTA

At the end of the Peloponnesian War Lysander was in a strong position,[26] but before long there was a reaction against him. He imposed 'decarchies', rule by cliques of ten men, on several cities, and was behind the institution of the Thirty in Athens;[27] but soon the decarchies were replaced by 'traditional constitutions', and king Pausanias facilitated the restoration of democracy in Athens and when put on trial was acquitted. It was alleged that Lysander had plans for replacing Sparta's hereditary kings with elected kings, and that he tried to buy the support of oracles, but it is not clear how far these allegations were justified. When king Agis II died, c.400, Lysander encouraged rumours that his son Leotychidas was in fact the son of Alcibiades,[28] and the throne went to Agis' brother Agesilaus II, who became a strong-minded king not at all inclined to let Lysander rule through him. Soon afterwards a man called Cinadon, an 'inferior' (perhaps downgraded from full citizenship because he could not pay his mess dues), plotted to unite all the other classes against the full citizens; but he was dealt with before the trouble could spread. When Agesilaus was sent to Asia in 396 Lysander was one of the citizen advisers sent with him, but he got Lysander out of his way on separate missions. In 395 Lysander was back in Greece. At the beginning of the Corinthian War he and Pausanias were sent into Boeotia by separate routes: they failed to combine their forces; Lysander fought on his own at Haliartus and was defeated and killed;[29] Pausanias after making a truce to extricate his army was convicted and retired into exile.

Agesilaus was ambitious to expand Sparta's power in Asia, and after their interference with his sacrifice[30] he was vindictively hostile to the Boeotians. But Sparta's wars did not go well, and they were ended by diplomacy, when Antalcidas obtained the King's Peace in 387/6. Agesilaus saw how the Peace could be exploited to Sparta's advantage, and is said to have replied to a complaint that the Spartans were 'medising' (serving Persia's interests)[31] that in reality the Persians were 'laconising' (serving Sparta's interests). Agesilaus backed the Spartan occupation of Thebes in 382, and after Thebes' liberation in 379/8 he was energetic in action against Thebes until he was taken ill. By the end of the decade he was active once more, and it was his confrontation with Epaminondas which led to Thebes' exclusion from the treaty which preceded the battle of Leuctra in 371.

Sparta's defeat there in a full-scale pitched battle was a shocking revelation that Sparta was not as strong as had been supposed. Citizen numbers were suffering an irreversible decline:[32] in contrast to approximately 8,000 full citizens at the beginning of the fifth century Sparta had perhaps about 1,300 before Leuctra and about 900 after, and by now the 'citizen' army perhaps comprised 90% *perioikoi* and only 10% full citizens. The men's lifestyle was not conducive to the fathering of children, and it did not occur to the citizens that they should make up their numbers by promoting men from other categories. One consequence of this drastic reduction was that in the fourth century one in three or four of the citizens had to serve for a year as one of the five ephors.

The 360s saw a decline with which the Spartans could not come to terms. They were no longer able to enforce their will across the Peloponnese; they lost Messenia in 370/69, and the peace treaty of 365 in which some other Peloponnesian states participated but Sparta did not marked the end of the Peloponnesian League. With Thebes now the Greek friend of Persia, Sparta and Athens supported the disaffected satraps in the Satraps' Revolt; and after the battle of Mantinea in 362, when the other Greeks agreed not to support them, Sparta sent Agesilaus to command Greek mercenaries in support of Tachos in Egypt. He died in 360/59, ending his reign as he began it by fighting against the Persians, but now less gloriously. He was a strong king and believed in a strong Sparta, but he was too willing to alienate other Greeks, and Sparta's inherent weakness made his ambitions unrealistic.

## ATHENS

Athens' democracy had lost the Peloponnesian War, and while the demagogue Cleophon remained opposed to peace the settlement followed discussions between Theramenes and Lysander.[33] It is not surprising that there was again a movement towards oligarchy, and under pressure from Lysander the Thirty were instituted in the summer of 404 (the term Thirty Tyrants, commonly used later, seems not to have been used in fourth-century Athens). Theramenes probably thought that, with memories of 411–410 fresh and his own position strong, he would this time be able to achieve a moderate oligarchy, but he was outmanoeuvred by the extremists led by Critias (a relative of Plato).

The Thirty began moderately, but after they had obtained a garrison from Sparta the régime became increasingly violent, and when Theramenes protested he was condemned. A body of 3,000 men with some rights was established, and the others were expelled from the city. But during the winter a growing body of democrats led by Thrasybulus began to fight back, first occupying Phyle, in the northwest of Attica, and then moving to Piraeus. After a battle in which Critias was killed the Thirty were deposed and replaced by a board of Ten, who were perhaps expected to be more tractable but turned out not to be. In summer 403, when Pausanias came with an army from Sparta, he first made a show of force against the democrats but then helped to arrange a reconciliation. Democracy was restored in Athens, and there was an amnesty except for the men most deeply implicated, but a semi-independent state was established at Eleusis for men unwilling to live under the democracy. That lasted until 401/0, when the men at Eleusis hired a mercenary force which the Athenians defeated, and Eleusis was then once more incorporated into Athens.

The slogan 'traditional constitution' (*patrios politeia*) had been deployed for propaganda purposes by men of various shades of opinion, but it now became accepted that for Athens the traditional constitution was democracy. After two bitter experiences of oligarchy nobody active in politics would admit to being an oligarch; but, whereas in the fifth century anybody opposed to the current form of democracy was seen as an oligarch, it now became possible to suggest changes of more or less significance while still professing allegiance to democracy, and this perhaps helped Athens to enjoy stability in the fourth century when many other states did not.

In various ways Athens in 403 self-consciously made a fresh start. The first bout of oligarchy had revealed that there was great uncertainty about the current law on various matters, and in 410 a re-editing of the laws was begun. That was interruptd by the Thirty (who at first had their own plans for legal reform) but resumed afterwards, and the new code and the associated religious calendar were completed in 400/399. A new distinction was now made between 'decrees' of the assembly, on particular matters in particular circumstances, and 'laws', which were intended to be permanent and to apply to all Athenians, and for enacting which a new procedure was introduced. This was intended partly to make it harder for the democracy to vote itself out of existence, as it had done in 411 and 404, and partly in reaction against the view propounded by some of the sophists that law (*nomos*) was mere human convention, to be contrasted with the eternal realities of nature.[34]

Various changes were made in the working of the democracy in the course of the fourth century: on the whole those made in the earlier part of the century can be regarded as in the spirit of the fifth-century democracy. The system of payment for performing the civilian duties of a citizen[35] was completed *c*.400 by the introduction of payment for attending the assembly, perhaps another measure to strengthen the restored democracy. After losses from the Peloponnesian War and the plague Athens had perhaps about 30,000 adult male citizens at the end of the war, in contrast to about 60,000 before the war.[36] But the Athenians reaffirmed Pericles' citizenship law;[37] and, rather than abandon the rule forbidding reappointment to civilian offices (but in the fourth century men could serve twice in the council, and that concession may not have been needed earlier), they stopped enforcing the ban on office-holding by members of the lowest of Solon's four classes,[38] though the ban was not formally rescinded.

Another change was made perhaps in response to the need for economy in an Athens which no longer received tribute from the Delian League. In the fifth century there was a single state treasury into which revenue was paid and from which expenditure was disbursed. In the fourth there was a rudimentary system of budgeting: separate spending authorities were instituted (e.g. the assembly, the council, the fund for paying jurors, the fund for building triremes) and given a regular grant. In principle this made good sense, but the system was inflexible, and if there was no money left in a particular fund money could not be transferred from elsewhere (there were occasions when the lawcourts were suspended because there was no money to pay the jurors). In the first half of the century Athens did not reduce its military ambitions to match its reduced funds, and repeatedly experienced financial difficulties.

There were various changes in the running of the lawcourts. The thirty travelling magistrates who decided lesser private cases[39] had stopped travelling in the last years of the Peloponnesian War, and the oligarchy of 404–403 had made 30 an inauspicious number: in the fourth century their number was increased to 40, and they continued to work in Athens. A new system was introduced for the greater private cases: these went in the first instance to an arbitrator, who was one of the 59-year-old men in their last year on the military registers. Thus no private cases went to a jury except on appeal against the original decision, and this will have saved the state money. Probably by gradual development, though consolidated by law in the end, there was increasing use of writing in the judicial process: prosecutors were required to submit a written document, and witnesses no longer gave their testimony orally but a document was drawn up in advance and in court they had simply to acknowledge or deny it.

There was an increasing desire to guard against the bribery of jurors (there had been a notorious instance in 410 or 409). Six thousand jurors were enrolled each year. In the fifth century each presiding official had a panel of jurors assigned to him for the year, so it was easy to know in advance which jurors would decide which case. In the early fourth century the jurors were divided into ten sections for the year, but sections were allotted to courts day by day.

From the 380s or 370s each juror had a ticket (*pinakion*) bearing his name and other details, and on each day when the courts sat there was an elaborate procedure to assign jurors to courts, involving the placing of the tickets in allotment machines (*kleroteria*). A little later the tickets and allotment machines were used for appointment to offices too. Many Athenians had their tickets deposited in their tombs, and so many of the tickets have survived. Also about the 380s a new body was created to take over from the prytany, one tribe's 50 members of the council,[40] the duty of presiding in the council and assembly: these *proedroi* ('presidents') were appointed day by day, one from each tribe in the council except the current prytany, and the result was that nobody could know in advance which men would preside on a particular day.

Another change foreshadows though only slightly the greater value placed on expertise in the second half of the century.[41] Until the mid 360s the principal secretary of the Athenian state was a member of the council, elected to serve for one prytany in such a way that each tribe provided one secretary during the year. From the mid 360s this secretary was appointed from the citizen body as a whole and served for a whole year; but the appointment was now made by lot, repetition was banned, and from the mid 350s the tribes took it in turn to provide the secretary.

In politics a tendency which had begun in the late fifth century continued in the fourth, by which some men were politically active in Athens while others were military men who commanded armies and navies;[42] the latter sometimes took employment abroad when not commanding Athenian forces.[43] Politicians who dominated the assembly but held no office could not be held to account as office-holders could, so lawsuits were developed through which they could be prosecuted on such charges as making an unlawful proposal or giving bad advice to the people, often coupled with an accusation of taking bribes, since there was no concept of a 'loyal opposition' and it was assumed that no Athenian would work against the interests of Athens unless some enemy had bribed him to do so.

The amnesty of 403 forbade prosecution directly for acts committed before then, but, nevertheless, which side a man had been on in the time of the Thirty could be cited to his advantage or disadvantage for some time afterwards. When Socrates[44] was condemned in 400/399, the formal charge was that he failed to conform to the city's religion and corrupted the young men, but behind the second point was the fact that some men who had associated with him, such as Alcibiades and Critias, had been involved in the oligarchic movements. The vetting process which men had to undergo before entering an office to which they had been appointed[45] provided an opportunity to invoke their record in 404–403. The man originally appointed as archon for 382/1, Leodamas, had been on the oligarchic side, and was successfully challenged; the man appointed in his place, Evandrus, had been on the oligarchic side also, and he in turn was challenged,[46] but his appointment was upheld.

As in the fifth century, political attachments were primarily to individuals, though policies espoused by an individual could be one (but only one) reason for supporting him or opposing him. We have no evidence of fundamental disagreement on internal matters in this period. In foreign policy most Athenians had the same hopes for Athens most of the time, but there were two major turning-points where some men made the turn earlier than others, and some kept to the old policy after it had gone out of fashion: in the 390s, on accepting the position of subordination to Sparta imposed in 404 or pursuing an independent foreign policy once more; and in the years around 371, on recognising that Thebes rather than Sparta had come to pose the greatest threat to Athens. Prominent politicans included Thrasybulus, leader of the returning democrats in 403; Agyrrhius, from the restoration to the 370s (but he spent some time in prison after being convicted of embezzling public money), and his nephew Callistratus, in the 370s and 360s. The end of Callistratus' career is puzzling: in 361 he was prosecuted, we do not know why, and in his absence was condemned to death; he escaped into exile; later he risked returning to Athens, but he was still unpopular and was put to death then. Among leading generals were Conon and his son Timotheus; Iphicrates, who for many years was an enemy of Timotheus, but they were reconciled in the 360s; and Chabrias, who seems to have been particularly close to Callistratus.

## THE WEST

Our main source here is Diodorus Siculus, in book XIV (to 386) detailed and hostile to Dionysius, in book XV much less detailed and uncommitted on Dionysius. After the defeat of Athens' Sicilian expedition of 415–413,[47] Hermocrates of Syracuse in 412 took a small Sicilian contingent to support Sparta in the Aegean, but in his absence Diocles headed a revolution which resulted in a more extreme democracy. Egesta, which the Athenians had failed to help against Selinus, in 410 appealed to Carthage, and for the first time since 480[48] the Carthaginians accepted an invitation to greater involvement in Sicily. In 409 they captured Selinus and Himera, and Diocles failed to save Himera. In 407 Hermocrates returned to Sicily: when he tried to fight his way back into Syracuse he and several of his supporters were killed, but one who survived was Dionysius, who was to form marriage links with Hermocrates' family.

In 406 the Carthaginians invaded again, and besieged and captured Acragas. In Syracuse Dionysius complained of the generals' failure to save Acragas, and a new board of generals was appointed which included him. In 405 he quarrelled with his colleagues, had himself appointed 'general with full powers', and from this point onwards can be regarded as a tyrant. But he failed to save Gela and Camarina when the Carthaginians advanced on them, and he had to fight to re-establish his position in Syracuse. However, after a lacuna in Diodorus' text we find the Carthaginians suffering from a plague (perhaps on account of the marshy land outside Syracuse), and returning home with a treaty by which they were to possess the west of the island and the Greek cities which they had captured were to be unfortified and tributary to them. After subsequent wars there were changes in detail, but the Carthaginians were to retain their presence in Sicily until they were driven out by the Romans in the third century.[49]

Dionysius consolidated his position, and in 402–400 fought successfully against the Greek cities of the East Coast, and Rhegium on the toe of Italy. In preparing for a war against Carthage he is credited with the introduction to the Greek world of catapults (at this stage, probably arrow-firing mechanical bows) and of quadriremes and quinqueremes (ships broader than triremes,[50] with more than one man to an oar). The war began in 397, with the expulsion of Carthaginian traders from the Greek cities and an attack on the Carthaginians' possessions in the west of the island; in 396 the Carthaginians fought back (and Dionysius faced another challenge in Syracuse); they were again hit by a plague but resumed the war, and in 392 the war ended with a treaty similar to that of 405. In the next few years Dionysius fought successfully against Rhegium and other cities in southern Italy, and developed more extensive ambitions, with interventions in Epirus and Illyria, colonies in the Adriatic and a raid on an Etruscan temple, and in Syracuse grand public works. He sent chariots and poems to compete at the Olympic games of (probably) 384, but Lysias in his *Olympic Speech* (XXXIII) called him 'tyrant of Sicily' (he seems to have favoured the title *archon*, 'ruler', of Sicily) and urged that he should be excluded, his poems were laughed at, his chariots were involved in accidents and the homeward-bound ship was hit by a storm. About this time he had trouble with some of his supporters, and, while he tried to build up a court circle, he had to face criticisms of his poetry from a poet and of his tyranny from the Athenian Plato.

From 386 onwards we have much more meagre information in book XV of Diodorus. Dionysius provoked another war with Carthage. It began in the late 380s and perhaps continued into the 370s, and involved Carthaginian support for Dionysius' enemies in southern Italy; it ended with a treaty similar to the previous ones. In 368 Dionysius again started a war against Carthage by invading the west of the island. From time to time Sparta had given him some support, while in the 390s an attempt by Athens to win him over was unsuccessful. He sent help to Sparta in Greece in 372 and again in 369 and 368, and in 368 Athens, now on the same side as Sparta, made him an ally but could not persuade the League to accept him as a member. At the Lenaean festival in Athens at the beginning of 367 his tragedy *The Ransom of Hector* was awarded first prize, and it may be true that he died shortly after he had in that way 'defeated his betters'. It is hard to make a fair assessment on the basis of the evidence which we have. Dionysius came to power on the pretext that others were not resisting Carthage successfully, but although Syracuse itself was never captured his own campaigns against Carthage never ended with success. He was ambitious, militarily and culturally. He relied on mercenaries, and subjected the other Greek cities in the West to wars and population movements, as the tyrants of the early fifth century had done before him;[51] but the Carthaginians were cruel towards their enemies, and most of the western Greeks preferred subjection to him to subjection to Carthage.

He was succeeded by his son Dionysius II, who made peace with Carthage. Dion, a man with philosophical leanings who was both a brother-in-law and a son-in-law of the elder Dionysius, on two occasions had Plato brought back to Syracuse to attend to the younger Dionysius' education, but this led only to friction and the exile of Dion.

# 9

# THE RISE OF MACEDON, *c.*360–323

## PHILIP II, 359–336

Lower Macedonia, the area around the Thermaic Gulf which contained the old capital at Aegeae (modern Vergina) and the fourth-century capital at Pella, and the southern part of Upper Macedonia, were within the present-day boundaries of Greece; the northern part of Upper Macedonia was within the present-day Republic of Macedonia and the western fringe of Bulgaria. Upper Macedonia contained peoples with their own rulers, whom the kings of Lower Macedonia hoped to control. The Macedonian language was a dialect of Greek. The kings were recognised as Greek for the purpose of competing at Olympia on the basis of a (probably invented) claim that they belonged to the branch of descendants of the legendary Heracles which had provided the kings of Argos. The people could be regarded as Greek by Greeks who wished to be polite to them and as barbarian by Greeks who did not, and Thucydides at one point distinguishes them both from Greeks and from 'real' barbarians.[1] The kings ruled, rather as Homeric kings were imagined to have ruled, by tacit understanding rather than explicit laws about what their powers were; they could be referred to as kings by the Greeks, but probably did not use *basileus* as a formal title before the time of Alexander the Great; succession was within the family but not always from father to son.

In 480–479 Alexander I was king, nominally on the Persian side but in contact with the Greeks.[2] From before the Peloponnesian War until *c.*413 Perdiccas I manoeuvred between the Athenians and the Spartans;[3] Archelaus, who ruled from then until 399,[4] was a strong king and a moderniser, and attracted a cultural court circle. His death was followed by a period of instability; the longest-reigning king, Amyntas III (392–370/69), at one stage lost territory to the Chalcidians, to the East, and was driven out by the Illyrians, to the West. In the 360s Thebes became involved with Macedon, when both were interested in Thessaly, and so did Athens, when it tried to recover Amphipolis.[5] Philip II came to the throne in 359, after his brother Perdiccas III was killed in a war against the Illyrians; Perdiccas had a son, Amyntas, but he was too young to rule.

Book XVI of Diodorus Siculus is detailed (based on the work of Ephorus with a supplement by his son) to the end of the Sacred War in 346, but much less detailed after that; there is a shorter account of Macedon before and during Philip's reign in Justin VII–IX (in Latin, c.200–400 AD, an epitome of Pompeius Trogus, *Philippic History*, first century BC).[6] We also have evidence – plentiful but to be read with care – in the speeches of the Athenians Demosthenes and Aeschines. We have inscriptions from Athens and elsewhere, and archaeological evidence includes the city of Olynthus, destroyed by Philip, and Pella and Aegeae in Macedon.

Philip proved to be effective both in fighting and in diplomacy; he was skilful at conveying hints which he did not regard as firm promises but other people did. To gain time he made peace with the Illyrians and with the Paeonians, to the North; and by detaching their backers he dealt with two other claimants to the throne. One of these was supported by the Athenians, and to them he suggested that he would enable them to regain Amphipolis. Meanwhile he began a reform of the army: in addition to its traditional strong cavalry he gave it for the first time a capable infantry phalanx, armed more lightly than Greek hoplites and with a spear, the *sarissa*, which at 18 feet = 5.5 m was twice the length of Greek hoplites' spears. In 358 he was able to fight successfully against the Paeonians and Illyrians, and made his first contact with Thessaly. In 357 he made an alliance with the Molossians of Epirus, and married Olympias, who in 356 bore him Alexander; and he captured Amphipolis, and kept it for himself. The Athenians indignantly declared war, but were distracted by events elsewhere. He captured Potidaea, expelled the Athenian settlers[7] and gave the site to Olynthus. Beyond

Amphipolis he captured Crenides in Thrace and refounded it as Philippi; he now controlled the gold and silver mines of the region, and his currency was to supplant Athenian as the most desirable currency in the Greek world.

In the 360s Athens had been pursuing its own interests in ways which were worrying to members of its League, and towards the end of the decade Thebes had tried to exploit the worries.[8] Since Leuctra the cities of Euboea had been aligned with Thebes, but in 357 Athens took advantage of disagreement between pro-Theban and pro-Athenian parties to regain their allegiance. However, probably in 356 and 355, several of the League's Aegean members were incited to revolt in the Social War (war 'against the allies') by Mausolus of Caria:[9] shockingly, the Athenians were defeated in naval battles, and the rebel states left the League.

Although Pelopidas and Epaminondas had died in 364 and 362, Thebes was still powerful and ambitious. It had begun to take an interest in Delphi, where the temple of Apollo had been destroyed in 373/2 and the collection of funds for a new temple had begun in 366 (cf. figure 6). A new Theban treasury was built there to commemorate the victory at Leuctra, and c.360 Thebes was granted *promanteia*, precedence in the consultation of the oracle. In 363/2 some aristocrats of the city of Delphi were expelled, and Athens took them in and denied the legitimacy of their expulsion. In the early 350s the Amphictyony[10] imposed fines on two enemies of Thebes: on Sparta, for sacrilege committed during the occupation of Thebes between 382 and 379, and on Phocis, which had been allied to Thebes in the 360s but had not been sufficiently loyal. Both refused to pay, and in 356 the Phocians under Philomelus seized Delphi. Thus began the Third Sacred War.

The Phocians defeated attempts to evict them, gained support from Athens, Sparta and a few other Peloponnesian states, and built up a mercenary army. In 355 the Thebans appealed to the Thessalians, who dominated the Amphictyony, and a formal sacred war was declared, supported by most of central Greece. The Phocians had several successes; in 354 Philomelus committed suicide after a defeat, but the Phocians fought on, again successfully. Philip intervened on the side of the Amphictyony for the first time in 353, and was twice defeated (which encouraged Greeks to think that he would present no more of a challenge than his predecessors); but in 352 he returned, was appointed *archon* of Thessaly, and was victorious in the major battle of the 'Crocus Field'. He advanced through Thessaly to Thermopylae, but the Athenians sent a force promptly and he did not try to fight his way through. Under the cover of the Sacred War, in the Peloponnese Sparta hoped to recover Messenia, and from 353 to 350 fought a war against Megalopolis; but the war ended with a truce which changed nothing.

Philip had in the meantime been advancing eastwards through Thrace, and he returned there in 352 after leaving Thermopylae, attacking a fortress near the Propontis in the territory of the east Thracian ruler Cersebleptes. Cersebleptes had already allowed Athens to send cleruchs to the Chersonese, and Athens now voted to send support to him, but delayed on hearing that Philip was ill; in 351 Cersebleptes was made a vassal of Philip. The Chalcidians, earlier allied to Philip, now felt threatened by him and inclined to Athens; and he sent naval expeditions into the Aegean, even raiding Marathon. Although in fact he was probably not specifically targeting Athens, he could now be perceived as posing a serious threat to Athens, and it was probably in 352/1 that Demosthenes recognised that in his *First Philippic* (IV), and urged Athens to campaign as near to Macedon as possible. His advice was not taken, and it was now too late to pursue this strategy which might have been effective early in Philip's reign.

In 349 Philip began a war against the Chalcidians, and Demosthenes in his *Olynthiac* speeches (I–III) urged support for them, in accordance with the strategy of his *First Philippic*. But early in 348 Athens was called on to intervene in rivalries in the Euboean cities, and most Athenians thought that more important, since if Euboea were on Philip's side he could use it to bypass Thermopylae if he wanted to move southwards. In the event, things went badly for Athens in both areas: Euboea apart from Carystus passed out of the Athenian orbit, and the Chalcidian war ended with Olynthus betrayed and destroyed. Demosthenes seems for a time to have favoured peace, since the Athenians would not follow his recommendations, but other Athenians were alarmed and tried to assemble an alliance against Philip.

The Sacred War was continuing, and in 348 the Phocians were getting the better of it. But they had been using Delphic funds to pay their mercenaries, and in winter 348/7 the latest general, Phalaecus, was deposed, and an enquiry found against the successive generals other than Philomelus. In 347 Philip sent a token force to support Thebes; he was expected to take part again in 346, and the Phocians appealed to Sparta and Athens. But early in 346 Phalaecus returned to power and, probably encouraged by hints from Philip, rejected the help of Sparta and Athens. For Athens to help Phocis was impossible if the Phocians refused to be helped; it turned to negotiation with Philip, and other states sent envoys also. He prepared a large army but kept everybody uncertain as to his intentions. In July, when he was at Thermopylae and it was too late to stop him, he made it clear that he was on the side of the Amphictyony as he always had been; the Phocians capitulated, and Phalaecus and his mercenaries were allowed to escape; at a special meeting of the Amphictyony Phocis and Sparta (but not Athens) were expelled, and Phocis was split into villages and ordered to repay Delphi's money in instalments. Philip was admitted to the Amphictyony, and in the autumn presided at the Pythian games. Thebes though on the winning side was exhausted after ten years of damaging warfare.

Athens' negotiations with Philip concerned not only the Sacred War but the war over Amphipolis which had been declared in 357. Demosthenes and Aeschines have each left us two accounts, from 343 and from 330, and it is difficult to make out what actually happened. It seems that before Athens sent its first deputation to Philip Aeschines had been one of those wanting to resist him, while Demosthenes had wanted peace so that the sequel would show that his distrust of Philip had been justified. Both men served on that deputation, with Demosthenes sceptical but Aeschines wishfully believing the hints that Philip might change sides. Philip sent envoys to Athens, who arrived in April. The assembly met for two days: on the first it considered a common peace treaty which all the Greeks could join or a treaty which would explicitly exclude the Phocians (the second was proposed by Philocrates, and the treaty finally made is referred to as the Peace of Philocrates); on the second day Demosthenes interrogated Philip's envoys, and they made it clear that

Athens could have peace on Philip's terms or no peace.

That led to a treaty with Philip for Athens and 'its allies', which meant Athens and its League, but was potentially ambiguous in that Phocis was an ally of Athens. The Athenian envoys went back to Macedon so that Philip could swear to the treaty, and had to wait while he was in Thrace fighting against Cersebleptes. Cersebleptes tried unsuccessfully to join the League in time to be included in the peace, and Philip did not allow Phocis to be included. He then marched to Thermopylae and obtained the Phocians' surrender. The Athenians were afraid that Philip might attack them, but he did not; they boycotted the Pythian games; some Athenians wanted to fight immediately, but Demosthenes, while expecting another war with Philip, in his speech *On the Peace* (V) warned that if Athens fought now it would be alone and clearly in the wrong. Almost certainly, despite his hints, Philip had no intention of deserting the Amphictyony, and there is no good evidence that, as urged by Isocrates in his *Philip* (V), he was yet contemplating a war against Persia for which the Athenian navy would be valuable. He took his commitment to Delphi seriously, and for a Macedonian king the recognised position in the Greek world which he gained in 346 was a worthwhile objective in its own right.

Philip consolidated his position, with a war against the Illyrians and further interventions in Thessaly. Demosthenes planned to prosecute Aeschines for treason in the negotiations,[11] and to win support in Athens and elsewhere in Greece for his hostile view of Philip, while Philip offered to amend the treaty. In 344, when there was no consensus, Athens neither responded favourably to Philip nor sent help to Persia for its latest attempt to recover Egypt (cf. Demosthenes' *Second Philippic* [VI]).[12] Between 344 and 342, when Philip offered to 'give' Athens Halonnesus, an island in the north Aegean, Hegesippus insisted that by rights it belonged to Athens and could only be 'given back', that Amphipolis and some places in Thrace also by rights belonged to Athens, and that the Peace of Philocrates ought to be expanded into a common peace (a speech by him survives as [Dem.] VII. *Halonnesus*). Philip eventually saw that he could exploit a common peace to his advantage, but he did not give way otherwise, and the negotiations collapsed. In various places in Greece there were local disputes in which Philip was invited to support one side and Athens the other. One place where he intervened was the Molossian kingdom, where he expelled Arybbas (who fled to Athens) and replaced him with Alexander, nephew of Arybbas and brother of Philip's wife Olympias. In Euboea his interventions were in support of unpopular leaders, and in 341 the cities there were brought back on to the Athenian side.

In 342 Philip returned to Thrace, finally expelling Cersebleptes. Athens sent further cleruchs and a garrison to the Chersonese, and they came into conflict with Cardia, on the isthmus and included as an ally of Philip in the Peace of Philocrates. The matter escalated; in support of an aggressive line by Athens we have Demosthenes' *Chersonese*, *Third Philippic* and *Fourth Philippic* (VIII, IX, X). In 340 Philip began to besiege Perinthus and Byzantium, using the latest machinery including torsion-powered catapults, while Demosthenes had persuaded other Greeks and the Persians to join in resisting him. When Philip captured Athenian merchant ships waiting to be convoyed from the Black Sea to the Aegean, Athens declared war. But his sieges did not go well, and in 339 he withdrew.

He was brought back into Greece by the Fourth Sacred War. Athens had been renewing at Delphi Persian War dedications which stressed the medism of Thebes; at the Amphictyony in 340 Amphissa objected on behalf of Thebes, and Aeschines as Athens' representative complained that Amphissa was cultivating the sacred land of Cirrha, below Delphi. This led to the declaration of a sacred war against Amphissa, in which Thebes and at Demosthenes' insistance Athens refused to join. In 339 Philip was invited to command, and, after beginning to take the direct route south from Thermopylae towards Amphissa, he turned eastwards in the direction of Boeotia. He and Athens both sent deputations to Thebes; Demosthenes succeeded in making an alliance between Thebes and Athens, and several other Greek states supported them. During the winter Philip failed to break through his opponents' line in the north of Boeotia, but in 338 after feigning withdrawal he advanced to take Amphissa and reach the Gulf of Corinth. In August he encountered his opponents at Chaeronea in Boeotia, and defeated them (his son Alexander on his left wing annihilated the Thebans' sacred band). Afterwards he commissioned the Philippeum at Olympia, to house statues of himself and his family.

As in 346 there was panic in Athens, but Philip did not attack. It would have been hard to take Athens by storm, and by now he was contemplating a Persian war. He was more vindictive towards Thebes, as a former ally which had turned against him. His settlement included a garrison and a pro-Macedonian régime in Thebes, and garrisons in Corinth (on Acrocorinth, the hill towering over the city: figure 4) and (near Epirus) Ambracia. In winter 338/7 at a meeting in Corinth he imposed a common peace treaty on the mainland Greeks (except Sparta, which could be left in isolation) and organised them under his leadership in what is called the League of Corinth (and the inclusion of Athens meant the end of what remained of the Second Athenian League). His dominant position was clothed in familiar Greek garb, and the combination of a league with a common peace treaty provided a more effective, though not impartial, means of enforcement than the previous common peace treaties had had. For Athens this was a major loss: after being able to give orders to other states for a century and a half, it now had to take orders from Philip. But for most Greek states being beholden to Philip was no worse than being beholden to Athens, Sparta or Thebes, and Philip from his greater distance and with his wider concerns was less likely to interfere with them. Because of the position which Athens claimed in the Greek world, Demosthenes had been right to see Philip as a threat to Athens, but he had been wrong to represent him as a threat to the whole of Greece. The League decided on a war against Persia, which could be sold to the Greeks as a war of revenge for 480–479, and advance forces were sent out in 336.

Philip's reign ended with dynastic trouble. There were many women in his life, and it is not profitable to distinguish between wives and mistresses. His first son, Philip Arrhidaeus, was mentally defective. Alexander, born in 356 to his Molossian wife Olympias, was regarded as his heir. But in 337 he took a Macedonian wife, Cleopatra, who might bear a son to supplant Alexander. Alexander and Olympias fled to the Molossians. A reconciliation with Alexander was arranged, and to placate Olympias and her brother, the Molossian Alexander, Philip arranged for him to marry the Cleopatra who was Philip's daughter by Olympias. At the celebration of that marriage at Aegeae in 336 Philip was stabbed to death by a member of his bodyguard. Officially the ruling family of Lyncestis in Upper Macedonia was blamed; there were various rumours, some pointing to Olympias and/or her son Alexander, but the truth cannot be recovered. One of the royal tombs at Aegeae is best identified as that of Philip and one of his wives, with a skull reflecting his loss of an eye in one campaign (figure 21). In two and a half decades Philip had brought Macedon from a position on the margins of Greece to a dominant position in Greece, but he was killed in circumstances which might plunge Macedon back into its previous turmoil.

## ALEXANDER III, 336–323

But there was no turmoil. Alexander was presented to the Macedonians as the new king by Antipater, one of Philip's generals; Philip's new wife Cleopatra and the daughter to whom she had given birth were put to death, and so was Cleopatra's uncle Attalus, in Asia Minor with Philip's advance force. Alexander marched South through

Figure 21. Aegeae: reconstructed head of Philip II of Macedon, Manchester Museum, The University of Manchester.

Greece, to be greeted with protestations of loyalty, and the League of Corinth appointed him as commander of the war against Persia. In 335 he campaigned in Thrace and Illyria; rumours that he had been killed prompted a revolt in Thebes, but he arrived there all too quickly, and shocked the Greek world by capturing and destroying one of its major cities.

There were various accounts of Alexander's reign by contemporaries or near-contemporaries, but none have survived. A Greek who went on the campaign as official historian, Aristotle's nephew Callisthenes, ended his life in trouble.[13] The five major accounts which do survive are, in chronological order, Diodorus Siculus XVII (first century BC), Q. Curtius Rufus (in Latin, first century AD), Plutarch, *Alexander* (first/second century AD: the Roman parallel is *Caesar*), Arrian, *Anabasis* (second century AD), Justin XI–XII (*c*.200–400 AD, epitomising the earlier Pompeius Trogus). Arrian followed writers who had served under Alexander and were in a position to know the truth even if it might not always suit them to tell the truth, Ptolemy and Aristobulus. Diodorus, Curtius and Justin have material in common which is probably derived from Clitarchus, who wrote soon after Alexander's death, had a taste for the sensational and preserved details not always favourable to Alexander. Many recent studies have relied on this alternative and less favourable tradition, but it is unwise to assume that what is favourable is always fictitious and what is unfavourable is always true.

Persia had experienced dynastic problems, which ended with the accession in 336 of Darius III.[14] Philip's advance force was sent to Asia in 336, originally under Parmenio and Attalus, but Alexander had Attalus as the uncle of Philip's new wife Cleopatra killed. Parmenio was successful, and popular with the Greek cities, in 336, but in 335 Memnon of Rhodes struck back on behalf of the Persians, leaving Parmenio in control only of territory near the Hellespont. Alexander came in 334, with perhaps 4,500 or 5,100 cavalry and 32,000 infantry (later he received reinforcements on various occasions, but had to leave garrisons behind in many places); at the crossing of the Hellespont he identified his campaign with the legendary campaign against Troy (through his mother he was allegedly descended from the Trojan War hero Achilles). He fought and won his first major battle at the River Granicus, near Dascylium, but came close to being killed by one of the Persians; and he then proceeded down the Aegean coast. Miletus and Halicarnassus had to be taken by siege; Memnon, dislodged from Halicarnassus, took to the Aegean islands, but died in 333 before he could cause serious problems for Alexander. Alexander went inland to Gordium, and to indicate that he would become ruler of Asia he unravelled or cut the 'Gordian knot' which fastened a wagon to a plinth. In 333 he proceeded round the coast from Cilicia into Syria: Darius III took an inland route and arrived in his rear, and Alexander turned back to defeat him on a narrow coastal plain at Issus.

While Darius returned to the centre of the empire to prepare for another encounter, Alexander, not surprisingly for a man with a Macedonian and Greek background, began with the Mediterranean coast. In 332 after besieging Tyre and Gaza he advanced into Egypt, where he was welcomed as a liberator. He founded his first Alexandria on the coast, at the west end of the Nile delta, and in the winter visited the oracle of Ammon in the Libyan desert. In 331 he returned to Syria and then turned inland. Scorched earth in the Euphrates valley forced him to follow the Tigris, where Darius was waiting for him, but at Gaugamela he again defeated Darius. Darius fled to Ecbatana (Hamadan, in Iran). Alexander proceeded to Babylon, and then to the Persian palaces at Susa and Persepolis; Persepolis was destroyed, either as an act of revenge for the Persians' destruction of Athens in 480 or as the culmination of a wild celebration.

Meanwhile in 331 King Agis of Sparta had begun a rising against the Macedonians in Greece and laid siege to Megalopolis. The Athenians decided not to join in; and Antipater, left in charge of Macedon by Alexander, defeated the Spartans and killed Agis. Sparta was then probably enrolled in the League of Corinth.

In 330 Darius withdrew to the East. Alexander went in pursuit of him (the League of Corinth's war of revenge was officially ended, and Greek allies went home or re-enlisted as mercenaries). Before Alexander could reach him Darius was stabbed to death by Bessus; Alexander gave him a royal funeral, and afterwards increasingly represented himself as legitimate king of Asia. Pursuit of Darius turned into pursuit of Bessus; after difficult fighting against some of the satraps Alexander caught him in 329 in Bactria (Afghanistan), and convened a special court of Medes and Persians to condemn him for killing the king. After guerrilla warfare and the spectacular capture of mountain fortresses, Alexander reached the Indus in 326.

In the last of his major battles Alexander defeated an Indian prince, Porus, at the River Hydaspes (Jhelum), but considered him a worthy foe and left him in position as a vassal ruler. He then wanted to advance against a great kingdom and to what was thought to be the end of Asia, but at the easternmost tributary of the Indus, the Hyphasis (Beas), the army refused to continue, and he was forced to change his plan. He went downstream, and was seriously wounded in the attack on one town, but in 325 reached the mouths of the Indus. To return to the centre of the empire he divided his forces. Ships were built, and Nearchus sailed to the Persian Gulf; Craterus took veterans by an inland route; Alexander went through the desert of Gedrosia (the Makran, in Pakistan), but that proved even more challenging than he had expected, and there were heavy losses.

After the survivors had celebrated, in 324 Alexander returned to the great palaces. Many people had thought he would never return: now several leading men, specially Persians, were arrested and some were executed. Satraps were required to disband their mercenary armies, and, perhaps to address the problem of roaming mercenaries, Greek states were ordered to take back their exiles. Alexander and many of his officers married Persian wives. When 30,000 young Orientals who had been undergoing training since 327 were paraded, and he announced that he would send his European veterans home, at Opis there was a mutiny: it was quelled and there was a banquet of reconciliation, but he did not change his plans. Hephaestion, the man closest to him, died, and this was a great blow to him. In 323 he moved to Babylon: he had plans for expeditions to Arabia and to the Caspian, and other projects were talked of. Envoys came from Greek cities to pay him divine honours. But at the end of May he was taken ill after a party, and in mid June he died, not quite 33 years old. Inevitably there was talk of a plot, but probably Alexander's hard fighting and hard living had weakened him so that he could not throw off an innocent illness. He left two sons, by different Asiatic women. It was said that when asked who was to succeed him he replied, 'the best' or 'the strongest'.

Alexander had the infantry phalanx and cavalry he had inherited from Philip, and allied and mercenary forces of various kinds; in set-piece battles he stationed the infantry in the centre (with a special brigade of 'hypaspists' on the right of their line) and the allied cavalry on the left, and attacked with the Macedonian cavalry from the right. In the later part of the campaign, when there was more need for separate operations by separate units, the commanders of the separate cavalry regiments became more important; and Asiatic cavalry came to be incorporated in the army. In the first three of the great battles Alexander's army was better able to exploit gaps in the enemy's line than the enemy's army was in his; at the Hydaspes, after crossing the river at several points, he kept his left-wing cavalry concealed to mislead the enemy. He excelled also in sieges, using the latest machinery including stone-throwing catapults and portable machines as field artillery, and he showed tactical ingenuity in a variety of smaller episodes; we hear little of his supply train but it must have been well organised. The one area in which he did not have to prove himself was naval warfare. As a commander he was never at a loss, frequently surprised the enemy by his speed, and drove his men hard but won their support, but he sometimes took personal risks to a dangerous extent.

In administration Alexander was pragmatic; the Persian system of satraps and other provincial officials was retained. Island Greeks were added to the League of Corinth; Greek cities of Asia Minor were made allies but not enrolled in the League; and Alexander initially favoured democracies because the oligarchs had been pro-Persian. Western provinces could be 'liberated' from the Persians (while in practice experiencing little apart from a change of ruler), but the central, Persian, provinces could not, and there he appointed a series of Persian satraps. In India he returned to Macedonian satraps, but under them retained as vassals local rulers willing to cooperate with him. Only six Alexandrias can be regarded as cities certainly founded by him, but other existing towns were given European garrisons. Their purposes were administrative and military: while the European occupants took Greek culture with them, they did not mingle enthusiastically with the local population, and at the end of Alexander's reign many tried to return home. But these cities, and those founded later by the Seleucids,[15] did have a Hellenising effect, as Greek language and culture became attributes of the ruling class across the empire.

Alexander inherited not only Philip's army but Philip's officers, and Parmenio as second-in-command and various members of his family were particularly well placed. Some died or were demoted. There was a particular crisis in 330, when Parmenio's son Philotas was said not to have passed on information about a conspiracy: Alexander demanded the death penalty, and the army voted it; Parmenio, left in the centre when Alexander continued in pursuit of Darius, might not be trustworthy after that, so Alexander had him killed too. A group of men who supported Alexander on this occasion, including his favourite Hephaestion, were important afterwards. In 328 Clitus (who had saved Alexander's life at the Granicus) complained of Alexander's Orientalism and disparagement of Philip, and in a drunken argument Alexander killed him. In 327 opposition to Alexander's desire to introduce the custom of *proskynesis* among his European followers[16] was led by Callisthenes, and he was later blamed for a conspiracy among young men in Alexander's entourage and eliminated. In the mutiny at the Hyphasis in 326 the soldiers were championed by Coenus, one of the men who had backed Alexander against Philotas; he died soon afterwards, but no source alleges foul play. We have already noticed the purge after Alexander's return from India, and the mutiny at Opis.[17] Probably Alexander did not scheme to get rid of men he considered enemies but reacted impulsively to crises, but the overall effect was that many leading men did not survive to the end of his reign.

Alexander was a Macedonian, allegedly descended from legendary heroes, and given a Greek education, by Aristotle among others. For the Macedonians his war was a war of conquest; for the Greeks it was represented as revenge for 480–479, and it suited them and him to invoke the Trojan War as a precedent. By 330 he controlled the great palaces, and the object of the war of revenge had been achieved. Darius served as a further objective; after his death Bessus; after that an advance against a great Indian kingdom and to 'the end of

Asia'. He was a man motivated by strong urges and eager to rise to challenges.

After the death of Darius he saw himself as King of Asia; but, while offending conservative Europeans with items of Oriental clothing and custom, he did not adopt the titles or the religion and all the customs of the Persian kings, and so he failed to win over the Persians. Some have argued from a few texts that he originated the doctrine of the 'brotherhood of man', but the texts will not bear the weight that has been put on them. At most he envisaged a kingdom in which Greeks/Macedonians and Persians would be two dominant races; but his conquests created a cosmopolitan world unlike that of the Greek cities, in which the doctrine could and did develop.

Originally in Greek religion there was a clear division between gods and mortals, though some mortals, such as founders of cities, could become heroes and receive a lesser kind of veneration, and upper-class men might claim to be descended from gods or heroes. However, in the century before Alexander some men such as Lysander had pushed against the division,[18] none more than Philip (the city renamed Philippi and the Philippeum at Olympia[19] are two instances among several). Greeks had written of outstanding men as godlike, but without seriously implying that an exceptional man could become a god. Olympias had suggested to Alexander that his true father was Zeus. As pharaoh of Egypt he became a descendant of Ammon (identified by the Greeks with Zeus), and at the oracle of Ammon he was allegedly greeted as 'son of Zeus'. In 327 he tried (but abandoned it in the face of opposition) to extend to his European followers the Persian custom of *proskynesis* towards a superior, blowing a kiss, which could be accompanied by a bow or prostration. For Persians this was a social custom without religious implications, and Alexander must have realised that, but for Greeks it was appropriate only towards gods. The proposal does not prove that Alexander wanted to be treated as a god, but he no doubt liked being reverenced in that way. Hephaestion after his death was pronounced to be a hero; and at the end of Alexander's reign it does seem that the Greek cities (but no barbarians) were prepared to treat him as a god: there is little evidence that the initiative came from him, and more probably, though he had come to see himself as somebody special and enjoyed such honours, this was a way in which the Greeks thought it appropriate to honour him for his unprecedented achievements. The ruler cults of the Hellenistic world were a natural sequel.[20]

What might Alexander have done if he had not died when he did? Expeditions to Arabia and to the Caspian were being planned, and other more ambitious projects are mentioned;[21] after his death Perdiccas produced plans allegedly found among his papers and persuaded the army to disavow them.[22] It is at any rate credible that he envisaged a future of further expeditions and further conquests, rather than the consolidation and administration which what he had already conquered badly needed. But the conquests he had already made greatly enlarged and transformed the Greek world, as we shall see in the chapters which follow. He is called Alexander the Great in the Roman Plautus' comedy *Mostellaria* (third/second century BC).[23]

## PERSIA

Caria, in the south-west of Asia Minor, was *c*.392/1 detached from the satrapy of Sardis and placed under the local aristocrat Hecatomnos. He died in 377/6, and was succeeded by his sons and daughters: Mausolus married to Artemisia, Idrieus married to Ada, and Pixodarus. By the time of Pixodarus the family controlled Lycia too. In the eyes of the Persians they were satraps, but they presented themselves to the Greeks as independent rulers. Mausolus moved the capital from inland Mylasa to coastal Halicarnassus, and commissioned the Mausoleum there (figure 15).[24] In the 360s he dabbled in the Satraps' Revolt,[25] but did not lose his position; in the 350s he was behind the states which defected from Athens' League in the Social War. In 341/0 Ada was ousted by Pixodarus, and he was made to marry his daughter to a Persian, who took over after he died; in 334 Ada submitted to Alexander, and he reinstated her (but after her death he appointed an ordinary satrap).

Artabazus, whose claim to Dascylium was one of the triggers of the Satraps' Revolt of the 360s, himself revolted in the 350s; for a time in the 340s he was a refugee in Macedon. In the reign of Artaxerxes III there were two attempts to recover Egypt. The first, in the late 350s, was unsuccessful, and afterwards the revolt spread to Cyprus and Phoenicia, but they were regained, and in winter 343/2 Egypt was regained, after Mentor of Rhodes, commanding Greek mercenaries for the Egyptians, had defected to the Persians. Mentor's brother Memnon was in Macedon with Artabazus; Mentor was now able to arrange for their reconciliation with Artaxerxes, and after Mentor's death Memnon was active for the Persians in Asia Minor against Alexander.[26] In the early 330s Egypt revolted again and was recovered again.

Bagoas, the grand vizier, had played an important part in the recovery of Egypt, and the story is told that he came to fancy himself as a king-maker (in fact he may have played a lesser part and members of the royal family a greater). In November 338 he poisoned Artaxerxes and all his sons except the youngest, whom he put on the throne as Artaxerxes IV; in June 336 Bagoas killed him and his sons, and installed as Darius III a man from another branch of the royal family; later he tried to kill Darius, but Darius switched the cups and Bagoas died. Darius was not an unworthy king, but he had not expected to be king, and the Persian Empire which Alexander attacked was weakened by this upheaval.

## ATHENS

In the 350s a new generation of Athenian leaders came to the fore, and failure in the Social War prompted a reconsideration of policy. Isocrates, not an original thinker but a reflecter of others' thoughts, c.380 had defended the Delian League and reasserted Athens' claim to leadership,[27] but in *On the Peace* (VIII) after the Social War he wrote off Athens' League as a failure. Men such as Eubulus concentrated on financial recovery, which required not only increased revenues but also reduced expenditure, particularly on military adventures which did not justify their cost, and Xenophon in his *Ways and Means* (*Poroi*) reflected the thinking of these men. In the less prosperous Athens of the fourth century impositions on the rich which were continued from the fifth century[28] became more problematic: attempts were made to improve the collection of *eisphora*, the *ad hoc* property tax, to spread more evenly the costs of financing ships in the navy and to reduce the number of men exempted from liturgies.

It was probably in the late 350s and by Eubulus and Diophantus that the theoric fund was introduced, ostensibly to cover the cost of citizens' theatre tickets at major festivals. It received not only a regular allocation but also any surplus revenue (surpluses had previously gone to the military fund), and by controlling whatever surplus money Athens had and joining the council in the oversight of the old financial boards this fund's treasurer (elected and eligible for reelection, by analogy with that of the military fund), for a time Eubulus himself, became very influential. At the end of the 340s, as support for Demosthenes' hard line against Macedon grew, supporters of his controlled the fund, and in 337/6 he was treasurer himself. His opponents now saw this powerful position as undemocratic (cf. below), and to weaken it the single treasurer was made a board and tenure was limited; but financially the position had been a success, and between the mid 330s and mid 320s a similarly powerful position 'in charge of administration' (*epi tei dioikesei*) was held by Lycurgus and associates of his. In the third quarter of the century Athens became prosperous again; there was building activity, for civilian and for military purposes; but some of the money was wasted. After the humiliation of the Social War Athens modernised its navy, in the 320s building quadriremes and quinqueremes,[29] and made it larger than ever before, but it had no need of so many ships and no possibility of manning them.

It had become possible to suggest changes in the democracy without being perceived as a dangerous oligarch,[30] and some changes now – such as the institution of powerful, elected financial officials – were not in the spirit of the earlier democracy. From c.440 exceptions had been possible to the rule that each tribe had to supply one of the ten generals,[31] and between the 350s and the 330s the link between generals and tribes was abandoned altogether. Isocrates c.354 in his *Areopagitic* (VII) conjured up a vision of a better, earlier democracy, in which the council of the Areopagus[32] had played a large part. From the mid 340s the Areopagus did play a larger part in Athenian affairs, intervening in judicial and other matters, usually by submitting a report to the assembly on its own initiative or the assembly's, and usually in support of Demosthenes and his associates. After Chaeronea it was enabled to condemn men accused of cowardice or treason. When a law of 337/6 threatened the Areopagus with suspension if the democracy were overthrown,[33] this was probably a reaction from Demosthenes' opponents who saw the powerful Areopagus as undemocratic.

For Eubulus and his associates the need for financial recovery conditioned attitudes on other matters; when Demosthenes came to see resistance to Philip as paramount that conditioned attitudes on other matters; and at this time we come nearer than usual to party politics, with groups of men holding a shared position on a range of issues. And Demosthenes tended to redefine 'democracy' to mean freedom from subjection to an outsider, i.e. Philip, while his opponents claimed that he was undemocratic in the normal sense of the word. At first Demosthenes was in a minority, and his opponents rejected his plans for resistance to Philip but not any resistance; but after the Peace of Philocrates, while Demosthenes expected further conflict, they wanted to accept the Peace and make the best of it. Demosthenes' first attack on Aeschines for his part in the negotiations misfired, since the intended prosecutor, Timarchus, was vulnerable to an attack by Aeschines (in his I. *Timarchus*). In 343 Aeschines was prosecuted by Demosthenes and was narrowly acquitted (Dem. XIX. *Embassy*, Aeschin. II. *Embassy*), while Philocrates was successfully prosecuted by Hyperides. Hegesippus responded obstructively to Philip's offer to renegotiate the Peace ([Dem.] VII. *Halonnesus*);[34] Lycurgus was another supporter of Demosthenes; and from then until Chaeronea support for Demosthenes increased.

After Chaeronea there were swings of the pendulum and prosecutions of opponents in response to the latest news. Among men favouring cooperation with Macedon were Demades and Phocion, the latter a man who tried to combine a political and a military career in the older manner, and who is said to have served as general for 45 years. Prosecutions were launched by Diondas against Hyperides for proposing honours for Demosthenes before the battle, and by Aeschines against Ctesiphon for proposing honours for him early in 336. They were brought to court in 334 and 330, when the prosecutors thought the political climate was favourable (from the latter we have Aeschin. III. *Ctesiphon* and Dem. XVIII. *Crown*), but they both failed: even when resistance to Macedon was not feasible, the jurors supported Demosthenes and the policy which he had urged when it was feasible.

Alexander's destruction of Thebes in 335 finally showed that for the time being resistance was not feasible. From the mid 330s to the mid 320s Demosthenes and his associates, apart from Lycurgus, were not prominent. The Athenians focused on rebuilding their morale, on celebrating their heritage and on erecting new buildings; but they also developed a programme for *epheboi* (men aged 18 and 19) which included hoplite training, and as we have noticed they modernised and enlarged their navy. They hoped when the occasion was right to recover from Chaeronea as they had recovered from the Peloponnesian War; but they decided not to join Agis' rising in 331, though Lycurgus probably did want to join.

One consequence of Alexander's order to the Greek cities to take back their exiles would be that Athens would lose its cleruchy on Samos,[35] and it tried to negotiate about that. One of the men facing trouble from Alexander was his treasurer Harpalus. In 324 he fled to Greece with ships, mercenaries and money; after leaving the ships and mercenaries at Taenarum in Laconia, where a body of mercenaries was assembling, he went with money to Athens and was placed under arrest, but after a time he escaped and half of the money was found to be missing. An enquiry by the Areopagus named both Demosthenes and Demades among the offenders; prosecutors came from both sides of the old divide; Demosthenes when sentenced to a large fine went into exile. Then Alexander died, and the old political alignments resurfaced.

## THE WEST

Diodorus' narrative continues in book XVI, now based on a mixture of sources; and there are lives of *Dion* and *Timoleon* by the Latin biographer Nepos (first century BC) and Plutarch. The Platonic *Letters* vii and viii, purportedly addressed to Dion's friends after his death, whether written by Plato or not, seem to be well informed.

By the end of the 360s Dion of Syracuse[36] was in exile in Greece; he met Plato at the Olympic festival of 360, and began to plan his return. He crossed to Sicily with a small force in 357, while Dionysius II was away from Syracuse, and was followed by Heraclides, another exile, in 356. Dionysius returned and tried to negotiate, but then departed to Locri in Italy (his mother's city), leaving his son and a garrison in the inner city, Ortygia. After a period of turmoil, in 355 Dion gained control of the whole city. He perhaps hoped to set up a kind of Platonic aristocracy, but he fell out with Heraclides and had him killed, and in 354 he was himself killed by an Athenian, Callippus. Callippus was followed by two half-brothers of Dionysius in succession, until in 346 an embittered Dionysius, expelled from Locri, recaptured Syracuse.

Hicetas, a friend of Dion ruling in Leontini, encouraged the Syracusans to appeal to their mother city, Corinth, and to Carthage. In 344 Corinth sent Timoleon, who had been living in a kind of limbo since, twenty years earlier, he had helped to kill his own brother when that brother tried to make himself tyrant there. The Carthaginians sent a large force, which failed to intercept Timoleon. The course of events is hard to recover, but by 343/2 Timoleon controlled the whole of Syracuse, and he dispatched Dionysius to retirement in Corinth. Syracuse was given a new constitution, though Timoleon retained a powerful position, perhaps as 'general with full powers'. During the previous dozen years those who could leave Syracuse had done so, but Timoleon inspired enough confidence to attract settlers, more from the West than from the rest of the Greek world, and the archaeological record points to a revival throughout Greek Sicily.

From 342 to 337 he fought a series of wars against the Carthaginians and against tyrants in other cities. Perhaps in 341, he won a major victory over the Carthaginians at the River Crimisus, and in 339 he made a treaty by which the Carthaginians retained the western part of the island. Andromachus of Tauromenium, father of the historian Timaeus, was not overthrown as other rulers were, either because he was virtuous or because he had been the first to welcome Timoleon when he arrived in Sicily. Timoleon was going blind, and in 337 he resigned his position, and soon afterwards died. His propaganda attributed his success to good fortune and the favour of the gods; he does seem to have disapproved of despotic rule, but he was prepared to hold a powerful position and to beat the tyrants at their own tricks. We hear virtually nothing of Sicily during the reign of Alexander the Great, and Timoleon appears to have given it a generation of peace and prosperity.

# Hellenistic Greece, 323–146

# 10

# ALEXANDER'S SUCCESSORS, 323–272

## JOCKEYING FOR POSITION, 323–301

'Hellenistic' is a convenient label (derived from the noun 'Hellenismus' coined by the Prussian J. G. Droysen in the nineteenth century) for the Greek world and its history between the death of Alexander and the Roman conquest. It was an enlarged Greek world, not only including places inhabited by and places in contact with Greeks since the Archaic period but, as a result of Alexander's conquests, extending into the western part of Asia (though the more easterly parts of the region conquered by Alexander returned in due course to an Asiatic orbit, and were never conquered by Rome); and it was a world dominated by kingdoms which developed out of Alexander's empire. Different parts of this Greek world came under Roman control at different times, from southern Italy in the early third century and Sicily in the mid third century to Egypt in 30; but in this book the dividing line is set at 146, when Rome acquired mainland Greece (and also finally destroyed Carthage, its main rival in the western Mediterranean). In the Hellenistic world there was a plurality of great powers, contending against one another, and Greek cities could still have a foreign policy at least in so far as there were times when they could or had to choose between one leading power and another; but after conquest by Rome that freedom disappeared, except on a few occasions when a city might support a rebel against Rome or one political leader in Rome against a rival.

The history of Diodorus Siculus[1] is preserved intact to the end of book XX (302/1); in books XVIII–XX his main source for Greek

163

history was Hieronymus of Cardia, who served under the Antigonids who became rulers of Macedon; although not unprejudiced, he was well informed. Polybius, a prominent citizen of Megalopolis in Arcadia, lived from the beginning of the second century to *c*.118, was taken to Rome as a hostage, and wrote a history to recount and explain how Rome rose to dominate the Greek world, originally between 220 and 168, but extended to range from 264 to 146. He too was not unprejudiced, but in his attitude to the writing of history he approached Thucydides. Out of 40 books only I–V survive intact; we have an abridgment of I–XVIII and 'fragments' of the remainder; and much of Polybius' narrative was used by the Roman historian Livy (first century BC – early first century AD), from whose work books I–X and XXI–XLV survive, taking the narrative to 167. For the first three quarters of the third century the only narrative of Greek history which survives to give us a framework is Justin's epitome of Pompeius Trogus[2] (books XIII–XL cover the history of Greece and the successor kingdoms to their conquest by Rome, interrupted at the year 279 by XVIII. 3 – XXIII. 2, on Carthage from the beginning and Sicily from *c*.480 to that point).

Plutarch[3] continues to give us *Lives* of a number of leading men in the Greek world. Appian of Alexandria in Egypt (second century AD) wrote a history of Rome organised by the different peoples with whom Rome had dealings: what survives includes parts of books IX ([Macedon and] Illyria) and of XI (Syria); Greece and Ionia were covered by the lost book X. Two other writers important for the hellenistic period are the geographer Strabo and the traveller through central and southern Greece Pausanias, both of whom included a good deal of historical information.[4] Literature of other kinds from the Hellenistic period is important for the light which it sheds on social and intellectual life,[5] but not for the history of public events. On the other hand, we have an increased volume of epigraphic material for the Hellenistic period, as a growing number of states developed the habit of inscribing documents on stone; and there is a very large body of papyrus documents generated by the administration of Egypt.

When Alexander died in 323 he left his half-brother Philip Arrhidaeus,[6] and sons Heracles, born in 327 to his mistress Barsine (who had been married to Mentor and to Memnon),[7] and Alexander IV, born after his death to his Bactrian wife Rhoxana. At Babylon Arrhidaeus was declared king, and when Alexander IV was born he became joint heir. Of the generals, Perdiccas, who probably had succeeded Hephaestion as second in command, took charge in Babylon, and made Seleucus his second in command. Craterus was returning to Macedon with veterans; Alexander had intended him to replace Antipater there and Antipater to come to Asia,[8] but Craterus had not gone further than Asia Minor and Antipater had not left Macedon. In a distribution of satrapies Phrygia in Asia Minor was assigned to Antigonus Monophthalmus ('one-eyed': he had been there since 333), the Greek Eumenes, of Cardia in the Chersonese, who had been Alexander's secretary, received north-eastern Asia Minor, Lysimachus, a Thessalian, received Thrace, Ptolemy received Egypt;[9] and Antipater was to retain Macedon and Greece. So that nobody could claim a particular right to act on plans of Alexander, Perdiccas produced plans which he claimed to have found among Alexander's papers, and persuaded the army to renounce them as over-ambitious.[10]

Athens, threatened with the loss of Samos under Alexander's order for the return of Greek exiles,[11] and in the west the Aetolians, who had captured the Acarnanian city of Oeniadae, took advantage of Alexander's death to lead a coalition of mostly central and northern Greeks against Macedon in the Lamian War. In winter 323/2 they besieged Antipater in Lamia, in Thessaly. In spring 322 Leonnatus, from Dascylium, went to support Antipater, and the siege was abandoned though he was killed. The Athenian fleet was defeated in two battles; in the summer Craterus arrived and joined Antipater, and they defeated the Greeks at Crannon. Thanks to Demosthenes, in Athens democracy had come to be associated with opposition to Macedon,[12] and Antipater's settlement with Athens involved a change of constitution.[13]

Meanwhile there was conflict between the generals. While Perdiccas and Eumenes took action against a man who tried to set up an independent kingdom in eastern Asia Minor, Antigonus refused to work with them and joined Antipater in Macedon. In 322, when Perdiccas preferred marriage with Alexander's sister Cleopatra (whose husband Alexander of the Molossians[14] had died) to marriage with Antipater's daughter Nicaea, Antipater and his allies decided to cooperate with Ptolemy (who had hijacked Alexander's body, and had added Cyrene to his own territory)[15] against Perdiccas and Eumenes. Craterus was killed in battle against Eumenes, but Perdiccas was killed by disaffected officers including Seleucus when his invasion of Egypt proved disastrous. At Triparadisus in Syria, in 321, Antipater was confirmed in his control of Macedon, and became regent for the two kings, Antigonus was made 'general of Asia', with the job of fighting against Eumenes, Ptolemy was confirmed in Egypt, Seleucus was given Babylon. Antigonus' son Demetrius, Ptolemy and Lysimachus all married daughters of Antipater.

When Antipater went to Asia for the war against Perdiccas he left as his deputy in Macedon Polyperchon, who had served under Alexander and returned with Craterus; and when Antipater died in 319, at the age of 80, he appointed Polyperchon to succeed him as regent, and his own son Cassander as deputy. Cassander was offended and looked for support in Greece and elsewhere, gaining the backing of Antigonus. Greek cities in which Antipater had installed garrisons and congenial régimes after the Lamian War were likely to favour Cassander, so Polyperchon in the name of Arrhidaeus issued what was to be the first of a series of proclamations of the freedom of the Greeks, undertaking to restore men exiled under Antipater and the constitutions which the cities had had under Philip and Alexander.[16] The result was a period of turmoil in Greece. In Athens, for instance, the oligarchy installed at the end of the Lamian War was replaced in 318 by a democracy, but in 317 Cassander instituted a new oligarchy presided over by Aristotle's pupil Demetrius of Phalerum. In the Peloponnese Polyperchon besieged Megalopolis but failed to take it. He then brought back Alexander's mother Olympias (who after quarrelling with Antipater had withdrawn to Epirus). That prompted Eurydice, the ambitious wife of Arrhidaeus, to appeal to Cassander and take an army to confront Polyperchon; but her troops deserted, she and Arrhidaeus were placed under arrest, and soon Arrhidaeus was put to death and she was forced to commit suicide. Olympias then conducted a purge of Antipater's family and supporters. In 316 Cassander returned to Macedon: Olympias was besieged in Pydna, and captured and put to death; Rhoxana and Alexander IV were kept alive but under arrest. Cassander married a half-sister of Alexander, made his mark by refounding Potidaea[17] as Cassandrea (as Philip had founded Philippi and Alexander had founded various Alexandrias)[18], and in honour of his wife refounding Therma on the Thermaic Gulf as Thessalonica; and in Greece he restored Thebes, destroyed in 335.[19]

In Asia Antigonus was besieging Eumenes in a Cappadocian fortress when Antipater died. He then came to terms with Eumenes; and in 318, since Antigonus was supporting Cassander, Polyperchon gave Eumenes the title 'general of Asia'. Eumenes made his way to Phoenicia and then to Iran, where in 316 he was finally surrendered to Antigonus and executed. Antigonus thus had access to the wealth of the empire, and he seems to have been the only general still ambitious to control not just a part of it but the whole. Seleucus refused to acknowledge his supremacy, and went from Babylon to Ptolemy in Egypt; and the result was a coalition of Ptolemy, Cassander and Lysimachus against Antigonus, and a war which lasted from 315/4 to 311. Seleucus' return to Babylon then forced Antigonus to agree to a peace treaty: Cassander retained 'Europe' and the regency (but in 310 he had Rhoxana and Alexander IV killed), Lysimachus Thrace, Ptolemy Egypt and Cyrene; Antigonus retained 'all Asia' (and in an inscription claimed to have upheld the freedom and autonomy of the Greeks),[20] but was still in conflict with Seleucus, not included in the treaty. By 308 Antigonus had withdrawn to Syria (where he founded Antigonea near the mouth of the Orontes), and Seleucus was in control of the east: he founded a new capital north of Babylon at Seleucea on the Tigris; but *c.*305 he ceded some Indian territory to a prince called Chandragupta in exchange for a force of elephants.

In the North Lysimachus remained largely undisturbed in Thrace, while the other generals were focused on one another; he refounded Cardia, on the neck of the Chersonese, as Lysimachea. Polyperchon was still at large in southern Greece, and controlled Corinth and Sicyon. In 309 he took Alexander's surviving son Heracles[21] to Macedon, with the result that Cassander had Heracles killed, thus finally extinguishing the royal line, and he acknowledged Polyperchon as general in the Peloponnese. Polyperchon remained active but not seriously important in southern Greece; we do not know when he died.

In Egypt Ptolemy had moved the capital from Memphis (south of Cairo) to Alexandria, and built Alexander's tomb there, but otherwise represented his rule as a resumption of pre-Persian rule. He had gained possession of Cyprus, which he controlled through a brother, and made an alliance with Rhodes, and he coveted the Syrian coast and other territories. In 309–308 he advanced to Asia Minor, the Aegean and Greece, and took over Megara, Corinth and Sicyon. But in 307 Antigonus sent his son Demetrius to the Aegean, and he 'liberated' Athens from Cassander and Demetrius of Phalerum (Demetrius of Phalerum later advised Ptolemy on the foundation of his Museum and library),[22] and took Megara (Cassander had already recovered Corinth). In 307/6 he continued to Cyprus, besieged Salamis, won a naval battle and took control of the island from Ptolemy. However, in 306 Antigonus invaded Egypt but was driven back; and in 305–304, when Demetrius besieged Rhodes after its refusal to support the attacks on Cyprus and Egypt, that siege (which earned him the title Poliorcetes, 'besieger') was a failure. After gaining Cyprus Antigonus and Demetrius took the title *basileus* ('king'), which presumably represented a claim to the whole of Alexander's empire; and in 305–304 Ptolemy, and after him Lysimachus, Cassander and Seleucus, also took the title, though their claims were not to the whole empire (Cassander called himself 'king of the Macedonians').

Following the example set at the end of Alexander's reign,[23] the kings came to be revered as gods. Already in 311 Scepsis in the Troad founded a sanctuary with an altar and a cult statue for Antigonus, with a festival which seems to have been instituted even earlier.[24] In Athens in 307/6 new tribes were created and named after Antigonus and Demetrius, and they themselves were acknowledged as *Soteres* ('saviours'), with a priest and games in their honour.[25] In 304 Rhodes with the approval of the oracle of Ammon acknowledged Ptolemy as a god after he had supported it against Demetrius.[26] The League of Islanders (below) c.306/5 already had a biennial festival called Antigonea, and added the Demetriea in the

alternate years;[27] but *c*.280 it reflected its new alignment by insti-
tuting the Ptolemea.[28] Particularly in Egypt, a king or queen could
become a *synnaos theos* (temple-sharing god) with an established
deity: this is first attested posthumously for Arsinoe II, daughter of
Ptolemy I and eventually wife of Ptolemy II,[29] but it was physically
anticipated in Athens in 304/3 when Demetrius installed himself in
the Parthenon. Allied to that is the cult of a whole dynasty promoted
by the dynasty, as opposed to the cult of an individual ruler instituted
by a city: in Alexandria there was already a cult of Alexander early
in the third century; Ptolemy I and subsequent members of the
dynasty were added, and there were cults of the Ptolemies in Egyptian temples too.[30] When republican Rome entered the Greek world
it could not generate dynastic cults in the same way, but cults developed of the personified Roma.[31]

In 304 Demetrius returned to Greece, set about winning over and
'liberating' the cities, and in 302 organised the cities in a revival of
Philip's League of Corinth (in the Aegean a League of Islanders had
been founded, probably in 314 and with the support of Antigonus,
after the liberation of Delos from Athens; *c*.286 it came under the
influence of Ptolemy).[32] But in 301 he had to return to Asia Minor
to support Antigonus against a combined onslaught by the other
kings, and at Ipsus on the Anatolian plateau the kings were victorious and Antigonus was killed. After this separate kingdoms were
to survive in Macedon, Egypt and the Near East; Greece, the Aegean
and Asia Minor were contested, while the cities maintained such
autonomy as they could, and the Syrian coast was claimed by the
Egyptian kingdom as well as the near-eastern kingdom.

## CONSOLIDATION, 301–272

From just before Ipsus we have no general narrative except that of
Justin, but in this period we see the Hellenistic world settling into
the pattern which was to last until the Roman conquest. Ptolemy
was secure in Egypt and Seleucus in part of the near east; Cassander
was currently ruling in Macedon. After Ipsus Lysimachus took much
of Asia Minor, Ptolemy Cyprus and the Syrian coast, and Seleucus
inland Syria. Demetrius was a disruptive force, with a navy but no

kingdom: he was refused entry to Athens, which under Lachares aligned itself with Cassander and Lysimachus, and he was then attracted by the prospect of a marriage alliance with Seleucus. But in 297 Cassander and his eldest son died, and rivalry between his other two sons gave Demetrius the opportunity to return to Europe. He regained control of Athens in 295; in 294, after one of the sons had been successfully supported by Pyrrhus of Epirus,[33] while Lysimachus had done little to help the other, Demetrius enticed the successful son to a meeting, had him killed and himself took over Macedon. However, his ambitions were not limited to Macedon. He attacked Thrace but was defeated by Lysimachus. He enlarged his navy, and founded a base for it at Demetrias in southern Thessaly. To oppose him, in 288 Lysimachus and Pyrrhus (from Epirus) invaded Macedon, and Ptolemy sent a fleet into the Aegean. The Macedonians refused to fight for Demetrius; Macedon was divided between Pyrrhus and Lysimachus; in 287 Athens rebelled against him with support from Ptolemy (but his garrison remained in Piraeus); and in 286 he turned his attention to Asia Minor, where Lysimachus had been gradually and pragmatically taking control (Ephesus after a flood was refounded on a new site, to be Lysimachus' principal city there). Demetrius landed near Miletus and gained the support of some cities, but when confronted by Lysimachus' son Agathocles he withdrew to the East, was captured by Seleucus, and died in 283 or 282. Meanwhile Lysimachus expelled Pyrrhus from Macedon, and came to control the whole of Macedon and Thessaly apart from Demetrias. Demetrius had left his son Antigonus Gonatas in Greece, and Pyrrhus failed to expel him from there.

The kings were now growing old, and after multiple marriage alliances succession could be problematic. Seleucus had a son, Antiochus, by an Iranian wife, and he was designated as co-regent (Antiochus also took over a daughter of Demetrius whom Seleucus had married after Ipsus). Ptolemy had a son, Ptolemy Ceraunus ('thunderbolt'), by Antipater's daughter Eurydice; but his preferred heir was Ptolemy Philadelphus ('sibling-lover'), by another wife, Berenice, who was made co-regent in 285 and succeeded when he died in 283, and Eurydice with her family including Ceraunus had gone to Asia Minor. A daughter of Eurydice was married to Lysimachus, and she managed to incite him against his son Agathocles, so that in 283/2 Agathocles was assassinated and Lysimachus was left with no viable heir. In 282, therefore, Seleucus invaded Asia Minor, and early in 281 at Corupedium west of Sardis he defeated and killed Lysimachus. Hoping to lay claim to Macedon, he proceeded to the Hellespont and crossed into Europe, but he was then assassinated by Ceraunus. Within two or three years, Demetrius, Ptolemy, Lysimachus and Seleucus had all died.

At Lysimachea Ceraunus had himself proclaimed king of the Macedonians. With ships taken over from Seleucus he defeated Antigonus Gonatas, the most likely challenger, and he supplied forces to Pyrrhus for an Italian venture which would keep him out of the way. However, for some time Celtic tribes and the peoples whom they displaced had been pushing through Europe to the South and East. Lysimachus had managed to keep them out of his kingdom, but Ceraunus could not, and in 280/79 he was defeated and killed by a body of Gauls. A brother of his and a grandson of Antipater lasted only for short times; a more successful general, Sosthenes, refused to become king. Another body of Gauls, led by Brennus, moved into Greece in 279; but an army from central Greece held Thermopylae against them, an invasion of Aetolia was repulsed, Delphi was saved allegedly by a miraculous snowstorm, and Brennus died on the return to the North. Some Gauls returned to the Danube, some established the 'kingdom of Tylis' in Thrace, some moved into Asia Minor.

In Asia Minor Antigonus Gonatas and Antiochus both hoped to fill the vacuum left by the deaths of Lysimachus and Seleucus. But in 278 the two men were reconciled and Gonatas returned to Europe. Early in 277 he managed to enhance his reputation by ambushing and destroying a body of Gauls near Lysimachea, and by the end of the year he was king in Macedon. Various rival claimants were quickly dealt with. More seriously, Pyrrhus returned from Italy in 275, and in 274 defeated Gonatas and made himself king (a garrison of Gauls which he installed at Aegeae plundered the royal tombs); but after his death at Argos in 272 Gonatas was secure. Disputed areas remained, and lesser powers were to arise, but now all three of the great dynasties which were to rule until the Roman conquest were established: the Ptolemies in Egypt, the Seleucids in the Near East and the Antigonids in Macedon.

## ATHENS[34]

In Athens during this period we see a series of changes of régime. Demosthenes' association of democracy with freedom from Macedon[35] had taken hold: two of the régimes during this period (in 321–118 and 317–307) were technically oligarchic, with a restricted citizen body; they avoided the use of the word oligarchy, but throughout the period it was the régimes which were most determinedly anti-Macedonian which claimed most strongly to be democratic.

In the affair of Harpalus and the money which he brought to Athens both Demosthenes and Demades were among those found guilty and Demosthenes had gone into exile.[36] After Alexander's death in 323 old alignments resurfaced: Hyperides and Demosthenes (enabled to return from exile) led Athens into the Lamian War against Macedon, and Demades incurred *atimia* (loss of political rights). In 322 after the Macedonian victory Demades had his rights restored and joined with Phocion in negotiating peace; Demosthenes committed suicide and Hyperides was sent to Macedon for execution. The new constitution imposed by Antipater was described as 'the laws of Solon' or the 'traditional constitution',[37] but was based on a property qualification of 2,000 drachmae, and a Macedonian garrison was installed in the Piraeus; Demades was put to death when he went to Macedon on a deputation to protest against the garrison, because he had made approaches to Perdiccas. In 318, in response to Polyperchon's proclamation of freedom and the previous constitutions, the Athenians restored the democracy but could not get rid of the garrison; and Phocion was put to death. But in 317 they came to terms with Cassander, who imposed a property qualification of 1,000 drachmae, and Aristotle's pupil Demetrius of Phalerum as overseer. The régime of this Demetrius lasted until 307: he undertook various legal and institutional reforms, including the replacement of the liturgies through which the richer citizens had competed in spending their money in connection with festivals[38] by officials styled *agonothetai* ('contest-setters'), who were provided with public funds but could still add to them.

The year 307 brought liberation by Demetrius: the garrison was removed, and he restored the forms of democracy, describing that as the 'traditional constitution', but did not undo all the changes (*agonothetai* were retained, and a change was either made now or retained from the previous régime by which the training programme for *epheboi* was reduced to one year and made voluntary[39]). Acknowledging the realities of the new world, the Athenians duly showed their gratitude by worshipping Antigonus and Demetrius as Saviours and creating two additional tribes named after them. In 304/3 Demetrius took up residence in the Parthenon, and some opponents of his were exiled; in 302 the calendar was grossly distorted so that he could be initiated into the lesser Eleusinian mysteries and immediately afterwards into the greater. After the defeat of Antigonus and Demetrius at Ipsus in 301 Athens made a declaration of neutrality, and in the course of the following years a supporter of Cassander called Lachares gained a powerful position which enabled his opponents afterwards to call him tyrant; but in 295 Demetrius blockaded Athens until Lachares fled. Demetrius was now overbearing. He installed garrisons in Attica, including one inside the city wall, on the Museum hill (hill of the Muses, where the Philopappus monument was built in the second century AD); and at first there were departures from the normal pattern of office-holding. In 287 with the help of Ptolemy Athens regained internal freedom but not freedom from garrisons apart from that at the Museum (in the years which followed Eleusis and Rhamnus were recovered, but not Piraeus, Salamis or Sunium).

A series of decrees for important men adds to what we read in the literary narratives. Lycurgus, the financier of the 330s and 320s, was honoured for his services to the democracy with a statue in the agora in 307/6;[40] Demosthenes was similarly honoured on the proposal of his nephew Demochares in 281/0;[41] Demochares himself was active in the régime of 307/6 but was one of those exiled in 304/3 by 'those who overthrew the democracy'; he returned in 286/5, and in a decree of 271/0 was stated emphatically never to have been involved in anything contrary to the democracy.[42] In 283/2 there were honours for the poet Philippides, who was a friend of Lysi-machus, had interceded with him on various occasions since the battle of Ipsus (when many Athenians had fought on the side of Antigonus and Demetrius), and had never opposed the democracy.[43] Callias was honoured in a decree of 270/69 (when he was serving as an officer of Ptolemy II at Halicarnassus): he had done nothing contrary to the democracy but had suffered confiscation of his property under the oligarchy; he returned with the backing of Ptolemy I in 287 to support the overthrow of Demetrius' régime, and he cooperated with Ptolemy I and II to obtain money and grain for Athens (several decrees of the 280s show that the grain supply was problematic with hostile garrisons at Piraeus and on Salamis).[44] Callias' brother Phaedrus was honoured later, in 259/8, when Athens was under Antigonid control:[45] he had held office under Lachares and under the régime of Demetrius which followed, but he supported Athens in Demetrius' siege (the brothers cooperated in securing the harvest of 287 before the siege began), and was general in 287/6 and handed over the city free, democratic and autonomous.[46]

Athens was threatened with the loss of Samos by Alexander's edict for the return of exiles, and from 322 onwards there was an independent Samos again, from c.280 to 197 under the aegis of the Ptolemies. Polyperchon's proclamation of 319 would have allowed Athens to recover Samos, but it was never put into effect. Athens' north Aegean islands, Imbros, Lemnos and Scyros,[47] were taken by Antigonus in 318, but were in Athenian hands again for a few years from 307/6, for much of the third century and from 166 onwards. Delos[48] was liberated from Athens by Antigonus in 314, and remained independent until it was given back to Athens by Rome in 166.[49]

## EPIRUS

Sparta's king Archidamus III had gone to Italy to fight for Taras against the Lucanians, but had been killed in 338. In 334 Olympias' brother Alexander I, installed as king of the Molossians in 342,[50] likewise accepted an invitation to support Taras, but he was defeated and killed in 331. Kings continued to come from this family, but from this point onwards there was built up around the kingdom a broader Epirote Alliance. Alexander's son Neoptolemus II succeeded, at first under the guardianship of his mother Cleopatra and of Olympias, but the throne was claimed also by descendants of Arybbas, ousted in 342: his sons Aeacidas and Alcidas in turn, and then Aeacidas' son Pyrrhus. Claimants were backed at different times by the rulers in Macedon and by the Illyrians.

Pyrrhus, the best-known and the most able and ambitious of the kings,[51] was first installed, in 307/6 at the age of 12, by the Illyrians. In 302 he was expelled by Cassander and replaced by Neoptolemus, and then went to serve under Demetrius Poliorcetes (who had married his sister). In 298 he was sent to Ptolemy as a hostage, and in 297 after Cassander's death he returned with Ptolemy's support to Epirus; at first he ruled jointly with Neoptolemus but soon he had him killed. In 295 he married a daughter of the Syracusan Agathocles,[52] and received Corcyra as dowry. In 294 he backed one of Cassander's sons for the throne in Macedon, and gained for himself substantial territory in north-western Greece. However, Demetrius killed the son and took over Macedon (and Pyrrhus' Syracusan wife). In 288 Pyrrhus and Lysimachus attacked Macedon from West and East, and partitioned Macedon between them, but before long Lysimachus drove him out.

In 281/0 Pyrrhus received an appeal from Taras in southern Italy, which by now had come into conflict with Rome, and which recently had sent some support to him. He was about to challenge Ptolemy Ceraunus in Macedon, but made a treaty with him so that he could respond to this appeal. In 280 he crossed to Taras, where he was made commander in chief; and at Heraclea, near the coast between Taras and Thurii, the Romans refused his offer of arbitration but he was victorious though with heavy losses when he deployed elephants against them. This was the first direct intersection of Greek history and Roman history. Many of the Greek cities and southern Italian peoples now supported him, but when he advanced towards Rome he was driven back. Further negotiations with Rome broke down. Pyrrhus raised large sums of money from the Greek cities, and in 279 marched north again and was victorious, again with heavy losses, in a two-day battle at Ausculum, on the east side of Italy: this was the 'Pyrrhic victory' for which he became notorious.[53]

He then accepted an invitation to support Syracuse in a war against Carthage, while Rome gave its support to Carthage, and in 278 he went to Sicily while Rome regained some lost allies in Italy.[54] He began successfully, but could not take Lilybaeum from the Carthaginians, and while he planned to take the war to Africa he alienated the Greek cities in Sicily. In 276 he returned to Italy, attacked by a Carthaginian fleet *en route*, and in 275 was defeated in a last battle against the Romans at Malventum (which they subsequently renamed Beneventum), north-east of Neapolis.

In the meantime Ptolemy Ceraunus had been killed, the Gauls had invaded Macedon and Greece, and in 277 Antigonus Gonatas had made himself king in Macedon. In 275 Pyrrhus left a son and some forces in Taras but returned to Greece, and in 274 he won a battle and gained control of Macedon and Thessaly. In 272 he turned to the Peloponnese, failed to take Sparta, but forced his way into Argos. There he was trapped by Gonatas, and he was killed by a tile which a woman threw from a roof-top; he was succeeded in Epirus by his son Alexander II. For all his ability, he could not persevere with a policy: Gonatas compared him to a gambler who made many good throws of the dice but did not know how to use them.[55] In the same year Taras surrendered to the Romans (who called it Tarentum).

## SICILY

After the death of Timoleon in 337[56] we have 20 years of near-silence on Sicily. Diodorus resumes his account in the year 317/6,[57] but backtracks to give an account of the rise of Agathocles before then. Agathocles was of a family exiled from Rhegium, which went to Syracuse when Timoleon invited settlers; his father is described as a potter, but was more probably the owner of a workshop than a practising craftsman; Agathocles himself married the widow of one of the richest Syracusans.

Syracuse had come to be dominated by a body of six hundred men. After a campaign to support Croton in Italy Agathocles attacked the leaders of the six hundred but was himself forced into exile. He then took part in various conflicts in Italy, and successfully supported the democracy of Rhegium against an attack by the Syracusan oligarchs. Many of them were exiled and Agathocles returned; they gained the support of Carthage; Corinth sent a general, Acestorides, and he arranged a reconciliation but Agathocles went into exile again. Agathocles raised an army, attacked Syracuse and persuaded the Carthaginians to withdraw, and then, perhaps in 319/8, returned to Syracuse. Perhaps in 316/5, he invited members of the six hundred to a meeting, and aroused fury against them, so that allegedly four thousand oligarchs were massacred and six thousand others fled, mostly to Acragas. After offering to retire he had himself elected 'general with full powers', and undertook a cancellation of debts and redistribution of property.[58]

The next few years saw war in Sicily, with opposition to Agathocles headed by Acragas and Messana. Acrotatus, son of a Spartan king, was invited to command the opposition but made himself unpopular and had to flee, and in 314 the Carthaginians arranged a settlement under which Sicily was to be divided between Greeks and Carthaginians as before but the Greek part was to be subordinate to Syracuse. Agathocles continued fighting against his enemies, dealing savagely with cities which he captured, but in 311 after a heavy defeat he was driven back to Syracuse by the Carthaginians. While they blockaded Syracuse, in 310 he managed to sail out and take a force to attack Carthage, the first time Europeans had attempted that. He burned his boats, defeated a Carthaginian army and captured various lesser towns. He invited as an ally Ophellas, who had served under Alexander and since 322 had been governing Cyrene on behalf of Ptolemy, but in 308 after Ophellas arrived Agathocles fell out with him, had him killed and took over his army. He then returned to Sicily, leaving his son Archagathus in command in Africa, but the Carthaginians got the better of him; Agathocles came again in 307, but made no progress, and eventually returned to Sicily, abandoning his army to the Carthaginians.

Meanwhile in Sicily a Carthaginian army was heavily defeated by the Syracusans, but Agathocles' Greek opponents decided to continue fighting against both Syracuse and Carthage. This brought Agathocles back from Africa in 308, to join forces which were already getting the upper hand; in 306, after his final return, he made a treaty with Carthage by which Sicily was divided as before and he received an indemnity, and perhaps in the same year the Carthaginians made a treaty with Rome. After this he finally defeated his Greek opponents; and it was probably in 304 that he followed the example of the rulers in Alexander's empire and took the title of king.

Because we lack Diodorus' complete text after 302/1 information on the later part of Agathocles' rule is sparse. About 300 he went to Italy to support Taras against the Lucanians and others; it seems that he aspired to build up an alliance of all the Sicilian and Italian Greeks for another conflict with Carthage, and he captured some cities in Italy. He married a daughter or step-daughter of Ptolemy; and he captured Corcyra, giving that with his daughter as a dowry to Pyrrhus in 295 and to Demetrius Poliorcetes in 291. But before he could begin his Carthaginian war he was taken ill. His intended heir, his son Agathocles, was killed by one of his grandsons, another Archagathus. In disgust he resigned his position rather than let Archagathus succeed him, and in 289/8, though poison is alleged, he perhaps died a natural death.

There followed a period of upheaval, in which Syracuse lost its dominant position and tyrants seized power in various cities, in Syracuse first Hicetas and subsequently Thoenon. The Greeks' weakness was exploited by the Carthaginians and by the Mamertines, Italian mercenaries of Agathocles who had occupied Messana. In Syracuse Thoenon was driven from the outer city but held out in the fortress of Ortygia. The citizens appealed to Pyrrhus, who crossed from Italy to Sicily in 278, when a Carthaginian fleet was blockading Syracuse. The Carthaginians withdrew, and Pyrrhus gained control of the whole city and was given the title king. In 277 he moved against the Carthaginians in the west of the island, and had several successes but was unable to take the harbour town of Lilybaeum. He then planned to go to Africa, like Agathocles before him, but he became increasingly high-handed and unpopular in Sicily, and in 276 the Carthaginians sent a fresh army to Sicily but he returned to Italy.

# 11

## LIFE IN THE HELLENISTIC WORLD

### POLITICAL LIFE

In the heartland of Greece, comprising the Greek mainland, the Aegean and the West Coast of Asia Minor, Greeks and city states were long established, and in many respects the rise of the Successor kingdoms did not drastically change the lives of the individual cities. For a few major cities the need to manoeuvre between the kings and to seek their favour represented a serious loss of power and esteem; but for most cities manoeuvring between the kings was not very different from manoeuvring between the leading cities of the classical period, and a distant king with wider concerns might be less apt to interfere than an ambitious neighbouring city.[1] The cities continued to hold their own meetings and appoint their own officials, to enact their own laws and decrees, levy their own taxes and celebrate their own festivals, and to make alliances and pursue quarrels with other cities. In Macedon and other places where cities were founded (or existing settlements were refounded as cities) by a king, there was not the same tradition of civic life, and there decisions of a city might overtly conform to a king's policy, as when Philippi recognised the immunity of the sanctuary of Asclepius at Cos,[2] and we may find an *epistates* ('overseer') in a city as a king's agent and instructions to the city sent to him by the king, as in the case of a sanctuary at Thessalonica.[3] Kings were happy to grant freedom to some cities or all cities, on the understanding that the freedom had been graciously granted by them rather than forcibly asserted against them.[4]

179

Most cities were technically democratic or mildly oligarchic (in the latter case, with a low property qualification, or the right to make speeches and proposals in the assembly restricted); sometimes the term 'democracy' was still used to make a contrast with oligarchy as well as with monarchy, but on other occasions it was used to refer more generally to lawful constitutional government. There were, however, increasing opportunities for very rich citizens to act as benefactors of their cities and to gain influence in return, and the Romans when they entered the picture were happier dealing with the rich. The particularism of the individual cities was to some extent weakened, as increasing grants of *isopoliteia* ('equal citizenship') enabled citizens of one city to enjoy the rights of citizens when spending a shorter or a longer time in another city; and there was increasing use of 'foreign judges' invited from another city to settle disputes both between cities and in a city, on the assumption that their lack of involvement in the disputes would outweigh their lack of knowledge of local legal and other details. Cities seeking recognition of their sanctuaries (cf. above) built up networks of friends. Amalgamations of separate cities (now referred to as *sympoliteia*, 'joint citizenship', rather than as *synoikismos*),[5] and the dissolution of such amalgamations, continued from the Archaic and Classical periods. The two great leagues of mainland Greece in the Hellenistic period, the Aetolian and the Achaean,[6] differed from the leagues organised in the classical period by Athens, Sparta and Thebes in that they were not centred on a single, powerful and ambitious city to which the other member cities were subordinated.

In Egypt and the Near East Alexander's conquests and the subsequent development of the Successor kingdoms resulted in the arrival not only of Graeco-Macedonian rulers and their courts but also of Greek and Macedonian settlers and the foundation of Greek cities in the midst of a non-Greek indigenous population.

In Egypt there were only a few cities, the most important being Alexandria: only Greeks and Macedonians were citizens (but there were also other foreign settlers, such as Phoenicians and Jews), and there were royal officials in the cities. The temples with their lands and their priests provided another power structure. Elsewhere the population lived in towns and villages, which were grouped in *nomoi* ('nomes'), with a hierarchy of officials, as under previous régimes; many of the settlers there were ex-soldiers given land as 'cleruchs',[7] and often acted as absentee landlords while native Egyptians did the farming. There was some intermarriage between settlers and Egyptians, and many Egyptians took a Greek name in addition to their Egyptian name. Administrative documents on papyrus show that the authorities' attitude to agriculture was highly intervention-ist,[8] but the intention seems to have been to extract as much revenue as possible to support the royal court and its military undertakings rather than in a modern sense to control the economy. From the middle of the third century onwards we read of a series of native uprisings, and also of increasing feuding within the ruling dynasty; but in spite of that the dynasty remained in power for nearly three hundred years, and while certainly nationalist/social discontent sometimes surfaced Egypt does not seem to have suffered from gross mismanagement.

The Near East was the main part of the Persian Empire conquered by Alexander, and most of it for most of the time came under the Seleucids; it contained a mixture of lands and peoples. Coastal Asia Minor and the 'fertile crescent' from the Mediterranean to Meso-potamia were well urbanised. Beyond Mesopotamia mountains run north-west to south-east from eastern Turkey to Iran, and the main centres of the Persians were in the southern part of that region. Beyond that were the provinces towards Afghanistan and Pakistan, of which the Indus valley was ceded to Chandragupta *c.*305[9] and, north of there, a separate Indo-Greek Bactrian kingdom was emerg-ing by the middle of the third century.[10] The Seleucids had no single capital, but essential business would be referred to the king wherever he was; and they continued the non-interventionist administrative practices of the Persians, tolerating a mixture of satrapies, cities and local princedoms (and often giving a regional command to a member of the royal dynasty), using a variety of languages for official texts, but expecting military service and tribute from their subjects. Power lay with the king, his 'friends' and his armed forces.

Some land, and some categories of land such as forests and mines, was explicitly royal land (and the men working it were *basilikoi laoi*, 'royal people'). There were also temple properties and private estates, with their own *laoi*. Often rural land would be attached to a city; and more generally the king could make gifts of land and issue instructions for its use.[11] Seleucus I and Antiochus I were both active founders of cities, sometimes planting settlers at a new site, sometimes refounding and giving Greek institutions to a well-established town, and sometimes establishing a colony of veterans with a military purpose. Established cities tended to be less subject to royal interference than new ones.

## CULTURAL LIFE[12]

The religion of the Greeks continued very much as it had earlier, with the cults of rulers and dynasties grafted on to it.[13] The importation into the Greek heartland of deities and cults from outside continued from the classical period; the Egyptian Sarapis (the Greek form of Osiris–Apis) and Isis, and some near-eastern deities, became popular beyond their home territory. There was a development across the whole Greek world of new deities, without the anthropomorphic trappings of the older ones, such as Tyche (fortune). Public observances remained important, but the number of cults focused on an individual's relationship with a deity may have increased. As noted above, a number of cities sought recognition from cities across the Greek world of the inviolability of a sanctuary of theirs.

In cultural as in political matters Athens lost the predominance which it had enjoyed in the fifth and fourth centuries. Institutions of Greek culture, such as the gymnasium and the theatre, like the institutions of Greek politics spread to the new or refounded cities of the enlarged Greek world, and among the writers of literature in Greek there came to be some men of non-Greek origin and some women. Of particular importance were the Museum (a community of salaried scholars) and library at Alexandria, founded by Ptolemy I on the advice of the Athenian Demetrius of Phalerum.[14] This not only provided a centre for literary activity, but encouraged the scholarly editing and interpreting of older literature and a more learned approach to the writing of new literature. One Alexandrian achievement was the Septuagint, said to be a translation into Greek of [the first five books of] the Jewish scriptures made by seventy[-two] scholars for Ptolemy II,[15] but in fact a translation of the whole completed over some centuries.

Poetry tended towards polished works on a small scale. The following writers were all active in Alexandria about the second quarter of the third century. Callimachus, from Cyrene, wrote prose works which have not survived, including the *Pinakes* ('tablets'), a catalogue of writers of Greek literature; his poetry included the *Aitia* ('origins' of customs, sayings and works of art), which survives only in fragments, six *Hymns* and some epigrams. Theocritus, from Syracuse, wrote *Idylls*, of which some imitated the archaic Alcaeus,[16] but the best known are the pastoral mimes for which he used the epic hexameter (these were in turn imitated in Latin by Virgil in his *Eclogues*). Apollonius of Rhodes is best known for his *Argonautica*, an epic poem on the legend of Jason and the golden fleece, which is learned and episodic rather than a grand whole. Herodas wrote *mimiamboi* (iambic 'mimes'), short dramatic pieces on themes similar to those of new comedy, some of which have survived on papyrus. Aratus, from Soloi in Cilicia and not associated with Alexandria, wrote didactic poetry: his *Phaenomena* gave an account of the constellations and of the signs of the weather.

In the next generation the greatest name is that of Eratosthenes, who succeeded Apollonius as Librarian at Alexandria and wrote not only poetry but works of literary criticism, chronology, mathematics, geography and philosophy. History continued along the paths established in the fourth century, with some works wide-ranging and others narrowly focused, some serious and others rhetorical and dramatic. The most outstanding historian was Polybius (*c*.200–118), from Megalopolis in Arcadia, who wrote of the rise of Rome to dominate the Greek world, professed serious intentions and methods comparable to those of Thucydides and was very willing to criticise writers whom he considered inferior.[17]

The hellenistic period saw considerable achievements in science. There were some technical improvements with practical benefits. Archimedes (third century), of Syracuse, is credited with the 'Archimedean screw' for raising water and the compound pulley, as well as with exclaiming [*h*]*eureka* ('I have found it') when he realised how the water was displaced as he stepped into a bath. Ctesibius (third century), of Alexandria, invented mechanical water-clocks and machines powered by air under pressure. In military machinery the most important developments took place in the fourth century,[18] but these were built on in the Hellenistic period. In botany and zoology the work of Aristotle was continued (as it was in other subjects too) by his pupil Theophrastus of Eresus on Lesbos, whose *Enquiry into Plants* and *Causes of Plants* survive. In medicine Hippocrates (late fifth century), of Cos, was a celebrated early figure; but what have been preserved as the 'Hippocratic' writings in fact accumulated over a longer period; the greatest of the later writers was Galen (second century AD), of Pergamum. How medicine developed between these two points, and how far temple medicine (there was a sanctuary of Asclepius at Cos) and 'Hippocratic' medicine complemented or opposed each other is hard to determine; but Praxagoras (late fourth century), of Cos, was an important anatomist, Herophilus (early third century), of Calchedon, discovered the nerves, and he and Erasistratus (early third century), of Iulis, both practised dissection.

In astronomy Meton (late fifth century), of Athens, had worked out a 19-year cycle to keep years of lunar months in step with the sun,[19] and the historian Thucydides knew that eclipses of the sun happen at the new moon.[20] In the enlarged Greek world of the Hellenistic period there was more access to Babylonian observations. Aristarchus (early third century), of Samos, suggested that the earth revolves around its own axis, and that it revolves around the sun rather than the sun around the earth. Hipparchus (second century), of Nicaea in Bithynia, invented several instruments,[21] produced a catalogue of the stars, and discovered the 'precession of the equinoxes' (by which the appearance of the stars in the night sky shifts extremely gradually through the seasons of the year). Eratosthenes (above) worked with latitude and longitude, and calculated the circumference of the earth. Agatharchides (early second century), of Cnidus, explained the annual flooding of the Nile. In mathematics Euclid (*c*.300), perhaps working in Alexandria, in his *Elements* consolidated previous work to produce a systematic geometry based on axioms, theorems and proofs, which remained the basis of geometry to the twentieth century AD. Archimedes (above) calculated the value of π, the ratio between the diameter and the circumference of a circle. Hipparchus (above) invented trigonometry.

Fifth-century philosophers had questioned a wide range of accepted beliefs and explanations. In the fourth century, in a quest for new certainties, Plato had tried to distinguish true knowledge from delusive appearances and Aristotle in various fields had sought to generalise from a multitude of observed instances. In the Hellenistic period Athens remained a major centre for philosophy; though Aristotle's school (known as the Peripatetics, because of the custom of walking around, *peripatein*, while discussing) continued to range widely, other philosophical schools were concerned particularly with how people ought to live their lives. The Cynics, of whom the best known was Diogenes (late fourth century), of Sinope, rejected all the general standards and conventions of life in society. The Epicureans, founded in his *kepos* ('garden') at Athens by Epicurus (late fourth century, originally from Samos), had an atomic view of the universe, and taught that the chief aim of human life should be a kind of pleasure which results from *ataraxia* ('avoidance of trouble'). The Stoics, founded by Zeno (*c*.300), from Citium in Cyprus, and named after the Painted Stoa in Athens, where he taught, concerned themselves with logic, physics and ethics, and believed that the world is rational and that true happiness results from acting rationally in accordance with human nature; this was the only philosophical school which was happy with engagement in political life. Scepticism had begun under Pyrrhon (fourth century), of Elis, and as the name implies emphasised that we should admit to uncertainty rather than pretend to know what we cannot know; in the third century this position was adopted by the successors of Plato in the Academy. Some writers conjured up fictional utopias: Euhemerus (*c*.300), of Messene, and Iambulus (perhaps third century), wrote of islands on the edge of the world where everything was perfect and many of the normal human institutions were not needed.

In architecture, more complex structures were produced which continued the general style of earlier Greek buildings. As already in the Mausoleum at Halicarnassus, there was some use of *motifs* from outside the Greek repertoire, such as palm-leaf capitals at Pergamum. Alexandria had tall tenement buildings, and its lighthouse (early third century) in some versions of the list joined the Mausoleum among

Figure 22. Louvre: statue of *Victory from Samothrace* (*c*.200).

the seven wonders of the Ancient world. Hellenistic sculpture, again following the lead of the Mausoleum, moved from the idealised figures of the classical period towards representations of identifiable individuals, and the same tendency can be seen in the portraits which the Hellenistic kings placed on their coins. Other notable works of the period include two sets of statues (one from Athens and the other perhaps from Pergamum) commemorating the defeat of the Gallic invaders of the third century;[22] *the Victory from Samothrace* (*c*.200: figure 22); *the great altar of Zeus at Pergamum* (early second century), in a style which has been described as Baroque, with a frieze at the ends of which the figures reach out beyond their frame to the actual steps; the Laocoön group (what survives is a Roman version of a

Hellenistic original: figure 23). The Colossus of Rhodes, a statue about 105 feet = 32 m high of the sun god Helios by the Rhodian sculptor Chares, another of the seven wonders, was set up at the entrance to the harbour *c.*300 to commemorate Rhodes' survival of the siege of Demetrius,[23] but brought down by an earthquake in 227/6.

For painting and mosaic we have to imagine what lay between the Macedonian tomb paintings of the fourth century and the wall paintings of Roman houses. A mosaic from Pella with a stag hunt and a floral border is of *c.*300; the Alexander Mosaic from Pompeii (figure 24) is a work of the second century, copied from a wall painting of *c.*300, and shows skilful use of perspective, lighting and shadows. In pottery, after the gaudier versions of the red-figure style in the late fifth and the fourth centuries had gone out of fashion, such painted pottery as was still produced had simpler decoration, as in the 'west slope' style, with a limited range of geometric and floral designs, and the *lagynoi,* narrow-necked jugs with decoration on the shoulder.

Figure 23. Vatican Museum: Laocoön statue group (perhaps a Roman work based on a Hellenistic original).

Figure 24. Naples, Museo Nazionale: part of Alexander Mosaic from Pompeii (second century, probably copied from a wall painting of *c*.300).

# 12

## UNTIL THE ROMAN CONQUEST, 272–146

### GREECE AND MACEDON TO 217

A prominent part was played in Greece in the third and second centuries by two leagues of states which were not based on a powerful and ambitious city but were regional federations which expanded beyond their own region. One of the peoples of north-western Greece was the Aetolians: in the time of Thucydides they were primitive and not urbanised,[1] but already then they could organise themselves effectively for war, and in 367 when one city imprisoned heralds announcing the truce for the Eleusinian Mysteries Athens protested to the federation.[2] They still had a reputation for piracy in the Hellenistic period. At the end of the Lamian War in 322[3] they survived technically undefeated. In the early third century they began gaining league members outside Aetolia through arrangements based on *isopoliteia* (equal citizenship),[4] an early instance being Heraclea in Trachis, near Thermopylae, in 280.[5] The league's principal officer was a general (who could be re-elected after a lapse of time); it had a council, which was executive rather than probouleutic, and a smaller body known as the *apokletoi* ('called out'); an assembly had two regular meetings a year and could have additional meetings. In 281 the Aetolians beat off an attack by the Spartan king Areus who claimed to be fighting for Delphi,[6] and in 279 they were active in opposition to the Gallic invaders.[7] After that they acquired two seats on Delphi's Amphictyonic council, and in the years which followed they gained more seats and supplanted the Thessalians as the dominant people in the Amphictyony. In 278 the Pythian games included thanksgiving sacrifices for the salvation (*soteria*) of Delphi,[8] and later the Soteria became a separate four-yearly festival.

The Achaeans, on the Peloponnesian coast of the Gulf of Corinth, had a federation of 12 cities in the fifth century,[9] and expanded to the north of the Gulf in the early fourth century.[10] The federation broke down *c.*300, but a revival began in 281/0; expansion beyond Achaea began in 251/0 when Aratus of neighbouring Sicyon added that city to the league.[11] The league had one general (from 255/4), eligible for reappointment after a year out of office, and a body of ten *damiourgoi*. At first it had four regular *synodoi* ('meetings') each year at Aegium of a probouleutic council and an assembly, and could hold additional *synkletoi* ('summoned' meetings) anywhere; after 217 *synkletoi* were used for specified major items of business, and after 188 *synodoi* did not have to be held at Aegium.

Sparta became assertive again under king Areus I (309–265). In 281 he attacked the Aetolians;[12] in 272 he returned from a campaign in Crete to contribute to the defeat and death of Pyrrhus.[13] In 269/8 he combined with Athens and Ptolemy II in the Chremonidean War against Antigonus Gonatas. The Athenian decree proposed by Chremonides refers to a combination of Athens with Sparta and its allies (in the Peloponnese and Crete), supported by Ptolemy, in defence of the freedom of the Greeks as in the glorious past. How far the war was in fact instigated by Ptolemy is not clear, but although he sent ships he did not make a substantial contribution to the fighting. Macedonian occupation of Corinth hindered cooperation between Athens and Sparta; Areus was killed in 265, and Athens capitulated in 263/2. For Athens this was the last attempt at an independent foreign policy, and in the years which followed Gonatas intervened in Athens' internal affairs to an exceptional extent.[14] A naval victory off Cos for Gonatas over Ptolemy possibly followed this war; and during the war Gonatas defeated an attack by Pyrrhus' son Alexander II.

After the war our attention is focused on the Peloponnese. The war left Gonatas in control of Corinth, and there was a pro-Macedonian tyrant, Aristodemus, in Megalopolis. In 251/0 Aratus liberated Sicyon from the latest in a series of tyrants and attached the city to the Achaean League; he then gained support from Ptolemy. About the same time Aristodemus in Megalopolis was assassinated, but another pro-Macedonian tyrant seized power there a few years later, and in the meantime Gonatas gave his support to a new tyrant, Aristomachus in Argos. Gonatas' nephew Alexander, commanding Gonatas' garrisons on Acrocorinth and in Euboea, revolted against Gonatas, withdrawing the garrisons and taking the title of king, but Gonatas regained control when Alexander died in 245. However, in 243/2 Aratus as general of the Achaean League liberated Corinth and gained that for the league, and the league also gained Megara, and Troezen and Epidaurus in the Argolid. Ptolemy III (who had succeeded his father in 246) was made *hegemon* (honorary 'leader') of the league, while Gonatas and the Aetolians made an agreement to divide Achaea between them if they defeated it.

In Sparta Areus' son Acrotatus had died in the 250s in an attack on Megalopolis, but c.244 Agis IV acceded to the other throne. Sparta's decline in full citizen numbers and concentration of wealth in a few families had continued since the fourth century,[15] and Agis in order to restore Sparta's military strength (rather than from egalitarian motives) planned a social reform, with a cancellation of debts and redistribution of land among citizens and *perioikoi*, and a revival of the training system and messes.[16] Proposals were put forward by Lycurgus, one of the ephors of 243/2, but rejected in the *gerousia*, where the opposition was led by the other king, Leonidas II. Lycurgus had him deposed and replaced by his son-in-law, Cleombrotus II. The ephors of 242/1 reinstated Leonidas, but Agis and Lycurgus had them deposed, and Leonidas fled into exile. A cancellation of debts was enacted but not the rest of the programme. Then in 241 the Aetolians invaded the Peloponnese by way of the isthmus of Corinth, Aratus called on Sparta as an ally to support the Achaeans against them, and Agis with a Spartan army joined the Achaeans at Corinth. However, Aratus was alarmed by the revolutionary Spartans and dismissed both armies. In Sparta Leonidas was reinstated again, and Agis fled to a sanctuary but was tricked into leaving and was executed. The Aetolians continued to the Achaean city of Pellene, where they were defeated by Aratus; but they seem to have attacked other places in the Peloponnese too. In 241/0 peace was made between Achaea and Gonatas, and between Achaea and the Aetolians, though Aratus afterwards attacked Argos and Athens. In 240/39 Gonatas died and was succeeded by his son Demetrius II, who had been co-regent for some time: after long upheavals he had given Macedon a period of stability.

We then see a change in alignments, with the Aetolians becoming allies of the Achaeans and Demetrius supporting Epirus against the Aetolians. The Achaeans and Aetolians continued to attack Athens and Argos, and the Achaeans extended their power into Arcadia until in 235 the current tyrant of Megalopolis, Lydiades, resigned his tyranny and brought Megalopolis into the Achaean League; but that had a destabilising effect, as Megalopolis was opposed to Sparta. Demetrius invaded and won over Boeotia and neighbouring regions, which had previously been aligned with Aetolia; but in 234/3 a series of deaths brought the ruling family of Epirus to an end, to be succeeded by a federal republic. This came to terms with the Illyrians, who in 229 defeated a fleet of the Achaeans and Aetolians off the Paxi Islands south of Corcyra and themselves occupied Corcyra and attacked other places. In the course of this they attacked Italian traders and perhaps killed a Roman deputation, and this led to Rome's first venture across the Adriatic, in the First Illyrian War.[17]

Early in 229 Demetrius died, perhaps in a war against the Dardanians, to the north of Macedon. His son Philip V was a child, so his cousin Antigonus Doson was appointed regent and soon took the title of king. He continued the war against the Dardanians, and had to put down a revolt in Thessaly which was prompted by the Aetolians. Further south Boeotia defected from Macedon to the Achaeans and Aetolians; and Athens with the help of Aratus bought out its Macedonian garrisons, but instead of joining the Achaean League it maintained a neutral position in friendship with Ptolemy III.[18]

In the Peloponnese Aristomachus of Argos and some neighbouring tyrants resigned their positions and brought their cities, and their anti-Spartan leanings, into the Achaean League. In Sparta Cleomenes III, who had succeeded Leonidas c.235, came into conflict with the Achaeans in Arcadia, and in 229/8 the Achaeans declared war on Sparta. In 227 Cleomenes was victorious at Mount Lycaeum but Aratus captured Mantinea. At home Cleomenes attacked the ephors and seized power, bringing in Agis' programme of reforms and the Macedonian infantry phalanx,[19] weakening the *gerousia* and abolishing the ephors, and in breach of Sparta's practice of maintaining two distinct royal families installing his own brother Euclidas as his fellow king. As the war continued with successes for Cleomenes, the Achaeans made approaches to Antigonus Doson. At a conference in Argos in 225 the Achaeans made demands which Cleomenes refused, the Achaean League fell into factional divisions, and Cleomenes first seized Pellene and other places in Achaea, and then occupied Argos, Corinth and other cities. In 224 Doson marched South, and Aratus agreed to hand the fortress of Acrocorinth to him. Cleomenes had a strong position near Corinth, but after Argos defected from him he was driven back to Sparta. While he appealed to Ptolemy III, and perhaps sold freedom to helots for money to be spent on mercenaries, Doson with the Achaeans instituted a league of leagues (an alliance composed of leagues rather than of individual cities) to oppose Sparta and the Aetolians. In 223 Cleomenes captured and destroyed Megalopolis, but in 222 he was defeated at Sellasia in northern Laconia, and then fled to Egypt (where he was killed in 219). The political part, at least, of his reforms was annulled, and Doson appointed an *epistates*.

Doson himself had to return home to beat off an Illyrian attack; he died in 221 and was succeeded by Philip V, the son of Demetrius II, still only 17 years old and given a body of 'friends' as guardians. The new reign began with the Social War (war 'of the allies' united in Doson's league of leagues). The Aetolians had been raiding Epirus and Greece, capturing a Macedonian warship near Cythera, defeating an Achaean army under Aratus and massacring the inhabitants of Cynaetha in Arcadia. In 220 the league declared war against the Aetolians, and stated its intention of freeing Delphi from Aetolian domination; but Sparta and some other Peloponnesian states favoured Aetolia. In 219 the allies fought in the Peloponnese and Philip in north-western Greece, but in the winter he had a successful campaign in the Peloponnese. In 218 an agreement was made by which the Achaeans would pay for Philip's campaigns in the

Peloponnese (which would allow Philip to revive the Macedonian navy: he rid himself of advisers opposed to that). In 217 news arrived that Hannibal of Carthage had defeated the Romans at Lake Trasimene in Italy: this gave Philip the opportunity to turn his attention to Illyria, and in a conference at Naupactus, at which the Aetolian Agelaus warned that the Greeks should resolve their differences before 'the clouds in the west' descended on Greece,[20] peace was made on the basis of a *status quo* which left Philip stronger than he had been at the beginning of the war. From this point onwards the history of Greece and Macedon is bound up with the advance of Rome.[21]

## ATHENS

The Chremonidean War enabled Athens and Sparta for the last time to see themselves as leading the Greeks against a foreign enemy.[22] Sparta was to assert itself later in the third century, but for Athens defeat on this occasion was a turning-point, and it no longer sought to be a major player in Greek affairs. Immediately after the war Athens was subject to direct Macedonian interference: not only were there garrisons on the Museum hill and in various places in Attica, but according to the second-century writer Apollodorus 'the offices were abolished and all deliberation was entrusted to one man'.[23] That is an exaggeration, and Athens' constitution remained technically democratic, but one inscription shows a general appointed by Antigonus Gonatas but given his particular posting by the assembly, and it is possible that Demetrius the grandson of Demetrius of Phalerum was appointed as Gonatas' agent with the title *thesmothetes*.[24] But in 256/5 or 255/4 Gonatas 'gave the Athenians freedom', withdrawing his Museum garrison (but not his other garrisons) and presumably ending his internal appointments.[25] Although it no longer had a foreign policy of its own, Athens was drawn into the wars of Gonatas and Demetrius II on their side, and at times there was fighting in Attica.[26]

In 229 after the death of Demetrius Antigonus Doson was preoccupied in the North, and Athens took advantage of this to buy out the Macedonian garrisons. Aratus of Sicyon, though previously hostile, contributed to this, and Polybius reflects the Achaeans' annoyance that Athens did not then join the Achaean League but adopted a policy of neutrality in friendship with Ptolemy III. Its leaders were the brothers Euryclides and Micion, who had already held important positions in the time of Gonatas and Demetrius: Euryclides lived almost until the end of the century, and a decree of *c.*215 in his honour listed his achievements before, during and after the liberation.[27] At first there was not a total breach with the Antigonids, and in 224/3 the festival of the Ptolemea was instituted and another additional tribe, Ptolemaïs, was created but Antigonis and Demetrias were not abolished. In 218 when Megaleas, one of the advisers who had fallen out of favour with Philip V, sought asylum in Athens, the generals rebuffed him.

Athens remained uninvolved in the First Macedonian War of 214–206:[28] Livy names it among the participants in the Peace of Phoenice at the end of the war, but that is a fiction to justify Rome's involvement in the Second Macedonian War of 200–196.[29] In 201 Athens executed two Acarnanians who while uninitiated had taken part in the Eleusinian mysteries; and Acarnania with support from Philip raided Attica. In 200 Athens declared war on Macedon, abolished the two Macedonian tribes and resolved to obliterate all references to the Antigonids in public documents (many instances of erasure have been found,[30] but also some texts which the erasers overlooked). Rhodes and Attalus I of Pergamum were at war with Philip, and invited Athens to join them: it did so, and created the new tribe Attalis. An Athenian deputation went to Rome, which had already decided to embark on the Second Macedonian War againt Philip but now cited the attack on Athens among its pretexts.

After the war Athens remained firmly pro-Roman, and perhaps became a formal ally of Rome during the war of 192–188. After that war Athens along with Thessaly played a leading role in re-establishing the Delphic Amphictyony.[31] Athens remained loyal to Rome in the Third Macedonian War of 171–167 against Perseus, and was then rewarded with Lemnos, Imbros and Scyros, the north Aegean islands which it had possessed in the fifth and fourth centuries,[32] Delos, which was made a tax-free port (its citizens took refuge in Achaea and were replaced by Athenian settlers), and more strangely Haliartus in central Boeotia. In Asia the rulers with whom the Athenians maintained the strongest links were the Attalids of Pergamum, who erected stoas below the acropolis and in the agora, and who in return were honoured with statues on the acropolis. Trouble arose when in the 150s the Athenians tried to annex Oropus, lying between Boeotia and Athens and currently independent:[33] eventually they occupied Oropus and expelled the inhabitants, but the threat of an attack by the Achaean League induced them to withdraw.

## EGYPT AND ASIA

In Egypt Ptolemy I was succeeded by Ptolemy II in 283, and in the near east Seleucus I was succeeded by Antiochus I in 281: each had already been designated heir and took over without difficulty.[34] The Ptolemies were secure in Egypt from the beginning, and regarded Cyrene, Cyprus and southern Syria (Coele Syria, 'Hollow Syria') as essential to their security against possible attackers,[35] and the Seleucids had become secure in the Near East away from the Mediterranean; but the Mediterranean coast of Syria and Asia Minor were contested; the Ptolemies took an interest in Greece; the Antigonids from Macedon took an interest in Asia Minor, and much of Asia Minor had been controlled by Lysimachus until he was killed by Seleucus at Corupedium early in 281.

After Corupedium Antiochus and Antigonus Gonatas both tried to establish themselves in Asia Minor, while Ptolemy II had some interests there too. A ruler in Bithynia on the North Coast, Zipoetes, refused to acknowledge either; he soon died, and his eventual successor Nicomedes I aligned himself with Gonatas. In 278 Gonatas and Antiochus were reconciled and Antiochus was left to take over Asia Minor, but in 277 Nicomedes enlisted a body of invading Gauls as mercenaries to fight against his brother (another Zipoetes), and later they asserted their independence and roamed destructively over much of Asia Minor. This allowed Antiochus to present himself as a champion of Greek civilisation against the barbarians. Perhaps c.270 he defeated them in a famous 'battle of the elephants', and eventually they were settled in Galatia, in central Asia Minor.

Lysimachus when he controlled western Asia Minor had established a local man, Philetaerus, in the fortress of Pergamum, north of Sardis; but Philetaerus fell out with Lysimachus, and when Lysimachus' son Agathocles was killed in 283/2 he transferred his allegiance to Seleucus and after Seleucus' death to Antiochus. He gradually took a more independent stance, but did not assume the title of king, and this tendency was continued by his successor, now designated Eumenes I (263–241).

Ongoing conflict, primarily between the Seleucids and the Ptolemies, is conventionally divided into a series of wars. In the First Syrian War (274–271) Magas, a half-brother of Ptolemy II, ruling Cyrene, but married to a daughter of Antiochus, unsuccessfully attempted a rising against Ptolemy and also incited Antiochus to make war on him. The upshot was a return to the *status quo ante*, to the advantage of Ptolemy. In 261, after an alleged plot by Antiochus' son Seleucus, a younger son, Antiochus II, succeeded, and that triggered the Second Syrian War (260–*c*.253), by which Ptolemy lost ground while Antiochus made gains in Asia Minor (and married a daughter of Ptolemy, and his sister married Gonatas' son Demetrius). In 246 Ptolemy II and Antiochus II died: Ptolemy was succeeded by his son Ptolemy III (who was married to Magas' daughter), and Antiochus was said to have named on his deathbed his son Seleucus II as his heir. Seleucus was challenged by Antiochus' Ptolemaic wife on behalf of the son she had borne him, and Ptolemy III began the Third Syrian War (246–241) by invading Syria in support of him. He advanced successfully into northern coastal Syria.[36] By then the wife and son had been murdered, though Ptolemy may for a time have concealed the fact. He then marched East to the Euphrates, and claimed to have conquered the whole of the Seleucid Empire,[37] but he had to return (laden with booty) to deal with a rising in Egypt. Seleucus recovered in Syria and the East, but Ptolemy retained the Syrian harbour town of Seleucea in Pieria and gains in Asia Minor.

In order to concentrate on Syria Seleucus had made his brother Antiochus Hierax his deputy in Asia Minor, but Hierax then enlisted Galatian mercenaries and challenged Seleucus in the War of the Brothers, defeating him near Ancyra in 240 or 239. In Pergamum Eumenes had been succeeded in 241 by his nephew and adopted son Attalus I: Hierax and the Galatians attacked him, but he won several victories, gaining control of Seleucid Asia Minor for himself, and taking the title of king as his predecessors had not.[38] Hierax eventually fled to Thrace and was murdered there. Antigonus Doson advertised an interest in Asia Minor with a naval expedition to Caria in 227. Another state which benefited from the uncertainties in Asia Minor was Rhodes, which was well placed for trading connections, maintained friendly links with the Ptolemies and itself built up a substantial navy. In 227/6 it was hit by a serious earthquake (which demolished the colossal statue of Helios),[39] but afterwards attracted gifts from many rulers and cities. In 220 it responded to pressure from others to head a war against Byzantium over the tolls which it levied on Black Sea trade.

Seleucus II died in 226/5, and was succeeded briefly by his elder son Seleucus III (226/5–223) and then by his younger son Antiochus III (223–187). Ptolemy III was succeeded by his son Ptolemy IV (221–204), who was uninterested in ruling and during whose reign affairs were in the hands of two courtiers, Sosibius and Agathocles. In the Fourth Syrian War (221–217) Antiochus recaptured Seleucea in Pieria and advanced southwards through coastal Syria, but in 217 he was defeated at Raphia in southern Judaea,[40] and the southern part of the Syrian coast remained Ptolemaic. Meanwhile Antiochus' relative Achaeus had been given the task of recapturing the Seleucid territories in Asia Minor from Attalus. He quickly succeeded in that despite Ptolemaic support for Attalus, and in 220 he took the title of king; but in 218 Attalus regained part of the lost territory, and from 216 to 214 Antiochus made an agreement with Attalus and fought against Achaeus, capturing Sardis and having him executed there. Sardis was then occupied by Zeuxis on behalf of Antiochus. In the East at the beginning of Antiochus' reign Molon, who was appointed as his deputy, rebelled, but was defeated in 220. From 212 to 205 Antiochus campaigned in the east, where separate kingdoms in Parthia (east of the Caspian) and Bactria (east of that) had been emerging, and he obtained formal submission from the Parthians and, after Bactra had withstood a two-year siege, from the Bactrians. He then returned to Asia Minor, where he was making some gains when in 204 Ptolemy IV died, leaving a six-year-old son to succeed as Ptolemy V. Antiochus took advantage of that, and in the Fifth Syrian War (201–199) he at last gained southern Syria for the Seleucids, and the Ptolemaic possessions in the Aegean and Asia Minor were lost too.

Attalus joined in the Second Macedonian War on the Roman side,[41] and in 198 while he was in Greece Antiochus' commander Zeuxis began an attack on Pergamum. In 197 Attalus died and was succeeded by his son Eumenes II; Antiochus came to Asia Minor and made further gains there, and in 196 crossed the Hellespont to the Chersonese. At the end of the Macedonian War the Romans originally spoke of the freedom of the Greeks in Europe and in Asia, but Antiochus insisted that the Romans had no right to interfere in his affairs. Prompted by Eumenes, the Romans persisted, but Antiochus, mourning the death of his son, did not give way, and in 195 he provided a refuge for the fugitive Hannibal of Carthage (Hannibal later went to Prusias I of Bithynia and eventually committed suicide). In 190 Roman soldiers entered Asia Minor, at the end of that year they defeated Antiochus' larger numbers near Magnesia by Sipylus, and in 188 by the Peace of Apamea Antiochus had to give up all of Asia Minor except the south-east coast and pay substantial reparations. Land to the North was given to Pergamum, land to the south to Rhodes, with cities on good terms with Rome declared free. In need of money, Antiochus tried to confiscate temple properties in the east of his kingdom, and in 187 was lynched in Susa; his son Seleucus IV ruled until 175. Eumenes duly extended his power, and rebuilt the city of Pergamum on a grand scale;[42] Rhodes encountered particular resistance in Lycia, to the east of Caria.

Later, however, Rhodes failed to back Rome in the Third Macedonian War against Perseus, and a treaty in 164 left Rhodes deprived of Lycia and Caria. In 166 Delos, independent since 314,[43] was given back to Athens by Rome and made a tax-free port, so that it supplanted Rhodes as the main trading centre of the southern Aegean. Eumenes' relations with Rome became cool; in Asia he fought against the Galatians and eventually defeated them, but the Romans ruled that they should be autonomous rather than subject to Pergamum. Eumenes died and was succeeded by his brother Attalus II in 159/8. Prusias II of Bithynia attacked Pergamum in

P. J. Rhodes

156–154, but Rome backed Pergamum and exacted reparations from him.

In Egypt rebellions at the beginning of the reign of Ptolemy V were eventually put down; the Rosetta Stone (in the British Museum) is one copy of a document of 196 honouring him when he was crowned in that year,[44] and in 194/3 he married Cleopatra, the daughter of Antiochus III. He died in 180, to be succeeded by Ptolemy VI, who in 170–168 tried in the Sixth Syrian War to regain southern Syria. Antiochus IV succeeded his brother Seleucus IV in 175: he was a strong king, who took the title *Epiphanes*, 'illustrious' (but was characterised by opponents as *Epimanes*, 'madman'). In response to Ptolemy he won over Cyprus, invaded Egypt and laid siege to Alexandria until the Roman C. Popillius Laenas ordered him to desist – drawing a circle round him on the ground and demanding a response before he left it.[45]

Southern Syria, including Judaea, was left in Antiochus' hands. Antiochus III on taking this from the Ptolemies had allowed the Jews to follow their traditional laws[46] and to appoint a high priest, and a division arose between Jews eager to embrace Greek culture and Jews who saw it as a threat to their religion. In 174 the high priest was the traditionalist Onias, but his brother Jason offered money to Antiochus IV if he were made high priest and enabled to turn Jerusalem into a Greek city called Antioch. In 171 Menelaus outbid Jason, trouble erupted while Antiochus was fighting in Egypt, and he saw that as a rebellion, and in 168 garrisoned Jerusalem and replaced the worship of Jehovah with the worship of the Greek gods. This provoked resistance both from the ultra-pious and from men led by Judas Maccabaeus of the Hasmonean family who began a guerrilla war. Antiochus died in 164 and was succeeded by his young son Antiochus V; in 163 the Jews' traditional freedoms were restored. The garrison remained and feuding among the Jews continued; but in 142 the garrison surrendered and Judaea became an independent state under the Hasmoneans.

In the East the Bactrians were now totally independent and the Parthians were becoming stronger.[47] In 165 Antiochus IV set out to reassert his power in the east: he was successful in Armenia, but in 164 he died before he could attack the Parthians; and the Seleucid dynasty now began to disintegrate. Antiochus V was challenged by Demetrius, son of Antiochus IV's brother and predecessor Seleucus IV, who thought he should have succeeded Seleucus but for some years had been a hostage in Rome. The Romans refused to back his claim, but in 162 he escaped, occupied northern Syria, proclaimed himself king and had Antiochus V and his guardian executed. He interfered in Cappadocia (eastern Asia Minor), while Prusias II of Bithynia made war on Pergamum until he was forced by the Romans to withdraw. He then quarrelled with Ptolemy VI, who combined with Attalus II and the Cappadocian king in 153 to back a rival candidate, Alexander Balas, who claimed falsely to be a son of Antiochus IV. Rome added its support, and Demetrius was killed in 150 in a battle near Antioch and succeeded by Balas. He lasted until 145, when he was defeated by Ptolemy in another battle near Antioch and murdered soon afterwards. He was succeeded by Demetrius' son, another Demetrius, and soon after the battle Ptolemy died. For part of the time he had ruled jointly with but had quarrelled with his brother, who now succeeded him (as Ptolemy VIII: the son conventionally designated Ptolemy VII probably never reigned), and for its last century, while the machinery of administration continued to work, the dynasty was torn apart by family feuding.

## THE ROMAN CONQUEST

With the final defeat of Pyrrhus in 275 and the surrender of Taras in 272 Rome had come to control the whole of the Italian peninsula, either directly or through alliances.[48] In Syracuse, after Pyrrhus had abandoned Sicily in 276,[49] Hieron II (who claimed probably falsely to be descended from the fifth-century Gelon, and whose wife Philistis may actually have been related to Dionysius I and his supporter Philistus)[50] was appointed general and then seized power. In 265 he defeated the Mamertines who were occupying Messana, took the title of king, and joined the Carthaginians in besieging the city; but he withdrew when the Mamertines allowed the Carthaginians to install a garrison. However, in 264 Messana transferred its allegiance to Rome and expelled the garrison, and Rome then began its First Punic War (264–241) against Carthage. Hieron at first supported

Carthage, but in 263 when the Romans besieged Syracuse he came to terms with them, retaining most of his kingdom until his death in 215, and enjoying good relations with Carthage (after the war) and with Rhodes and the Ptolemies in the East. The war led the Romans to build a navy, and it ended with the Carthaginians defeated and Sicily apart from Hieron's kingdom established as Rome's first overseas province, under the command of a praetor. Hieron's son Gelon died before him, so in 215 (during the Second Punic War) he was succeeded by his grandson Hieronymus, who became unpopular; a tumultuous period in which Syracuse was torn between Rome and Carthage ended with a Roman siege of the city in 213–212, at the end of which it was captured and looted. Acragas, supported by Carthage, was captured in 210; and in 204–202 P. Cornelius Scipio set out from Sicily to defeat Hannibal in Africa.

Rome was drawn eastwards across the Adriatic by the Illyrians, who lived to the north of and sometimes intervened in Epirus. Under Agron and, after his death, his widow Teuta, they were energetic and made various raids to the south, capturing the Epirot city of Phoenice, and in 229 they defeated the Achaeans and Aetolians off the Paxi islands and occupied Corcyra.[51] Appeals were made to Rome by Italian traders from Phoenice and/or the island state of Issa (further North, settled from Syracuse in the fourth century), which the Illyrians were besieging; and a member of a Roman delegation sent to protest was killed. Rome sent both of that year's consuls with substantial forces to fight the First Illyrian War, and they quickly obtained a number of formal surrenders; the settlement was announced to the Aetolian and Achaean Leagues, and to the Greeks attending the Isthmian games in 228. Demetrius of Pharos, who had been rewarded for betraying Corcyra to the Romans, became regent in Illyria, in 222 made an important contribution to the victory of Antigonus Doson's alliance over the Spartan Cleomenes at Sellasia,[52] and in 221 joined another Illyrian, Scerdilaïdas, in raiding the Peloponnese and the Aegean. In doing that they crossed a line specified in Rome's treaty of 229, and in 219 in its Second Illyrian War Rome sent both consuls, and they ousted Demetrius, who fled to Macedon and became influential with Philip V.

From 220 to 217 Philip was engaged in the Social War against the Aetolians, and Demetrius of Pharos encouraged him to build up his naval power in the Adriatic,[53] while Rome began its Second Punic War (218–202) and the Carthaginians under Hannibal invaded Italy. In 217 Hannibal defeated the Romans at Lake Trasimene, leaving Philip free to end the Social War and retaliate in Illyria against attacks by Scerdilaïdas. As Hannibal's successes continued Philip made approaches to him, and in 215 the Romans captured a Carthaginian ship taking to Philip a draft treaty for cooperation against the Romans and for the liberation of the various places in the Adriatic which had come under the protection of Rome.[54] This led to the First Macedonian War (214–205). Philip sent ships into the Adriatic, but was caught by heavier Roman ships and destroyed his own; he then had some successes on land against Scerdilaïdas. In 212 the Romans made contact with the Aetolians,[55] and prompted what was in effect a renewal of the Social War, with Rome and Attalus of Pergamum supporting the Aetolians against Philip's alliance. In the Achaean League Aratus had died in 213; Sparta was in a turbulent state but joined the Aetolians; Messene was divided, and had suffered two Macedonian interventions, in one of which Demetrius of Pharos was killed, but also joined the Aetolians eventually. Aetolia made some gains in the war, but was unsuccessful against its main objective, Acarnania; in 210 the Romans captured Aegina and sold it to Attalus. After several attempts by uninvolved states to mediate, the Aetolians broke their alliance with Rome and made peace with Philip in 206; and the Romans made peace with Philip at Phoenice in Epirus in 205. Most significant for the long term was that allies on each side were 'written into' the treaty: on Philip's side the Achaeans, his allies in central Greece and his brother-in-law Prusias I of Bithynia in Asia Minor (who had not taken part in the war), on the Roman side Sparta and the other friends of the Aetolians in the Peloponnese, and Attalus.[56]

By this time the last major figure in Spartan history was in power: Nabis, descended from the Demaratus who was king at the end of the sixth century and the beginning of the fifth.[57] A king called Lycurgus had expelled his fellow king and reigned alone; when he died in 210 he was succeeded by his young son Pelops with Machanidas as regent; and when Machanidas was defeated and killed by the Achaeans in 206 Nabis took his place, and came to be regarded as king.[58] He went beyond the reforms planned by Agis and Cleomenes,[59] exiling the rich and redistributing their property, freeing many slaves but apparently not the helots, and enlisting a mercenary army.

After the Peace of Phoenice the Rhodians turned to suppressing piracy in the Aegean, and this brought them into conflict with the Cretans, who were backed by Philip and by Nabis. When Antiochus III embarked on the Fifth Syrian War against Ptolemy V, Philip made an agreement with Antiochus about the Ptolemaic possessions in and around the Aegean; and in 201 he campaigned successfully there, though he was unable to take Pergamum when he attacked that. At the end of the year Rhodes and Attalus appealed to Rome. The Romans wanted to bring Philip into line after his earlier support for Hannibal, and to win the support of Greeks opposed to him: they immediately sent an ultimatum to Philip, and in 200 formally began the Second Macedonian War. The Aetolians did not join in on the Roman side at first but did before long; the Achaeans, alienated by Philip, at first refused to suppport him and in 198 joined the Romans; Philip transferred Argos to Nabis on the understanding that he would return it if Philip won the war, but after entering Argos and introducing a revolution there Nabis too joined the Romans. Most of the fighting was in central and northern Greece. T. Quinctius Flamininus, one of the consuls of 198, aimed to liberate the Greeks entirely from Philip, and in talks at Nicaea near Thermopylae he formally demanded that Philip should give up the three fortresses which he still held as 'fetters of Greece', Demetrias (in Thessaly), Chalcis and Acrocorinth. The matter was referred to the Roman senate, and it endorsed that demand. Flamininus' command was prolonged, and in 197 he defeated Philip overwhelmingly at Cynoscephalae in Thessaly.

Rome sent ten *legati* to help Flamininus implement a settlement, and at the Isthmian games of 196 Flamininus proclaimed on behalf of the senate and himself that all the Greeks were to be free and independent (which displeased the Aetolians, who had hoped to gain from Philip's defeat).[60] A new Thessalian League was founded; in the Peloponnese in 195 at the prompting of the Achaeans, Flamininus liberated Argos from Nabis and reincorporated it in the Achaean League; but in Asia Antiochus insisted that the Romans had no right to interfere in his affairs.[61] In general, from now onwards problems arising from treaties and local problems between cities were referred to Rome for decision.

The dissatisfied Aetolians made contact with Nabis, Philip and Antiochus. An attempt by Nabis to retake Sparta's harbour at Gytheum (entrusted to the Achaeans by Flamininus) was resisted by the Achaeans under another prominent leader, Philopoemen; after which in 192 the Aetolians killed Nabis and ravaged Sparta, and then Philopoemen reincorporated Sparta in the Achaean League. In the north the Aetolians captured Demetrias and persuaded Antiochus to come to support them. This led to a new war in Greece, the defeat of Antiochus by the Romans at Thermopylae in 191 and the submission of the Aetolians in 188; their domination of Delphi came to an end and the older form of the Amphictyony was reestablished. Philip tried to encroach on both Thessaly and Thrace, but was forced to back down. In the Peloponnese the Achaeans' incorporation of Messene and Sparta provoked opposition; Philopoemen and Polybius' father Lycortas took a hard line, but after the death of Philopoemen in 182 in the war against Messene the affair ended with Messene and Sparta both in the league.

Philip died in 179, and was succeeded by his intended heir, his elder son Perseus, though his younger son Demetrius was in good standing at Rome. Eumenes II of Pergamum incited Rome to fight its Third Macedonian War against Perseus (171–167), which led to the defeat of Perseus at Pydna in 168. Rome's settlement was drastic: the Macedonian monarchy was abolished and Macedon was divided into four republics, designated simply by numbers (and Illyria, which had supported Perseus, was divided into three republics). In Greece the friends of Rome were invited to identify the enemies of Rome, of whom a large number, including the historian Polybius, were taken to Italy as hostages.

There were disturbances in Macedon, which came to a head in 150 when Andriscus, who claimed to be a son of Perseus, raised an army in Thrace and invaded Macedon. The four republics could not withstand him; in the Fourth Macedonian War he defeated a first

Roman army in 149 but was defeated and captured by Q. Caecilius Metellus in 148. Also in 150, the Senate finally allowed Rome's surviving hostages from Achaea to return. In Achaea Sparta was again resisting membership of the league. A Roman pronouncement in 147 that Sparta and some other cities were to leave the league was met with Achaean anger, and preparation for a war against Sparta; but in 146 the Romans declared war and in a series of battles the Achaeans were defeated, first by Metellus and afterwards by L. Mummius. Corinth was then destroyed; Macedonia was made a Roman province; 'Achaia' was not formally annexed but was made an appendage of the province, with the defeated league greatly reduced and the cities opposed to it technically free.

In the same year, 146, Rome finally destroyed Carthage. It thus had no rival in the western Mediterranean and had now taken direct responsibility for Macedon and Greece. Egypt and the kingdoms in Asia were still free, but the Romans had intervened there on various occasions and had grown to expect their wishes to be complied with. In little more than a century Rome's direct control was to be extended there too.

# 13

## EPILOGUE

In 155 the future Ptolemy VIII, currently ruling in Cyrene while his brother Ptolemy VI was ruling in Egypt, in order to deter assassins publicised a will in which he left his kingdom to the Romans if he were to die without an heir.[1] That will did not have to take effect, but the example was followed by Attalus III of Pergamum, and when he died in 133 his kingdom was bequeathed to Rome. After the Romans had put down the revolt of a claimant called Aristonicus, the Attalid kingdom became the province of Asia, with Pergamum itself a free city.

The last serious challenge to the Romans came from king Mithridates VI (120–63) of Pontus, in north-eastern Asia Minor. In Rome's First Mithridatic War (89–85) he ordered the massacre of the Romans and Italians in the province of Asia; Athens was among his supporters; Athens was besieged, and he was defeated but allowed to survive in Pontus, by L. Cornelius Sulla. He was finally defeated, and led to commit suicide (allegedly by asking a bodyguard to kill him since he had made himself immune to poison), in the Third Mithridatic War (73–63) by Cn. Pompeius, Pompey the Great. The Seleucid kingdom was brought to an end also, when Pompey refused to recognise either of the current claimants, and eastern Asia Minor and the Levant became a mixture of provinces and vassal kingdoms. Jerusalem was captured, but a Judaea cut down to size was allowed to continue under a Hasmonean high priest. Further East, Parthia had been securely in control of Mesopotamia and the provinces beyond it since the 120s, and in Armenia, between the Black Sea and Mesopotamia, Tigranes II (c.95–56) was powerful and ambitious. Pompey left Tigranes as a vassal ruler, and in practice left the

Parthians in control of Mesopotamia, though he refused to acknowledge their king as King of Kings. For a long time afterwards Rome's eastern policy was to be focused on Armenia and Parthia.

By 101 Egypt, Cyrene and Cyprus were ruled by three different members of the feud-ridden Ptolemaic dynasty.[2] Cyrene was bequeathed to Rome when its last ruler died in 96, and was organised as a province in 75/4. Cyprus was annexed in 58, and its ruler committed suicide. In Egypt Ptolemy XI, the last legitimate descendant of Ptolemy I, was installed by Sulla in 80 on condition that he bequeathed his kingdom to Rome, and almost immediately he murdered the wife he had been forced to marry and then was lynched. Rome did not immediately activate the bequest, but eventually recognised the claimant who became Ptolemy XII (known as Auletes, 'the piper'; his brother was the last ruler of Cyprus). When he died in 51 he was succeeded by his daughter Cleopatra VII. She captivated first Julius Caesar in 48/7 and bore him a son, and then Octavian's opponent Antony in and after 41 and bore him three children; but after Octavian's defeat of Antony she committed suicide in 30 and Egypt became a special possession of the Roman emperors. And Achaia was made an ordinary province in 27.

Mithridates gave the Greeks their last opportunity to choose between Rome and an alternative, but in Rome's civil wars the Greeks had to choose between contenders for power in Rome, and Greece was caught up in the fighting. In 48 Pompey was defeated by Caesar at Pharsalus in Thessaly; in 42 Caesar's assassins M. Iunius Brutus and C. Cassius Longinus were defeated by Octavian and Antony at Philippi in Thrace; in 31 Antony was defeated by Octavian at Actium, at the entrance to the Gulf of Ambracia in north-western Greece. After that there was no alternative to Rome and its emperor, and the Greek cities no longer had any scope for a 'foreign' policy. But they continued as self-governing municipalities, with differing formal statuses which marked differing levels of formal esteem rather than realities of power, and experiencing the intervention of Roman officials more often because they asked for it than because the officials insisted on it.

But 'captive Greece took its wild victor captive, and imported the arts into rustic Latium', as the Roman poet Horace wrote.[3] Greek remained the *lingua franca* of the eastern part of Rome's empire. Upper-class Romans learned Greek, and Roman religion (with Roman gods assimilated to Greek counterparts), literature, philosophy, architecture and visual arts were all built up on Greek foundations. By claiming that Rome or a forerunner of it was founded by Aeneas, a fugitive from Troy when that was destroyed by the Greeks, the Romans even linked their own origin with the Greeks' legendary past. Of the emperors, Nero in the first century AD and Hadrian in the second were particularly enthusiastic for Greece (signified in Hadrian's case by wearing a beard as Greeks did but Romans did not). From the late first century to the early third there was a general revival of Greek pride and Greek culture, typified by the flourishing of rhetoric in the movement known as the Second Sophistic.

In 293 the Emperor Diocletian gave the Roman Empire a new structure, with two higher-ranking Augusti and two lower-ranking Caesars, and the beginnings of a division into a Western half and an Eastern half. Constantine reunified the empire, but in 324 he refounded Byzantium as Constantinople, and in his last years he ruled from there. By the end of the fourth century there was an increasingly clear-cut distinction between West and East, and in a now Christian world this was reinforced by a distinction between Western and Eastern churches. The Western Empire fell to invaders from the North in the fifth century (symbolic dates are a sack of Rome in 410 and the deposition of the last Western emperor in 476), but the Eastern Empire continued for another thousand years, until Constantinople was taken by the Ottoman Turks in 1453. Monks fleeing from there contributed to a new interest in Greek culture in a Western Europe whose heritage had been more Roman than Greek. In the sixteenth and seventeenth centuries the Ottomans advanced into south-eastern Europe as far as Vienna, but they twice failed to capture that, and afterwards started to fall back.

The Greek War of Independence (1821–30), supported by Western Europeans who were eager to rescue Greece for Europe and for Christianity, resulted in the creation of a state of (southern mainland) Greece. This gradually expanded, until in 1919 at the end of World War I the Ottoman Empire was dismantled, and Greece reached in

Europe almost but not quite to Constantinople/Istanbul and the waters between the Aegean and the Black Sea, and was given a large enclave in western Asia Minor centred on Smyrna/Izmir. But after Greece was defeated by Turkey in a war in 1922 there was a drastic exchange of populations, and Turkey now has a slightly larger foothold in Europe while Greece has no territory on the mainland of Asia Minor but almost all the Aegean islands close to its coast. Istanbul is a form of the name Constantinople, and travellers through Athens airport will see that Constantinople is still that city's Greek name.

# Guide to Further Reading

Other recent short histories of Ancient Greece are P. Cartledge, *Ancient Greece: A Very Short Introduction* (Oxford University Press, 2011), which picks 11 cities as characteristic of Greece at 11 different times, and was originally published as *Ancient Greece: A History in Eleven Cities* (Oxford University Press, 2009); and R. Osborne, *Greek History* (Routledge, 2004). A longer single-volume history is V. Parker, *A History of Greece: 1300–30 BC* (see next paragraph). Limited to the Classical period, and focusing on a series of topics treated by different authors, is R. Osborne (ed.), *Classical Greece Short Oxford History of Europe.* (Oxford University Press, 2000). Another topic-centred book, in which the topics are interrupted by a historical outline outside the sequence of numbered chapters, is P. Cartledge (ed.), *The Cambridge Illustrated History of Ancient Greece* (Cambridge University Press, 1998; corrected 2002).

For those who would like a more detailed treatment, there are three multi-volume series on the ancient world as a whole which include volumes on the Greeks. *The Fontana History of the Ancient World* (now London: Fontana Press) includes O. Murray, *Early Greece* (1980; 2nd edition 1993); J. K. Davies, *Democracy and Classical Greece* (1978; 2nd edition 1993); F. W. Walbank, *The Hellenistic World* (1981; 2nd edition 1993). *The Routledge* (originally Methuen) *History of the Ancient World* (Routledge) includes R. Osborne, *Greece in the Making, 1200–479 BC* (1996; 2nd edition 2009); S. Hornblower, *The Greek World, 479–323 BC* (1983; 4th edition 2011); G. Shipley, *The Greek World after Alexander, 323–30 BC* (2000). *The Blackwell History of the Ancient World* (now Chichester: Wiley–Blackwell) includes J. M. Hall, *A History of the Archaic Greek World, ca. 1200-479 BCE* (2007; 2nd edition 2013); P. J.

211

Rhodes, *A History of the Classical Greek World, 478–323 BC* (2005; 2nd edition 2010); R. M. Errington, *A History of the Hellenistic World, 323–30 BC* (2008); and also a summary volume, V. Parker, *A History of Greece, 1300–30 BC* (2014). Those who wish to pursue particular topics will find further bibliographical guidance in these.

The most authoritative single-volume encyclopaedia of the Graeco-Roman world is S. Hornblower and A. J. S. Spawforth with E. Eidinow (eds), *The Oxford Classical Dictionary* (Oxford University Press, 4th edition 2012). The largest and most authoritative atlas of the Graeco-Roman world, austerely limited to topographical maps of larger or smaller regions, is R. J. A. Talbert (ed.), *Barrington Atlas of the Greek and Roman World* (Princeton University Press, 2000); smaller, but including maps focused on themes, battles or particular periods, is N. G. L. Hammond (ed.), *Atlas of the Greek and Roman World in Antiquity* (Park Ridge, New Jersey: Noyes, 1981).

# Glossary

Achaean League
: Regional alliance centred on Achaea in the northern Peloponnese, important in the Hellenistic period: p. 190.

Aetolian League
: Regional alliance centred on Aetolia in north-western Greece, important in the Hellenstic period: pp. 189–90.

amphictyony
: 'League of neighbours', in particular the amphictyony which had responsibility for the sanctuary and festivals at Delphi: p. 29.

*archon*
: 'Ruler': general term for an official; in particular Athens had a board of nine archons, one of whom was designated archon: pp. 38–9.

Areopagus
: 'Hill of Ares': in Athens the council which met there, comprising former archons: p. 39.

aristocracy
: *Aristokratia*, 'best-power': a favourable term used of régimes which were not democratic but gave more power to those considered more entitled to it: p. 74.

assembly
: *Ekklesia* or other words: a meeting open to all qualified citizens, in most cities the ultimate decision-making body; in Sparta and generally p. 34, in Athens p. 75.

*basileus*
: King: p. 21; title used by Hellenistic rulers p. 168; in some places, including Athens (where he was one of the nine archons: p. 39), retained as the title of an appointed official.

council
: *Boule*: a representative body in a *polis*, which typically worked with the assembly in decision-making and had administrative powers (pp. 33–4); in Sparta the *gerousia* (pp. 33–4), in Athens the Council of 500 (pp. 45, 75; larger in the Hellenistic period).

Delian League
: Alliance built up by Athens in the fifth century: pp. 66–8.

| | |
|---|---|
| deme | (A particular use of *demos*.) In some places, including Athens, a local community within the polis: p. 45. |
| democracy | *Demokratia*, 'people-power': used of régimes in which all free men of local origin had a share in political power: p. 74. |
| *demos* | 'People': used of the whole citizen body or of the unprivileged in opposition to the privileged. |
| *eisphora* | 'Paying in': at Athens the name of a property tax levied on the rich: p. 76. |
| ephors | *Ephoroi*, 'overseers': the five principal civilian officials of Sparta, elected annually: p. 34. |
| *gerousia* | 'Council of elders': in Sparta the main council of the city: pp. 33–4. |
| helots | *Heilotai*, 'captives' or perhaps 'slaves': a servile class in Sparta: pp. 32–3. |
| hoplites | *Hoplitai*: heavy infantry: p. 21. |
| League of Corinth | Alliance formed by Philip II of Macedon after 338: p. 145. |
| liturgy | *Leitourgia*, 'work for the people': at Athens, public duties which the rich were required to perform at their own expense; particularly *choregia*, responsibility for a team of performers in a festival, and *trierarchia*, responsibility for a ship in the navy: p. 76. |
| metics | *Metoikoi*, 'migrants' or 'those living with': term used in Athens and elsewhere for free men of non-local origin who were not citizens: pp. 75, 106, cf. 12–13. |
| oligarchy | *Oligarchia*, 'few-rule': unfavourable term used of régimes which were not democratic but gave more power to those considered more entitled to it: p. 74. |
| ostracism | *Ostrakismos*: procedure at Athens in which, by writing a name on a potsherd (*ostrakon*), citizens had the opportunity each year to vote to send one man into exile for ten years: p. 46. |
| Peloponnesian League | Alliance built up by Sparta from the sixth century: p. 37. |
| *perioikoi* | 'Dwellers around': term used in Sparta and elsewhere of local people dependent on a polis but not citizens of it: p. 32. |

| | |
|---|---|
| phalanx | Massed infantry formation: p. 21. |
| *phratria* | 'Brotherhood': kinship group within a polis: p. 13. |
| *phyle* | 'Tribe': large kinship group within a polis: p. 13. |
| *polis* | 'City', used particularly of one organised as a city state: pp. 4–5. |
| *proedroi* | 'Presidents': an Athenian board which c. 380 took over from the *prytaneis* the duty of presiding in the council and assembly: p. 133. |
| *prytaneis* | 'Presidents', used particularly in Athens of the fifty representatives of one tribe in the council, who formed the council's standing committee for a fraction of the year: p. 75. |
| sacred band | *Hieros lochos*, élite body of professional citizen soldiers in Thebes after 379: p. 124. |
| Second Athenian League: | Alliance built up by Athens in the fourth century: p. 123. |
| *trittys* | A 'third' of a tribe in Athens: p. 45. |
| trireme | *Trieres*: a warship with three banks of oars, the standard Greek warship from the late sixth century to the early fourth: pp. 23–4. For fourth-century quadriremes and quinqueremes see p. 136. |
| tyrant | *Tyrannos*: a man who usurped power in a city: p. 21. |

# Notes

## PROLOGUE / CHAPTER 1

1     E.g. Thuc. I. 1–21.
2     E.g. Arist. *Pol.* VII. 1327 B 20–33.
3     See p. 32.
4     Hdt. VIII. 144. ii.
5     See p. 15.

## CHAPTER 2

1     Cf. p. 66.
2     Thuc. II. 2. i dates the beginning of the Peloponnesian War in the systems of three cities.
3     Thuc. I. 89 – 118. ii.
4     Thuc. I. 1–21, 23. i.
5     Cf. p. 74.
6     Cf. p. 34.
7     Cf. pp. 36–7, 122, 124.
8     Cf. p. 33.
9     Cf. p. 40.
10    Cf. p. 32.
11    The expansion of Athens into Attica was probably a large-scale instance of this: cf. p. 38.
12    Such as those who were judged ineligible to share in Sparta's conquered land: cf. p. 33.
13    Hdt. IV. 152.
14    Cf. p. 6.
15    Fornara 24.
16    Cf. p. 33.
17    E.g. the story of the founding of Cyrene in Hdt. IV. 150–8.
18    Thuc. I. 13. i.
19    Cf. the laments of the poet Theognis of Megara, 53–68, 183–92.
20    Arist. *Pol.* IV. 1297 B 16–24.
21    Hdt. V. 68.

22  Cf. p. 6.
23  Fornara 11.
24  Cf. pp. 29–30.
25  Cf. p. 33.
26  Cf. p. 118.
27  Thuc. I. 13. ii–iii.
28  Cf. the Jewish Moses: *Exodus* i. 7 – ii. 10.
29  Cf. p. 39.
30  Cf. p. 10.
31  Hdt. V. 68.
32  Cf. p. 29.
33  Cf. pp. 44–6.
34  Cf. p. 36.
35  Hdt. III. 125. ii; for Syracuse see pp. 58, 82–3.
36  Cf. p. 36.
37  Thuc. I. 18. i.
38  Cf. pp. 37, 47.
39  Cf. pp 74–5.
40  Cf. pp. 5–6.
41  See pp. 42, 67, 122.
42  Fornara 140: cf. Chapter 5 n. 16.

## CHAPTER 3

1   Cf. Thuc. I. 10. ii.
2   Cf. p. 18.
3   Plut. *Lyc.* 6.
4   Cf. p. 128.
5   Fornara 39. B; cf. p. 25.
6   Cf. p. 52.
7   Cf. p. 52.
8   Cf. p. 26.
9   Cf. p. 26.
10  Cf. pp. 44, 46–7.
11  Cf. pp. 47, 54.
12  Cf. p. 56.
13  Hdt. V. 42. i, 48.
14  Cf. p. 59–60.
15  Solon fr. 4a (West) *ap. Ath. Pol.* 5. ii.
16  Cf. p. 118.
17  Cf. p. 25.
18  Cf. p. 87.
19  Solon frs. 5–6 (West) *ap. Ath. Pol.* 12. i–ii.
20  Solon frs. 34, 36, 37 (West) *ap. Ath. Pol.* 12. iii–v.

21  Cf. p. 30–1.
22  Cf. p. 25.
23  Cf. p. 25.
24  Cf. p. 26.
25  Cf. p. 36–7.
26  Thuc. I. 20. ii, VI. 54–8.
27  Cf. pp. 33 (Sparta), 25 (Corinth).
28  Cf. p. 13.
29  *Ath. Pol.* 21. ii.
30  Cf. pp. 73–4.
31  Cf. p. 37.
32  Cf. p. 38.
33  Cf. pp. 37, 54–5.
34  Cf. p. 37.
35  *Ath. Pol.* 22. vi.

## CHAPTER 4

1  Cf. p. 10.
2  Cf. p. 53.
3  The word 'tyrant' was probably applied to him before it was taken over by the Greeks: cf. p. 21.
4  Cf. p. 6.
5  Cf. p. 36.
6  Hdt. III. 80–3 cf. VI. 43. iii.
7  E.g. A. Kuhrt, *The Persian Empire* (London: Routledge, 2007), i. 141–57 = Chapter 5 no. 1.
8  Bisitun (n. 7) §70.
9  Cf. p. 26.
10  Bisitun (n. 7) §§74–5.
11  Cf. p. 43.
12  Hdt. IV. 98, 133, 136. iii – 142.
13  Hdt. III. 129–38.
14  Cf. pp. 37, 47.
15  Cf. p. 47.
16  Cf. pp. 37, 47.
17  Cf. p. 41.
18  Cf. p. 47.
19  Cf. p. 48.
20  Cf. pp. 67–9, 73–4.
21  Cf. p. 48: the ostensible purpose was to get the better of Aegina.
22  Cf. p. 79.
23  Cf. p. 83.
24  Cf. pp. 80–1.

25    Cf. p. 61.
26    Aesch. *Pers.* 353–471.
27    Cf. p. 48.
28    Cf. p. 48.
29    Hdt. VII. 139.

## CHAPTER 5

1    Thuc. I. 89 – 118. ii; on the causes of the Peloponnesian War see pp. 85–8.
2    On Thuc., Diodorus and Plut. cf. pp. 10–1.
3    Cf. p. 9.
4    Athens did not distinguish between the two until the fourth century: cf. p. 131.
5    Cf. p. 62.
6    Cf. p. 79.
7    Cf. p. 55.
8    Cf. pp. 42–3.
9    Cf. p. 30.
10    Cf. p. 48.
11    Cf. pp. 47–8, 54, 56–7.
12    Cf. p. 73.
13    Cf. pp. 37, 47.
14    Evidence translated Fornara 95.
15    Cf. pp. 122–3.
16    For the Eleusinian mysteries cf. p. 31.
17    Plut. *Per.* 17.
18    Plut. *Per.* 12–14.
19    Cf. p. 84.
20    Fornara 97.
21    Fornara 128. 34–41.
22    Allied resentment: e.g. Thuc. I. 75.
23    Cf. pp. 44–6.
24    Cf. pp. 47, 48.
25    Cf. p. 67.
26    Cf. p. 79.
27    Cf. p. 68.
28    Cf. pp. 68, 79–80.
29    Cf. p. 39.
30    Cf. p. 48.
31    Cf. those appointed by Pisistratus: p. 42.
32    For assembly pay see p. 131.
33    Cf. p. 76.
34    Cf. pp. 59–61.

35 Cf. p. 67.
36 Cf. p. 69.
37 For Sparta see pp. 33–4.
38 Cf. p. 45.
39 Cf. p. 40.
40 Cf. p. 45.
41 Cf. p. 155.
42 For Per. as a *choregos* for tragedies by Aeschylus cf. p. 74.
43 Cf. p. 41.
44 Cf. p. 73.
45 Thuc. II. 65. ix.
46 Cf. pp. 32–8.
47 Cf. pp. 55–62.
48 Cf. p. 66.
49 Cf. pp. 36–8.
50 Cf. p. 58.
51 Cf. p. 37.
52 Cf. pp. 11–2.
53 Cf. p. 73.
54 Cf. p. 68.
55 Cf. p. 129.
56 Cf. p. 68.
57 Cf. p. 68.
58 Cf. p. 69.
59 Cf. p. 71.
60 Cf. p. 72.
61 Hom. *Il.* II. 649.
62 Cf. pp. 33–5.
63 Extracts Fornara 88.
64 Hdt. VII. 169–71.
65 Fornara 89.
66 Cf. p. 15.
67 Pind. *Pyth.* ix.
68 Pind. *Pyth.* iv, v.
69 Cf. p. 68.
70 Cf. pp. 94–6.
71 Cf. p. 80.
72 Cf. pp. 16–18.
73 Cf. p. 58.
74 On these cf. p. 18.
75 Cf. p. 71.
76 Cf. p. 97.
77 Cf. p. 18.

## CHAPTER 6

1   Cf. p. 97.
2   Cf. pp. 10–1, 65–6.
3   Thuc. I. 23. iv–vi with the remainder of book I; for the *pentekontaetia* cf. p. 65.
4   Cf. p. 18.
5   On the Thirty Years' Peace cf. p. 71.
6   Thuc. I. 24–55.
7   Thuc. I. 56–66.
8   Cf. p. 68.
9   Cf. pp. 68, 71.
10  Cf. Thuc. I. 67–88.
11  Thuc. I. 118. iii – 146; for the curse cf. p. 39.
12  Cf. pp. 36–7.
13  Thuc. II. 2–6.
14  Thuc. I. 44. ii.
15  Fornara 119.
16  Fornara 124–5; cf. p. 84.
17  Cf. p. 68.
18  Cf. p. 76.
19  Extracts Fornara 136.
20  Cf. p. 96.
21  Cf. p. 87.
22  Cf. p. 80.
23  Cf. p. 100.
24  Cf. p. 80.
25  Cf. p. 86.
26  Cf. pp. 19, 71.
27  Cf. pp. 125, 139.
28  Cf. p. 71; he was recalled from exile in 427–426.
29  Cf. pp. 80, 91.
30  Cf. pp. 100–3.
31  Cf. p. 69.
32  Thuc. V. 84–116.
33  Cf. p. 221 with n. 19.
34  Fornara 132; but a second fragment has been added since that collection was published.
35  Cf. p. 72.
36  Thuc. V. 83. ii.
37  For Sicily in the 420s see p. 90.
38  Cf. p. 101.
39  Cf. pp. 90–1.
40  Cf. p. 128.

41    Cf. pp. 101–2.
42    Cf. p. 102.
43    Cf. p. 85.
44    Cf. pp. 103–4.
45    Cf. p. 102.
46    Cf. pp. 95, 101.
47    For the political repercussions of that see p. 103.
48    Cf. p. 102.
49    Cf. p. 88.
50    Thuc. II. 65; cf. pp. 77–8.
51    He may have been responsible for Thuc.' exile: p. 91.
52    Cf. p. 90.
53    Thuc. IV. 27–8.
54    Cf. p. 92.
55    Cf. p. 93.
56    Cf. p. 95.
57    Cf. p. 95.
58    Cf. p. 96.
59    Cf. p. 96.
60    Probably a different man from Antiphon the sophist, for whom see p. 112.
61    Cf. p. 97.
62    Cf. pp. 97–8.
63    Cf. p. 98.
64    Cf. p. 98.
65    Cf. p. 130.

**CHAPTER 7**

1    Cf. pp. 34–5.
2    Cf. p. 74.
3    Cf. pp. 32–3.
4    Cf. p. 40.
5    Cf. p. 45.
6    Cf. p. 87.
7    Cf. pp. 5–6, 28.
8    Asclepius, *Inscriptiones Graecae* ii$^2$ 4960; Bendis, Pl. *Resp.* I. 327 A–328 A.
9    Cf. p. 31.
10    Cf. p. 3.
11    Cf. pp. 10–1.
12    Cf. pp. 85, 97, 120, 127; he wrote on many other topics too, including *Ways and Means*, p. 154.
13    Cf. p. 11.

14    Cf. p. 77.
15    Cf. p. 99.
16    For the orator see pp. 102, 110.
17    Cf. p. 130.
18    Cf. pp. 136–7, 158.
19    Cf. pp. 21–7.
20    Cf. p. 74.
21    Cf. p. 70.
22    Cf. p. 153.
23    Cf. pp. 86, 141.

**CHAPTER 8**

1     On Xen. cf. p. 85; on Diodorus and Plut. p. 11.
2     For the Thirty see p. 130.
3     Cf. pp. 96–7.
4     Cf. p. 128.
5     Cf. p. 98.
6     Cf. p. 67.
7     Cf. pp. 36–7.
8     Cf. p. 130.
9     Harding 31.
10    Isoc. IV. *Panegyric* 117–20: cf. p. 69.
11    Cf. p. 79.
12    Harding 35.
13    Cf. pp. 69–70.
14    Cf. pp. 126–7.
15    Cf. p. 127.
16    Cf. p. 134.
17    Harding 53. 35 – end.
18    Cf. pp. 69–70.
19    Cf. p. 91.
20    Cf. p. 123.
21    Harding 35. 12–5 contr. 9–12.
22    Xen. *Hell.* VII. v. 26–7.
23    Cf. p. 154.
24    Cf. p. 124.
25    Cf. p. 153.
26    Cf. pp. 98–9.
27    Cf. p. 130.
28    Cf. p. 96.
29    Cf. p. 121.
30    Cf. p. 121.
31    Cf. p. 73.

32    Cf. pp. 79–80.
33    Cf. p. 104.
34    Cf. p. 112.
35    Cf. pp. 73–4.
36    Cf. p. 74.
37    Cf. p. 74.
38    Cf. p. 40.
39    Cf. p. 73.
40    Cf. p. 75.
41    Cf. p. 155.
42    Cf. p. 100.
43    Cf. p. 127.
44    Cf. p. 112.
45    Cf. p. 76.
46    Lys. XXVI. *Evandrus* is a speech against Evandrus.
47    Cf. pp. 94–6.
48    Cf. p. 83.
49    Cf. pp. 201–2.
50    For triremes see pp. 23–4.
51    Cf. pp. 82–3.

**CHAPTER 9**

1     Thuc. IV. 124. i, 125. i.
2     Cf. p. 59.
3     Cf. pp. 86, 91.
4     Cf. p. 94.
5     Cf. p. 125.
6     For Diodorus cf. pp. 11, 65, 85, 120, 135. Justin I–VI, on earlier Greek and Persian history, adds little to what we have in other sources.
7     Cf. pp. 123, 126.
8     Cf. p. 126.
9     On Mausolus cf. p. 153.
10    Cf. p. 29.
11    Cf. p. 156.
12    On Persia and Egypt cf. p. 154.
13    Cf. p. 151.
14    Cf. p. 154.
15    Cf. pp. 167, 179.
16    Cf. p. 142.
17    Cf. p. 149.
18    Cf. p. 99.
19    Cf. pp. 139–40, 144–5.
20    Cf. pp. 168–9.

21    Cf. p. 149.
22    Cf. p. 165.
23    Plaut. *Mostell.* 775.
24    Cf. pp. 113–4.
25    Cf. pp. 127–9.
26    Cf. p. 147.
27    Cf. pp. 122–3.
28    Cf. p. 76.
29    Cf. p. 136.
30    Cf. pp. 130–1.
31    Cf. p. 76.
32    Cf. pp. 39, 73.
33    Harding 101.
34    Cf. pp. 123, 125–6.
35    Cf. p. 137.
36    Cf. p. 137.

## CHAPTER 10

1    Cf. pp. 11, 65–6, 85, 120, 135, 139, 147, 157.
2    Cf. pp. 139, 147.
3    Cf. p. 11.
4    Cf. p. 11.
5    Cf. pp. 109–10, 182–3.
6    Cf. p. 145.
7    Cf. pp. 147–8, 154.
8    Cf. p. 148.
9    For Ptolemy cf. p. 147.
10    Diod. Sic. XVIII. 4. i–vi.
11    Cf. pp. 149, 157.
12    Cf. p. 156.
13    On Athens in this period cf. pp. 172–4.
14    Cf. pp. 144–6.
15    For Ptolemy's new, mildly oligarchic, constitution for Cyrene see Harding 126 = Austin$^2$ 29.
16    Diod. Sic. XVIII. 55–6.
17    Cf. p. 139.
18    Cf. for Philippi pp. 139–40, for Alexandrias pp. 148, 150.
19    Cf. p. 147.
20    Harding 132.
21    Cf. p. 164.
22    Cf. p. 182.
23    Cf. pp. 152–3.
24    Austin$^2$ 39.

# P. J. Rhodes

25 Diod. Sic. XX. 46. ii, Plut. *Demetr.* 10. iii–vi, cf. Harding 137 and the hymn of 291, Ath. VI. 253 B–F (Burstein 7 = Austin² 43).

26 Diod. Sic. XX. 100. iii–iv.

27 Harding 136.

28 Burstein 92 = Austin² 256.

29 The Mendes *stele*: translation in S. Birch (ed.), *Records of the Past*, viii (London: Bagster for Society for Biblical Archaeology, 1876), 91–102, accessible online at www.reshafim.org.il/ad/egypt/texts/great_mendes_stela.htm; (verified 9 July 2014) and for the cult of Arsinoe as assimilated to Aphrodite cf. Burstein 93 = Austin² 295, Burstein 94 cf. Austin² 296.

30 Alexandria, *Elephantine-Papyri* 2 (not in Burstein or Austin²); Egyptian temples, e.g. the Rosetta Stone, Burstein 103 = Austin² 283.

31 First attested for Smyrna in 195: Tac. *Ann.* IV. 56.

32 Harding 138; on Philip's League of Corinth cf. p. 145; on Delos and the Islanders cf. Harding 136, and on its liberation from Athens p. 174.

33 On Pyrrhus cf. pp. 175–6.

34 After the end of Diodorus' surviving text the assignment of Athenian archons to years has been problematic: difficulties are being resolved; I give what appear at the time of writing to be the correct dates, but further evidence may yet require some further changes.

35 Cf. pp. 156, 165.

36 Cf. p. 157.

37 For the 'traditional constitution' cf. p. 130.

38 Cf. pp. 76, 155.

39 For *epheboi* cf. p. 157.

40 *Inscriptiones Graecae* ii² 457; version quoted in [Plut.] *Ten Orators* 851 F – 852 E: cf. pp. 155–7. (*Ten Orators* is included in Vol. X of the Loeb edition of Plutarch's. *Moralia*.)

41 Quoted in [Plut.] *Ten Orators* 850 F – 851 C (date 847 D, where Gorgias is a corruption of Ourias).

42 Quoted in [Plut.] *Ten Orators* 851 D–F.

43 Burstein 11 = Austin² 54.

44 Burstein 55 = Austin² 55.

45 Cf. pp. 190, 194.

46 *Inscriptiones Graecae* ii² 682: part translated by M. J. Osborne, *Athens in the Third Century* B.C. (Athens: Greek Epigraphic Society, 2012), 168–70. Various passages were erased when traces of the Antigonids were obliterated in 200: cf. p. 195.

47 Cf. pp. 67, 121–2.

48 Cf. p. 122.

49 Cf. pp. 195, 199.

50 Cf. p. 144.

51 There is a *Life* of him by Plut..

52 On Agathocles cf. pp. 176–8.

53 'If we win another battle against the Romans, we shall be totally ruined' (Plut. *Pyrrh..* 21. xiv).

54 Cf. p. 178.

55 Plut. *Pyrrh..* 26. ii.

56 Cf. p. 158.

57 Diod. Sic. XIX. 2–9. Diodorus' account is derived from Timaeus, who was exiled by Agathocles and strongly hostile to him (cf. XXI. 17. i–iii).

58 Dates from an inscribed chronological table, the Parian Marble, B. 12, 14: Harding 1. A = Austin² 1.

## CHAPTER 11

1 Cf. p. 145.

2 Austin² 65.

3 Burstein 72.

4 Most clearly shown by Antiochus III and Smyrna: Livy XXXIII. 38. vi.

5 Cf. pp. 11–2. The terms *isopoliteia* and *sympoliteia* are not used as systematically in ancient texts as by modern scholars.

6 Cf. chapter 12, esp. pp. 189–90.

7 Cf. the fifth-century Athenian cleruchs, pp. 69–70.

8 E.g. Austin² 319, extracts Burstein 101; Austin² 315.

9 Cf. p. 167.

10 Cf. pp. 198, 200.

11 E.g. Burstein 21 = Austin² 164.

12 For the Archaic and Classical periods see chapter 7.

13 Cf. pp. 168–9.

14 Cf. p. 168.

15 *Letter of Aristeas*, translated in R. H. Charles, *The Apocrypha and Pseudepigrapha of the Old Testament* (Oxford U. P., 1913), ii. 83–122; cf. Jos. *A.J.* XII. 11–118.

16 Cf. pp. 10, 109.

17 Cf. pp. 164, 183, 205.

18 Cf. pp. 136, 144, 150.

19 Cf. p. 5.

20 Thuc. II. 28.

21 The Anticythera Mechanism, found in an ancient shipwreck and now displayed in the National Archaeological Museum in Athens, was an elaborate device which enabled various astronomical calculations to be made.

22 Cf. pp. 171, 189, 196.
23 Cf. p. 168.

## CHAPTER 12

1 Thuc. III. 94. iv–v; cf. for 322 Diod. Sic. XVIII. 24. ii.
2 Harding 54.
3 Cf. p. 165.
4 Cf. p. 180.
5 Paus. X. 20. ix.
6 Cf. p. 190.
7 Cf. p. 171.
8 Austin[2] 60.
9 Hdt. I. 145.
10 Xen. *Hell.* IV. vi. 1.
11 Polyb. II. 41–43. iii.
12 Cf. pp. 190–1.
13 Cf. pp. 171, 176.
14 A short account Paus. III. 6. iv–vi; Chremonides' decree Burstein 56 = Austin[2] 61, cf. a decree honouring Chremonides' brother, Austin[2] 63; Athens' capitulation Apollodorus (Burstein 58). For Athens after the war see p. 194.
15 Cf. p. 129.
16 Cf. pp. 34–5.
17 Cf. p. 202.
18 Cf. pp. 194–5.
19 On the Macedonian phalanx cf. p. 139.
20 Polyb. V. 104. x.
21 Cf. pp. 201–6. Polyb.' original plan had been to start his history with the Social War: I. 3. i–vi.
22 Cf. p. 190 with p. 228 n. 14.
23 Burstein 58.
24 A general, Burstein 61; Demetr., Ath. IV. 167 F (*thesmothetes*, 'statute-setter', was normally the title of six of the nine archons).
25 'Freedom' with dates, two versions of the *Chronicle* of world history by the Christian bishop Eusebius (not in Burstein or Austin[2]); Museum garrison, Paus. III. 6. vi.
26 Cf. pp. 190–2.
27 Polyb.' comment, V. 106. vi–viii; decree for Euryclides, Burstein 67 = Austin[2] 74.
28 For the wider context from 212 to 146 see pp. 203–6.
29 Livy XXIX. 12. xiv.
30 *Inscriptiones Graecae* ii[2] 682, the decree honouring Phaedrus in 259/8 (p. 174: with p. 226 n. 44), is a conspicuous instance.

31 Thessalians, Austin[2] 88; Athenians, *Inscriptiones Graecae* ii[3] 1288 (not in Burstein or Austin[2]).

32 Cf. pp. 67, 121–2, 174.

33 Cf. p. 126.

34 Cf. pp. 168–9.

35 Cf. Polyb. V. 34.

36 Reported in a papyrus text, Burstein 98 = Austin[2] 266.

37 Burstein 99 = Austin[2] 268.

38 Cf. Burstein 85 = Austin[2] 231, from the monument which perhaps included the Pergamene statues of dying Gauls (cf. p. 186).

39 Cf. p. 187.

40 Cf. Austin[2] 276.

41 Cf. p. 204.

42 For the altar of Zeus at Pergamum cf. p. 186.

43 Cf. pp. 169, 174.

44 Burstein 103 = Austin[2] 283.

45 Polyb. XXIX. 27. i–vii.

46 Joseph. *A.J.* XII. 138–46. The main sources for what follows are I *Maccabees* and II *Maccabees* in the Old Testament Apocrypha, and *Daniel* in the Old Testament; *A.J.* XII is mostly derived from I *Macc.* but has some additional material.

47 Cf. p. 198.

48 Cf. pp. 175–6.

49 Cf. p. 178.

50 On Gelon cf. p. 82–3; on Dionysius I cf. pp. 135–7.

51 Cf. p. 192.

52 Cf. p. 193.

53 Cf. p. 193.

54 Polyb. VII. 9.

55 Cf. Sherk 2 = Austin[2] 77. B.

56 Livy XXIX. 12. viii–xvi (for the false addition of Athens to the Roman side see p. 195).

57 Cf. p. 37.

58 Title of king used on bricks, *Inscriptiones Graecae* v. i 885.

59 Cf. pp. 191–3.

60 Polyb. XVIII. 46. v.

61 Cf. p. 199.

## EPILOGUE / CHAPTER 13

1 Burstein 104 = Austin[2] 289; for Ptolemies VI and VIII cf. pp. 200–1.

2 Cf. Sherk 55. A(B). 8–9, B. 38–40.

3 Hor. *Epist.* II. i. 156–7.

# Index

(Only the most important names and subjects, and
only the most important occurrences of them, are listed)

230